P9-CWE-959

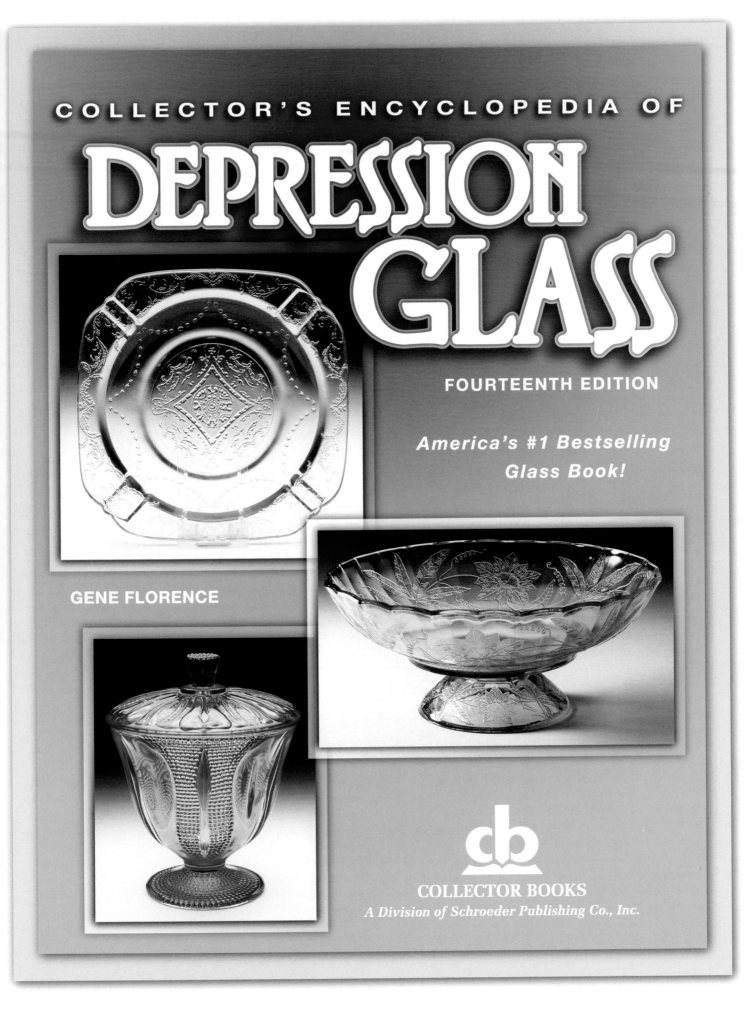

COLLECTOR'S ENCYCLOPEDIA OF

DEPRESSION GLASS

FOURTEENTH EDITION

America's #1 Bestselling Glass Book!

GENE FLORENCE

COLLECTOR BOOKS

A Division of Schroeder Publishing Co., Inc.

The current values in this book should be used only as a guide. They are not intended to set prices, which vary from one section of the country to another. Auction prices as well as dealer prices vary greatly and are affected by condition as well as demand. Neither the author nor the publisher assumes responsibility for any losses that might be incurred as a result of consulting this guide.

On the Cover: Green Madrid ash tray, $195.00; Blue Tulip candy, $135.00; Pink Floral ruffled comport, $895.00; Pink 3½" Cameo wine, $900.00; Pink Cupid cup, $75.00.

Cover design by Beth Summers
Layout by Terri Hunter

Searching For A Publisher?

We are always looking for knowledgeable people considered to be experts within their fields. If you feel that there is a real need for a book on your collectible subject and have a large comprehensive collection, contact us.

Collector Books
P.O. Box 3009
Paducah, KY 42002-3009

Gene Florence
P.O. Box 22186
Lexington, KY 40522
or
P.O.Box 64
Astatula, FL 34705

CONTENTS

ACKNOWLEDGMENTS

I appreciate all the extensive information dealers, collectors, and readers have shared with me through writing, calling, and talking to me directly at various areas around the country! Thanks for carrying those newly discovered pieces to shows for viewing and sending pictures confirming their existence.

By the way, if you have trouble photographing glass, take it outside in natural light, place it on a neutral surface (concrete works) and ignore the camera's flash attachment. A bright, but cloudy, day works best. Please enclose an SASE (self-addressed, stamped envelope) that is large enough to return your photos if you wish them back. Further, writing books from January through May (five last year) leaves little time for answering the piles of letters that arrive each week. I want to thank the thoughtful people who send postcards with the possible answers to their questions for me to check off the correct response! Those are a delight! I want to inform people who forget to include the SASE that they're wasting their time writing; they'll not be answered. I want to encourage you to send pictures of items you hope to have identified, or pencil rubbings of the pattern, rather than descriptions or personal drawings. I want to explain that my expertise, such as it is, lies in knowledge of the patterns presented in my books. I do not know enough about chinaware, iron dinner bells, pottery, antique furniture, radios, or violins to warrant your writing. Also, I do not send sheets of new pricing, to update your pattern in older books, though I'm grateful you bought that one; nor do I run a free personal appraisal service evaluating merchandise you're wanting to include in your next garage sale. I don't know the names, manufacturers, line numbers, and worth of every single piece of Depression glassware made. I know quite a bit about those collectible patterns presented to you in my various books and I will gladly help you in any way I can with those. Please know this is not so much "sour grapes" as self preservation! I'm suffering from an inundation of questions I have no knowledge of and it's a waste and frustration for both of us! I would abhor coming to the place where I'd discourage your writing me at all; but these questions on all and sundry are giving me pause to consider that.

I have relished the shows that Depression glass clubs and show promoters have invited me to attend. There is priceless information gathered there and hopefully, I helped to promote the glass and show to all our benefit, both material and esthetic. I'm beginning to cut back a bit on all the scurrying I've done in the past to attend as many shows as possible to keep current. Little health concerns are mounting up for both Cathy and me; I hope you will forgive me for slowing just a bit for both of us. Cathy's help is immeasurable and quite frankly, these books would not exist without her help. She has worked many long hours as chief editor, critic, proofreader and, lately, research assistant. She was always the labor end of unpacking, packing, sorting, labeling, etc. Unfortunately, as her job descriptions expanded, so did her stress levels! Imagine that!

Marc, my youngest, is overseeing my web page amongst a full-time work schedule teaching computer technology. No, I do not have much time to surf the net myself! These books take more of my time than I care to admit or than you could ever imagine! Chad, my eldest, is working in Florida drilling Team Mole's cable line holes for underground fiber optics. He likes it here better than trying to drill in frozen northern climes. Thanks, too, to Cathy's mom and dad, Sibyl and Charles, who have helped us wash, sort, pack, repack, shelve, measure, and otherwise do whatever was needed to be done both for photography sessions and shows. A new procedure has streamlined this process somewhat, though its enlarged the sorting that must be done at the annual, week-long photo sessions. Any way you slice it, its an enormous amount of work that must be accomplished before these books come to you neatly packaged between glossy covers.

As I write these acknowledgments, memories always surface of my mom, the original "Grannie Bear" for whom my shop was named, who really seemed to enjoy all the hustle and bustle of sorting and packing for photography sessions. Our job is more difficult without her hiding pieces away from customers in order to get them photographed — or her getting customers to lend their pieces for the camera.

Specific thanks need to go to Dick and Pat Spencer, Dan Tucker and Lorrie Kitchen, Matt and Angela Koester, Barbara Wolfe and Marianne Jackson at Anchor Hocking, and various readers throughout the United States and Canada for glass and information provided for this book. There have also been snippets of information forthcoming from readers in Australia, New Zealand, England, and Puerto Rico.

Photographs herein were crafted by Richard Walker of New York and Charles R. Lynch of Kentucky. They both labored long over multitudes of setups during one six-day session and five smaller sessions scheduled throughout the two year period. Glass arranging, unpacking, sorting, carting, and repacking was accomplished by Jane White, Zibby Walker, Dick and Pat Spencer, and Cathy Florence. Van loading and unloading was facilitated by Billy Schroeder and some other members of the Collector Books' shipping crew. In addition, Jane White and many of the crew previously mentioned helped on other photography shoots. They have dared me to express their unanimous opinion that we are all certifiably nuts to do what we do to get you these photographs. So done!

Thanks for the expertise of the editorial department at Collector Books (especially Terri Hunter, Della Maze, and Lisa Stroup) who know how to take my e-mailings and make them into a book!

This fourteenth book was written in Florida, sitting before my computer which faces the lake, where I can at least eye my fishing poles on the dock, watch the alligators cruise by, and see the fellow anglers motoring along and occasionally pulling up a fish! Oh, well; I wouldn't be fishing in Kentucky either!

As we go to press with this fourteenth edition, thank you, my readers, for making this America's #1 bestselling book on glass! Do enlighten your friends on Depression glass. In the grand order of things, it still appears that only a few of us realize its intrinsic, as well as monetary, value! I receive letters nearly every day from people who have just learned about Depression glass — or who just discovered they practically "gave away" some family pieces at a sale!

PREFACE

Depression glass as defined in this book is the colored glassware made fundamentally during the Depression years in the colors of amber, blue, black, crystal, green, pink, red, yellow, and white. There are other colors and some glass made before, as well as after, this time; but primarily, **the glass herein was manufactured from the late 1920s through 1940.** Further, this publication is mostly concerned with the **inexpensively made dinnerware turned out by machine** in bulk and sold through smaller stores or given away as publicity or premium items for other products of that time. Depression glass was often packaged in cereal boxes and flour sacks or given as incentive gifts for buying tickets or products at the local movie theaters, gasoline stations, and grocery stores. Wares were offered with magazine subscriptions, for buying (or selling) certain amounts of seeds or in return for amounts of coupons garnered with butter or soap purchases.

Collectors have also been seeking later made patterns encompassing the time from 1940 to the 1960s which has led to a companion book, entitled *Collectible Glassware from the 40s, 50s, 60s...*, now in its fifth edition. However, to correctly date glassware from this latter period, it was necessary to **move some patterns previously exclusive to this Depression glass book** into the time frame encompassed by the 50s book. If your pattern is no longer found within this Depression book, you should seek it in the 40s, 50s, 60s... book. Of course, there were more elegant, etched tableware's being manufactured during this 20s through 60s time frame which are highly collectible, today; but those are covered in my *Elegant Glassware of the Depression Era* book.

There have been major changes in collecting Depression glass since my first book was published on the subject in 1972. Prices have soared; seemingly plentiful patterns have been gathered into innumerable collections throughout the world and removed from the market. Collectors, rather than gathering the **sets** of dishes of old, have branched into collecting **items only** from many different patterns, i.e., cups and saucers, pitchers, shakers, tumblers, shot glasses, cruets, sugar and creamer sets, luncheon plates, etc. Smaller Depression patterns and previously ignored crystal and satinized ware have attracted clientele; collecting a "rainbow" (many colors) of one, or more, patterns is now in vogue, rather than the one color collecting of old. Truly, **anything that is Depression glass,** known pattern or not, suddenly has added significance and collectibility. Glass is sold on the Internet which has made great inroads into the collectibles market in just the two years since I last rewrote this book. Very knowledgeable glass collectors are more the norm than the exception, and they are crossing fields and branching into other areas of glass appreciation. This ever-broadening interest has prompted me to research eleven more books in the field of Depression glass, the Elegant and 50s previously mentioned, one on Kitchenware items of the Depression, six others on the Very Rare glassware of those times, not to mention the latest ones on Stemware Identification and Pattern Identification. Regarding these last two, I have actually had dealers write or seek me out lately at shows to give compliments and thanks (!) for saving them endless hours of searching through their libraries of books to identify some piece they've acquired! That's been a delightful bonus. Too, I've had some letters from readers recently who wanted nothing more than to say thanks for having written all these books and contributed to their pleasure in the glass. Words can't express the warm, fuzzy feeling one gets from these unexpected, but totally appreciated, thanks for our work. It's certainly not all mine anymore. Be sure and read the acknowledgments for the myriad people who contribute!

Twenty-nine previously uncataloged pieces have been added to the listings since the thirteenth edition as well as some previously unlisted colors. Those of you who feel nothing new is ever found should look closely at your favorite pattern. Similarly, there have been over 20 deletions of pieces that have never been found. These are due to original catalog misinformation or misinterpretation, entry mistakes, or errors of measurements in the past. My publisher has noticed that these mistakes were copied, along with the rest of this book, into another publication being sold as another author's work. We may soon be testing the copyright laws.

Information for this book comes from 30 years of research and selling experience, via communication with fellow dealers and collectors throughout the country, and over 1,325,000 miles of traveling the country, hunting and locating glassware. I must say that some of the most interesting (and surprising) information has come directly from readers, like you, sharing catalogs, magazines, photographs of glass, and their specific information with me. They may have a family member who worked at a plant, or talked with an engraver, or heard something at a market, or found something at a garage sale they thought significant. More importantly, they bothered to share it! It's invaluable and adds to the body of knowledge for us all.

PRICING

All prices in this book are retail prices for MINT CONDITION glassware. This book is intended to be only a GUIDE to prices as there are some regional price differences that cannot reasonably be dealt with herein! You may expect dealers to pay from 30% to 50% less than the prices quoted. Glass that is in less than mint condition, i.e., chipped, cracked, scratched, repaired or poorly moulded, will bring only a small percentage of the price of glass that is in mint condition.

Prices have become fairly well established due to national advertising by dealers, the Depression glass shows held from coast to coast, and the Internet. I have my own web page operated for books and glass (http://www.geneflorence.com). However, **there are still some regional differences in prices due partly to glass being more readily available in some areas than in others.** Companies distributed certain pieces in some areas that they did not in others. Generally speaking, however, prices are about the same among dealers from coast to coast.

Prices **tend to increase impressively** on rare items and, in general, they have increased as a whole due to more and more collectors entering the field and people becoming more aware of the worth of Depression glass.

One of the more important aspects of this book is the attempt made to illustrate as well as realistically price those items that are in demand. All items listed are priced. The desire is to give you the most factual guide to collectible patterns of Depression glass available.

MEASUREMENTS

To illustrate why there are discrepancies in measurements, I offer the following sample from just two years of Hocking's catalog references:

Year	Item	Ounces	Item	Ounces	Item	Ounces
1935	Pitcher	37, 58, 80	Flat Tumbler	5, 9, 13½	Footed Tumbler	10, 13
1935	Pitcher	37, 60, 80	Flat Tumbler	5, 9, 10, 15	Footed Tumbler	10, 13
1936	Pitcher	37, 65, 90	Flat Tumbler	5, 9, 13½	Footed Tumbler	10, 15
1936	Pitcher	37, 60, 90	Flat Tumbler	5, 9, 13½	Footed Tumbler	10, 15

All measurements in this book are exact as to some manufacturer's listing or to actual measurement. You may expect variance of up to ½" or 1 – 5 ounces. This may be due to mould variations or changes by the manufacturer as well as rounding off measurements for catalog listings.

ADAM JEANNETTE GLASS COMPANY, 1932–1934

Colors: Pink, green, crystal, some yellow, and Delphite blue. (See Reproduction Section.)

Today, very little Adam is being found at shows and not much is being advertised in the *Daze* or listed on the Internet. Even commonly found pieces from the past have vanished into collections. This makes prices escalate, with rarer pieces bringing whatever someone is willing to pay. Now, there are many advertisements for glassware on the "net." You can even find me at http://www.geneflorence.com if you search in cyberspace.

Generally speaking, green Adam remains more expensive than pink; green is less plentiful, so prices are routinely higher. Some increase has been observed in prices for butter dishes, candy jars, candlesticks, and shakers. If you are just beginning to collect green Adam, buy those pieces first — **if** you find them for sale!

With the increasing number of collectors searching for pink Adam, demand is causing prices to accelerate. Prices of pink have had a history of lagging behind green; but today, tumblers and serving pieces, are selling for as much as those in green! The pink vase is the most elusive piece of Adam unless you include the Adam/Sierra butter dish. Many pink vases tilt or appear lopsided! Some collectors are unwilling to pay a proud price for these flawed, but typically 30s, vases. You have to judge.

Sugar and candy lids are interchangeable, something Jeannette Glass did to save money, which is fortunate for collectors today. Sugar and candy lids are persistently harder to find than the bottoms in most Depression glass patterns.

Inner rim roughness (irr in ads) is a problem on nearly all Adam pieces. That is especially true of bowls. Damage to these came from both using and stacking them over the years. Even if you are willing to acquire **less than perfect glass,** don't pay mint condition prices. However, when it comes time to sell, you will receive a better price for mint glassware. Prices in this book are for mint **(like new)** glass. Admittedly, some damaged glass can be nicely repaired by competent artisans; but not all glass grinders and repairers are proficient! Some do more damage to the glass than if it had been left alone.

Adam lamps are rare. On page 74, you can see a pink Floral lamp that is designed the same way Adam lamps were. A sherbet was frosted to hide the wiring and a notch was cut into the top edge of the sherbet to position a switch. A metal cover was applied to the top of the frosted sherbet through which a tall bulb was connected to the switch. The prices listed are for working lamps. That **bulb attachment** is hard to find. The notched, frosted sherbets are available and could even be made today without much difficulty!

The **Adam butter dish** is the **only piece** that has been **reproduced! Do not use** the information given on this butter dish (in the Reproduction Section in the back of the book) **for any other pieces** in the pattern. This advise goes for all reproductions that I have listed in the back. Only use the revealing clues for the **piece** I describe. Substituting information to another piece in the pattern will not work.

The Adam/Sierra butter dish has **both** pattern designs on the **top.** Adam is found on the outside of the top and Sierra is found on the inside of this lid. These tops have been found on **both** Adam and Sierra butter bottoms; those respective butter bottoms, however, contain only **one** pattern. I have often seen an Adam butter top on a Sierra bottom or a Sierra top on an Adam bottom priced as the rare butter. **That is not it.** One is pictured with Adam and Sierra bottoms in the *Very Rare Glassware of the Depression Years, Fifth Series.* The price listed is the legitimate selling price these butter tops have brought recently.

	Pink	Green
Ash tray, 4½"	30.00	25.00
Bowl, 4¾" dessert	22.00	22.00
Bowl, 5¾" cereal	55.00	50.00
Bowl, 7¾"	30.00	30.00
Bowl, 9", no cover	45.00	45.00
Bowl, cover, 9"	25.00	45.00
Bowl, 9" covered	70.00	90.00
Bowl, 10" oval	35.00	40.00
Butter dish bottom	25.00	65.00
Butter dish top	60.00	330.00
Butter dish & cover	85.00	395.00
Butter dish combination with Sierra Pattern	1,500.00	
Cake plate, 10" ftd.	30.00	32.50
*Candlesticks, 4" pr.	95.00	115.00
Candy jar & cover, 2½"	100.00	115.00
Coaster, 3¼"	22.00	20.00
Creamer	25.00	25.00
**Cup	30.00	25.00
Lamp	295.00	325.00
Pitcher, 8", 32 oz.	45.00	45.00
Pitcher, 32 oz. round base	60.00	
Plate, 6" sherbet	11.00	11.00
***Plate, 7¾" square salad	18.00	18.00
Plate, 9" square dinner	35.00	30.00
Plate, 9" grill	28.00	25.00
Platter, 11¾"	33.00	33.00
Relish dish, 8" divided	20.00	25.00
Salt & pepper, 4" ftd.	90.00	115.00
****Saucer, 6" square	6.00	6.00
Sherbet, 3"	35.00	38.00
Sugar	20.00	32.50
Sugar/candy cover	25.00	45.00
Tumbler, 4½"	40.00	33.00
Tumbler, 5½" iced tea	75.00	70.00
Vase, 7½"	395.00	85.00

* Delphite $225.00   ** Yellow $100.00   *** Round pink $60.00; yellow $100.00   **** Round pink $75.00; yellow $85.00

AMERICAN PIONEER LIBERTY WORKS, 1931–1934

Colors: Pink, green, amber, and crystal.

Notice the American Pioneer design has vertical bands of hobs separated by two bands of horizontal ribs. If these ribs are missing, then the piece is not American Pioneer. That's as plain as I can say it. If the piece you have only has hobs, it is not a newly discovered piece of American Pioneer.

American Pioneer is preferred in green, but you need to be cognizant of the fact that there are three distinct tints available. Color discrepancies do not seem to bother collectors of American Pioneer as much as they do collectors of other patterns. Few green pieces are being found; collectors are just happy to attain any additional item no matter the shade.

Devotees who search for crystal or amber American Pioneer are having a difficult time finding new pieces. Only basic luncheon pieces are being found regularly in amber. Amber cocktails have been found in two sizes; none have been seen in any other color. One holds 3 oz. and stands 3¹³⁄₁₆" high while the other holds 3½ oz. and stands 3¹⁵⁄₁₆" tall. One set of amber covered pitchers (urns) has surfaced! I did have a report of an amber bottom being found. Liners for urns are regular 6" and 8" plates. That should make it easier to find those liners except for the 6" **pink** plate, which is rare.

Dresser sets are coveted pieces in American Pioneer. Two complete sets have been found in pink and a few more in green. Occasionally, an odd piece to these sets turns up; but attaining a complete dresser set is difficult. These have recently become even harder for Depression glass collectors to acquire due, in part, to the many perfume and cologne bottle collectors on a quest for them! Often items in a Depression glass pattern become more expensive because collectors from other fields are seeking them.

Two styles of American Pioneer cups are being found. Some have a more flared rim than others which makes one style have a 4" diameter (2¼" tall) and the other a 3⅜" diameter (2⅜" tall). Both cups take the same sized saucer; the flared version seems to predominate in both pink and green.

You may have difficulty in matching lids for covered bowls. I have been assured that there are three different covered bowl sizes instead of the two I have found. If you have a different size from those listed, please let me know the measurements. The same goes for any additional items in American Pioneer (or other pattern). I do relish the information you share with me; and I make a genuine effort to pass that knowledge along to collectors.

Candy jar lids are interchangeable in American Pioneer even though the jars are shaped differently. The 1½ pound candy is pictured with the lid in the top row of page 9. The taller, pound candy is on the right, but is shown topless. Often, these topless candy jars are marked as vases. The only vase in this pattern is round.

	Crystal, Pink	Green
* Bowl, 5" handled	20.00	20.00
Bowl, 8¾" covered	125.00	150.00
Bowl, 9" handled	22.00	27.50
Bowl, 9¼" covered	125.00	150.00
Bowl, 10¾" console	55.00	65.00
Candlesticks, 6½" pr.	100.00	125.00
Candy jar and cover, 1 lb	85.00	100.00
Candy jar and cover, 1½ lb.	100.00	135.00
Cheese and cracker set (indented platter and comport)	55.00	65.00
Coaster, 3½"	35.00	35.00
Creamer, 2¾"	25.00	20.00
* Creamer, 3½"	20.00	22.00
* Cup	15.00	15.00
Dresser set (2 colognes, powder jar, on indented 7½" tray)	425.00	395.00
Goblet, 3¹³⁄₁₆", 3 oz., cocktail (amber)	40.00	
Goblet, 3¹⁵⁄₁₆", 3½ oz., cocktail (amber)	40.00	
Goblet, 4", 3 oz. wine	40.00	55.00
Goblet, 6", 8 oz. water	45.00	57.50
Ice bucket, 6"	55.00	65.00
Lamp, 1¾", w/metal pole 9½"		75.00
Lamp, 5½" round, ball shape (amber $125.00)	150.00	
Lamp, 8½" tall	100.00	110.00
Mayonnaise, 4¼"	60.00	90.00
Pilsner, 5¾", 11 oz.	150.00	150.00
** Pitcher, 5" covered urn	175.00	225.00
*** Pitcher, 7" covered urn	195.00	250.00
Plate, 6"	12.50	15.00
* Plate, 6" handled	12.50	15.00
* Plate, 8"	13.00	15.00
* Plate, 11½" handled	30.00	35.00
* Saucer	4.00	5.00
Sherbet, 3½"	16.00	20.00
Sherbet, 4¾"	35.00	40.00
Sugar, 2¾"	20.00	22.00
* Sugar, 3½"	20.00	22.00
Tumbler, 5 oz. juice	35.00	40.00
Tumbler, 4", 8 oz.	30.00	50.00
Tumbler, 5", 12 oz.	45.00	55.00
Vase, 7", 4 styles	100.00	125.00
Vase, 9", round		235.00
Whiskey, 2¼", 2 oz.	50.00	90.00

* Amber — Double the price of pink unless noted **Amber $300.00 ***Amber $350.00

AMERICAN SWEETHEART MacBETH-EVANS GLASS COMPANY, 1930–1936

Colors: Pink, Monax, red, blue; some Cremax and color trimmed Monax.

More collectors of American Sweetheart are enamored of blue rather than red. The blue American Sweetheart (shown below) is becoming extremely elusive these days. Red is available, but that may also make the blue more desirable. There are two blue tid-bits pictured. One tid-bit consists of 8" and 12" plates while the other shows the 8" and 15". One of the reasons that I do not list many tid-bits in this book is that they are being newly made. A few may have been made at the factory, but most are recently assembled. Many date from the early 1970s when two plates and tid-bit hardware were all one needed to assemble any tid-bit you wished. I was at a flea market in Hartville, Ohio, last year where a seller was set up with tid-bits priced from $30.00 to $55.00. His $55.00 Monax American Sweetheart tid-bit I have seen advertised from $95.00 to $275.00. **Which would you buy?** In American Sweetheart I list the ones with 15½" plates, since it would be quite a costly risk to break one of those to make a tid-bit. Most original tid-bits in common colors (and in other patterns) sell in the $50.00 range for two tiers and $75.00 for three. Rarer colors, of course, bring more! Realize that there is no definite way to tell old from new when like hardware is used.

That 15½" plate pictured in the center was bought as "Cambridge" (priced $115.00 firm) in an antique mall. I am amazed by dealers who **identify** glassware when they have no idea what it is. Unfortunately, many shoppers believe anything on a tag. Remember, it is often buyer beware in antique buying any place except from reputable dealers.

Console bowls (18") increased rapidly in price recently, but have settled down at present. There has been at least one console bowl at the last four shows I have attended, and not one sold for the prices asked. Prices in the listing are actual prices received — not hoped for prices! There are **plain** (no pattern) red 18" console bowls being found. Conceivably, you **could** find a plain blue one. Remember though, it **has to have the pattern** to be American Sweetheart, no matter what you may be told in a sales pitch!

Red and blue American Sweetheart sets were originally sold in 15 piece settings consisting of four each cups, saucers, and 8" plates with a creamer, sugar, and 12" salver. Supplementary pieces in these colors were **very limited in distribution.** Notice on page 11 the latest price increases on the larger pieces in these colors.

If you are a new collector trying to master terminology, Cremax is a beige-like color made by MacBeth-Evans Glass Company in several patterns. Monax is the white made by MacBeth-Evans. The Monax with the grayish-blue/**black edge** pictured on the bottom of page 11 is being called "smoke" by collectors. Much of regular Monax American Sweetheart has a bluish cast to its edges. To be the rarely found "smoke" color, it will **always have a black trim** at the edge. (See photo.)

You will sometimes find pieces trimmed in pink, green, yellow, black, or 22K gold. Gold was often used as a glass trim. Unfortunately, today there is no premium for gold trim; in fact, many dealers have difficulty selling it because it is worn. The gold (only) can be removed by using a pencil eraser. Do not use a scouring pad since you will damage the glass! I only point this out because badly worn gold-trimmed items traditionally do not sell very well; plain Monax does. However, **some** collectors are charmed by the less than perfect gold trim remaining after 60 or 70 years of service — and have no wish to see it removed.

	Red	Blue	Cremax	Smoke & Other Trims
Bowl, 6" cereal			15.00	40.00
Bowl, 9" round berry			50.00	225.00
Bowl, 9½" soup				135.00
Bowl, 18" console	1,100.00	1,250.00		
Creamer, ftd.	150.00	175.00		100.00
Cup	110.00	145.00		100.00
Lamp shade			495.00	
Lamp (floor with brass base)			795.00	
Plate, 6" bread and butter				20.00
Plate, 8" salad	100.00	115.00		30.00
Plate, 9" luncheon				40.00
Plate, 9¾" dinner				95.00
Plate, 12" salver	185.00	250.00		115.00
Plate, 15½" server	325.00	425.00		
Platter, 13" oval				225.00
Saucer	20.00	25.00		15.00
Sherbet, 4¼" ftd. (design inside or outside)				100.00
Sugar, open ftd.	150.00	175.00		100.00
Tid-bit, 2 tier, 8" & 12"	250.00	335.00		
Tid-bit, 3 tier, 8", 12" & 15½"	625.00	750.00		

AMERICAN SWEETHEART (cont.)

American Sweetheart Monax and pink prices continue to slowly increase except for harder to find pieces which have raced wildly upward. Check prices for the small pink pitcher, small berry bowl, and shakers which have risen considerably. Monax (white color) shakers and the sugar lid have seen price jumps. Collectors, who avoided buying the higher priced pieces, have decided to take the plunge after watching **prices continue to rise.** The only problem with that is that there are now not enough pieces to go around; so prices escalate because of surge in demand. Too, advanced collectors, needing one or two pieces to complete a set, decide to pay whatever it takes. Some dealer is willing to raise the price to the "whatever it takes" level. Word always gets out that a piece sold for "X" dollars, and the next piece found is priced the same or higher. The price is thus established at the next level! Today, the popularity of auctions on the Internet are affecting price trends. At **any auction,** it only takes two people to run up a price; and there may be hundreds bidding on the Internet. I've seen rare pieces bought cheaply there, and common pieces not so cheaply.

Prices on American Sweetheart soup bowls and serving pieces have had only minor upward price adjustments. A pink cream soup can be seen on the left of the bottom picture. Soups of either style were not sold in basic sets which means that today, there are fewer of these unearthed. There is no sugar lid in pink to find; so collectors of pink only have to lose sleep over finding pitchers, tumblers, and shakers!

American Sweetheart comes with two sizes of pink pitchers and three sizes of tumblers. Some collectors buy only water tumblers since juice and tea tumblers are scarce. Please bear in mind that there are pitchers shaped like American Sweetheart that do not have the **moulded design** of American Sweetheart. You can see one of these on the left in the bottom photograph on page 13. It is not American Sweetheart (or Dogwood, which has to have the silk screened Dogwood design), but is the blank made by MacBeth-Evans to go with the plain, no design tumblers they made. The design has to be moulded into the pitcher for it to truly be American Sweetheart as is shown on the right of that photo. Plain pitchers without any pattern sell in the $35.00 – 40.00 range and plain tumblers $8.00 – 10.00 each. I have photos of a boxed set of American Sweetheart that had plain Dogwood shaped tumblers in the box and the MacBeth-Evans square ash trays that were packed with most boxed sets at that time. Unfortunately, today, those plain tumblers are not considered to be American Sweetheart; so the boxed sets suffer greatly in price because of this.

Demand for American Sweetheart continues even with the short supply of many pieces. Collectors are delighted with the numerous colors and with the fact that American Sweetheart has not been reproduced. (I had reports of reproduced sherbets, but I believe they were just weakly patterned pieces.) There is yet a copious supply of basic pieces in Monax (white color) such as cups, saucers, plates, sugars, and creamers that are still modestly priced. Monax pieces were widely distributed, and can be found in all parts of the country, making them an excellent starting point for new collectors. Just realize that locating rare pieces of Monax and pink American Sweetheart is a serious task for collectors who have already bought all the basics.

Sherbets are found in two sizes. The sherbet on the plate is ½" smaller in diameter than the larger one pictured behind it in the bottom photograph. The smaller, 3¾", is more difficult to find than the larger; but many collectors seek only one size, making price parity closer than rarity should demand. Rarity does not always set price. Demand does! A rarely found item that no one wants will remain reasonably priced because no one is buying it!

Sets of pink or Monax can still be collected with patience. Monax would be less expensive, and there would be fewer pieces to find in that color. **Collect what you truly like.** Ultimately, you will be able to gather a set.

	Pink	Monax
Bowl, 3¾" flat berry	85.00	
Bowl, 4½" cream soup	95.00	120.00
Bowl, 6" cereal	19.00	19.00
Bowl, 9" round berry	60.00	75.00
Bowl, 9½" flat soup	75.00	90.00
Bowl, 11" oval vegetable	75.00	80.00
Bowl, 18" console		495.00
Creamer, ftd.	15.00	11.00
Cup	20.00	11.00
Lamp shade		495.00
Plate, 6" or 6½" bread & butter	6.00	6.50
Plate, 8" salad	12.00	10.00
Plate, 9" luncheon		14.00
Plate, 9¾" dinner	42.50	27.50
Plate, 10¼" dinner		27.00
Plate, 11" chop plate		22.00
Plate, 12" salver	25.00	22.00
Plate, 15½" server		235.00

	Pink	Monax
Platter, 13" oval	60.00	75.00
Pitcher, 7½", 60 oz.	950.00	
Pitcher, 8", 80 oz.	750.00	
Salt and pepper, ftd.	575.00	450.00
Saucer	4.00	2.00
Sherbet, 3¾" ftd.	25.00	
Sherbet, 4¼" ftd. (design inside or outside)	24.00	22.00
Sherbet in metal holder (crystal only)	3.50	
Sugar, open, ftd.	12.00	8.00
* Sugar lid		450.00
Tid-bit, 2 tier, 8" & 12"	60.00	60.00
Tid-bit, 3 tier, 8", 12" & 15½"		325.00
Tumbler, 3½", 5 oz.	100.00	
Tumbler, 4¼", 9 oz.	90.00	
Tumbler, 4¾", 10 oz.	120.00	

*Three styles of knobs.

AUNT POLLY U.S. GLASS COMPANY, Late 1920s

Colors: Blue, green, and iridescent.

Aunt Polly blue continues to attract new collectors, although some people are turned off by the mould roughness found on most pieces. This is a very early pattern (late 1920s which has echoes of older pattern glassware of the 1890s). Mould refinements were made in the early 1930s that eliminated the rough mould seams found in this and other U.S. Glass Company's patterns. If you are inflexible about mint condition glass, I recommend you look for another pattern.

In the 21 years since I discovered that U.S. Glass was the manufacturer of Aunt Polly not one additional piece of blue has surfaced! A covered green candy is pictured, but this candy dish has never surfaced in blue. That candy lid is interchangeable with the sugar lid, giving sugar and creamer collectors an extra venue for finding lids in green and iridescent. This is an expensive candy dish because perfect lids are very difficult to find today!

Blue is still **the** most collected color of Aunt Polly, but a few collectors of iridescent and green endure. The quandary in collecting green relates to the diversified shades. Green is found from almost yellow in appearance to the vivid green you see in the photograph on the next page. Recently, I became aware of distinct color variations in the blue, also. I speak from the experience of buying a blue lid that did not match my blue sugar.

There are two variations of blue creamers shown. One has a more pronounced lip than the other. These lips were formed by hand using a wooden tool; that no doubt accounts for these irregularities. It is also one reason that ounce measurements are so difficult to list. The same piece can vary several ounces due to the shape of the lip. This is most conspicuous in water pitchers whose ice lips were created the same way!

The two-handled, footed candy without lid has increased in price more than any other piece since the last book. Everything else in Aunt Polly has remained rather steady. Collecting Aunt Polly is partially influenced by its lack of cups or saucers. Prices would soar if any were ever found. That predicament exists for other U.S. Glass patterns including Strawberry, Cherryberry, and U.S. Swirl.

There is an Aunt Polly look-alike shown in two colors. The brighter blue tumbler in the top picture and the Canary yellow in the bottom photo are moulded differently from the normally found tumblers. The paneled lines are wider and there is no design in the bottom. The ground bottoms on these items may indicate prototypes that were redesigned, because the Canary (Vaseline) colored tumbler is a typical U.S. Glass color of the late 1920s. Vaseline is a collectors' name for the glowing, yellow-green shown by that tumbler. It is yellow glass and not green, although both colors of glass from this era will glow under a black (ultraviolet) light. There is no such color as green Vaseline! Most companies had their own name for this color, be it Canary or yellow. A petroleum jelly product (first made in early 1930s) lent the glass this commonly mentioned color name.

The Aunt Polly oval vegetable, sugar lid, shakers, and butter dish are the magical finds for collectors wanting to acquire them. Obtaining only the blue butter top or bottom can create an aggravation, however. Butter bottoms in green or iridescent are plentiful since U.S. Glass butter bottoms are interchangeable. The starred butter bottom design also fits Cherryberry, Strawberry, and U.S. Swirl as well as Aunt Polly tops. That extra source of butter bottoms is the reason that the **butter top** prices are so much more than bottoms in green and iridescent. However, there is **no blue color** in those other U.S. Glass patterns mentioned; so, there have always been fewer butter bottoms to be discovered in blue!

	Green, Iridescent	Blue
Bowl, 4¾" berry	8.00	18.00
Bowl, 4¾", 2" high	18.00	
Bowl, 5½" one handle	15.00	25.00
Bowl, 7¼" oval, handled pickle	15.00	40.00
Bowl, 7⅞" large berry	20.00	45.00
Bowl, 8⅜" oval	55.00	125.00
Butter dish and cover	275.00	225.00
Butter dish bottom	100.00	95.00
Butter dish top	175.00	130.00
Candy, cover, 2-handled	75.00	
Candy, ftd., 2-handled	25.00	50.00
Creamer	30.00	55.00
Pitcher, 8" 48 oz.		215.00
Plate, 6" sherbet	6.00	15.00
Plate, 8" luncheon		20.00
Salt and pepper		250.00
Sherbet	10.00	14.00
Sugar	25.00	30.00
Sugar cover	60.00	165.00
Tumbler, 3⅝", 8 oz.		35.00
Vase, 6½" ftd.	35.00	55.00

AURORA HAZEL ATLAS GLASS COMPANY, Late 1930s

Colors: Cobalt blue, pink, green, and crystal.

Aurora used to be a pattern I recommended as economical when I was asked what cobalt blue pattern could be collected without taking out a second mortgage. Now, I cannot in good conscience call the 4½" small bowls selling at $60.00 each inexpensive! Creamers and tumblers are also vanishing from dealers' inventories. Even with the price of the little bowl now fetching $60.00, an eight place setting of Aurora would not require an equity loan as would some other cobalt blue sets. If you like cobalt blue, here is a smaller pattern to consider. In Texas recently, a collector confided that these were her special Sunday breakfast dishes.

Readers suggest that patterns with a tall creamer and no sugar, such as this one, should have the creamer listed as a milk pitcher. The reason I didn't list it as such was because milk pitchers usually held at least sixteen ounces; this one was a little small for that. However, lending credence to that idea, a collector reported that creamers were given away as premiums for buying a breakfast cereal in her home town. She remembers boxed displays on the counter from which the proprietor handed you one with your purchase. Unfortunately, she could not remember the name of the cereal, but thought it might have been Corn Flakes. Her grandmother had several of the creamer/milk pitchers in her attic!

A few pieces have been found in pink, and these command a price similar to the blue due to their scarcity. The small bowl, creamer, and tumbler have, so far, never been seen in that color. A Canadian reader says pink and green are more readily found there than in the States.

Both green and crystal cereal bowls, cups, and saucers have been found. So far, only collectors of cups and saucers have been very excited over this news. One expressed dismay that there were additional sets to find.

	Cobalt, Pink
Bowl, 4½" deep	60.00
* Bowl, 5⅜" cereal	18.50
Creamer, 4½"	25.00
** Cup	16.00
Plate, 6½"	12.50
*** Saucer	6.00
Tumbler, 4¾", 10 oz.	27.50

*Green $7.00 or crystal $5.00 **Green $7.50 ***Green $2.50

"AVOCADO" NO. 601 INDIANA GLASS COMPANY, 1923–1933

Colors: Pink, green, crystal, and white. (See Reproduction Section.)

Prices for "Avocado" green pitchers continue to escalate; but prices for tumblers have slowed, possibly because so few are being seen that they haven't had a chance to climb! Reproduced pink items have an orange cast to the color, but this does vary. Buyers beware! Prices for pink have finally recovered from those reproduced pitchers and tumblers introduced in 1974; but it is doubtful they will ever again catch the prices of green!

A few sets of milk glass pitchers and tumblers have been discovered. These are sought by both pitcher and "Avocado" collectors. These white items were a part of Indiana's experimenting with that color in the mid-1950s. You will also spot a few Pyramid and Sandwich pieces in white.

Prices for crystal "Avocado" are not advancing as are those for colors. So far, there have only been a few collectors for it. The deep bowl is the piece most often seen. Crystal pitchers have been found, but I have heard of no crystal tumblers, though I suspect they exist.

Reproduced green items are much darker than the original green shown here. Any color you find not in the listing below is a Tiara reproduction. See pages 228 and 229. Any pieces in yellow are of **recent** vintage! It's a pretty **1980s** yellow!

	Crystal	Pink	Green
Bowl, 5¼" 2-handled	10.00	30.00	35.00
Bowl, 6" ftd. relish	9.00	30.00	35.00
Bowl, 7" 1 handle preserve	8.00	30.00	35.00
Bowl, 7½" salad	12.00	45.00	65.00
Bowl, 8" 2-handled oval	11.00	22.00	35.00
Bowl, 9½", 3¼" deep	22.00	125.00	175.00
*** Creamer, ftd.	12.00	30.00	37.50
Cup, ftd., 2 styles		35.00	40.00
* Pitcher, 64 oz.	350.00	900.00	1,200.00
*** Plate, 6⅜" sherbet	5.00	16.00	18.00
** Plate, 8¼" luncheon	7.00	17.00	22.00
Plate, 10¼" 2-handled cake	14.00	40.00	60.00
Saucer, 6⅜"		22.00	24.00
*** Sherbet		55.00	65.00
*** Sugar, ftd.	12.00	32.00	37.50
* Tumbler	35.00	175.00	275.00

* Caution on pink. The orange-pink is new!
* White: Pitcher $400.00; Tumbler $35.00.
** Apple design $10.00. Amber has been newly made.
*** Remade in dark shade of green.

BEADED BLOCK IMPERIAL GLASS COMPANY, 1927–1930s

Colors: Pink, green, crystal, ice blue, Canary, iridescent, amber, red, opalescent, and milk white.

An upward surge in prices has brought Beaded Block out of the china closet. There were over 50 pieces for sale at a recent show I attended in Florida. In Houston, there were almost double that. The dilemma for collectors, now, is whether to pay the price being asked or do without. Patterns run in cycles and Beaded Block is hot now. Prices for colored and opalescent Beaded Block have risen rapidly and there have been few indications that that will change in the near future. Collectors seem to buy all colors and do not concentrate on only one as has been the tradition in other patterns.

The bountiful colors found in Beaded Block exceed most other patterns in this book. It is the **primary** Depression pattern that is mislabeled by unknowing dealers. I have seen crystal Beaded Block bowls labeled Sandwich glass and priced accordingly.

Square Beaded Block plates are commonly found while **round** plates are scarce. Most round "plates" were transformed into bowls. (The edges of plates were rolled up to make a bowl.) That made size variances in this pattern and a major headache for collectors. **The sizes listed here were all obtained from actual measurements of the pieces and not those listed in catalogs.** The two-handled jelly which most companies called a cream soup measures from 4¾" to 5". Be sure to read the section on measurements at the bottom of page 5! Company listings were more nearly approximations as I have discovered after nearly 30 years of research.

Imperial originally made Beaded Block in the late 1920s and early 1930s. I say "originally" because Imperial reissued pink and iridized pink in the late 1970s and early 1980s. These pieces are easily spotted since they are marked **IG** in the bottom. When I visited the factory in 1981, I was told that the white was made in the early 1950s and the **IG** mark (for Imperial Glass) was first used about that time. Only a few marked pieces of Beaded Block are found, but they include the white covered pear pictured below. This two-part candy in the shape of a large pear is found infrequently. Pears have been found in yellow, green, and amber. Amber seems to be the more easily found color and usually they are seen on the West Coast. These generally are priced in the $250 to $350 range; but I have seen them offered for as much as $695. The key word is offered.

Pink and white Beaded Block pitchers continue to be found, but not in the numbers of green and crystal. With all this collecting of Beaded Block, even the price of the green pitcher has increased.

A red Lily bowl (4½") is the only Beaded Block item found in that color! It is on every collectors wish list! Several of these were found in central Ohio years ago, but I have seen only one lately.

The 6" vases in cobalt and pink are really not Beaded Block. They have no beading and no scalloped edge as do all the other pieces except candy bottoms. Imperial called these tall pieces "footed jellies." These were attained at groceries with a product inside. One found with the original label read "Good Taste Mustard Seed, 3½ oz., Frank Tea & Spice Co., Cin., O." Remember, these are "go-with" pieces and not truly Beaded Block.

Beaded Block comes with both frosted and plain squares in the designs. Few Depression glass collectors make any distinction in price or collectibilty of the two styles.

	*Crystal, Pink, Green, Amber	Other Colors
Bowl, 4⅞"-5" 2-handled jelly	20.00	32.00
** Bowl, 4½" round lily	18.00	30.00
Bowl, 5½" square	20.00	32.00
Bowl, 5½" 1 handle	20.00	32.00
Bowl, 6" deep round	25.00	35.00
Bowl, 6¼" round	25.00	35.00
Bowl, 6½" round	25.00	35.00
Bowl, 6½" 2-handled pickle	30.00	40.00
Bowl, 6¾" round, unflared	25.00	35.00
Bowl, 7¼" round, flared	30.00	40.00
Bowl, 7½" round, fluted edges	30.00	40.00
Bowl, 7½" round, plain edge	30.00	40.00
Bowl, 8¼" celery	35.00	50.00
Candy, pear shaped	295.00	350.00
Creamer	25.00	45.00
*** Pitcher, 5¼", pint jug	85.00	
Plate, 7¾" square	20.00	30.00
Plate, 8¾" round	25.00	45.00
Stemmed jelly, 4½"	20.00	35.00
Stemmed jelly, 4½", flared top	20.00	35.00
Sugar	25.00	45.00
Vase, 6" bouquet	25.00	37.50

* All pieces 25% to 40% lower. ** Red $295.00 *** White $195.00, pink $175.00

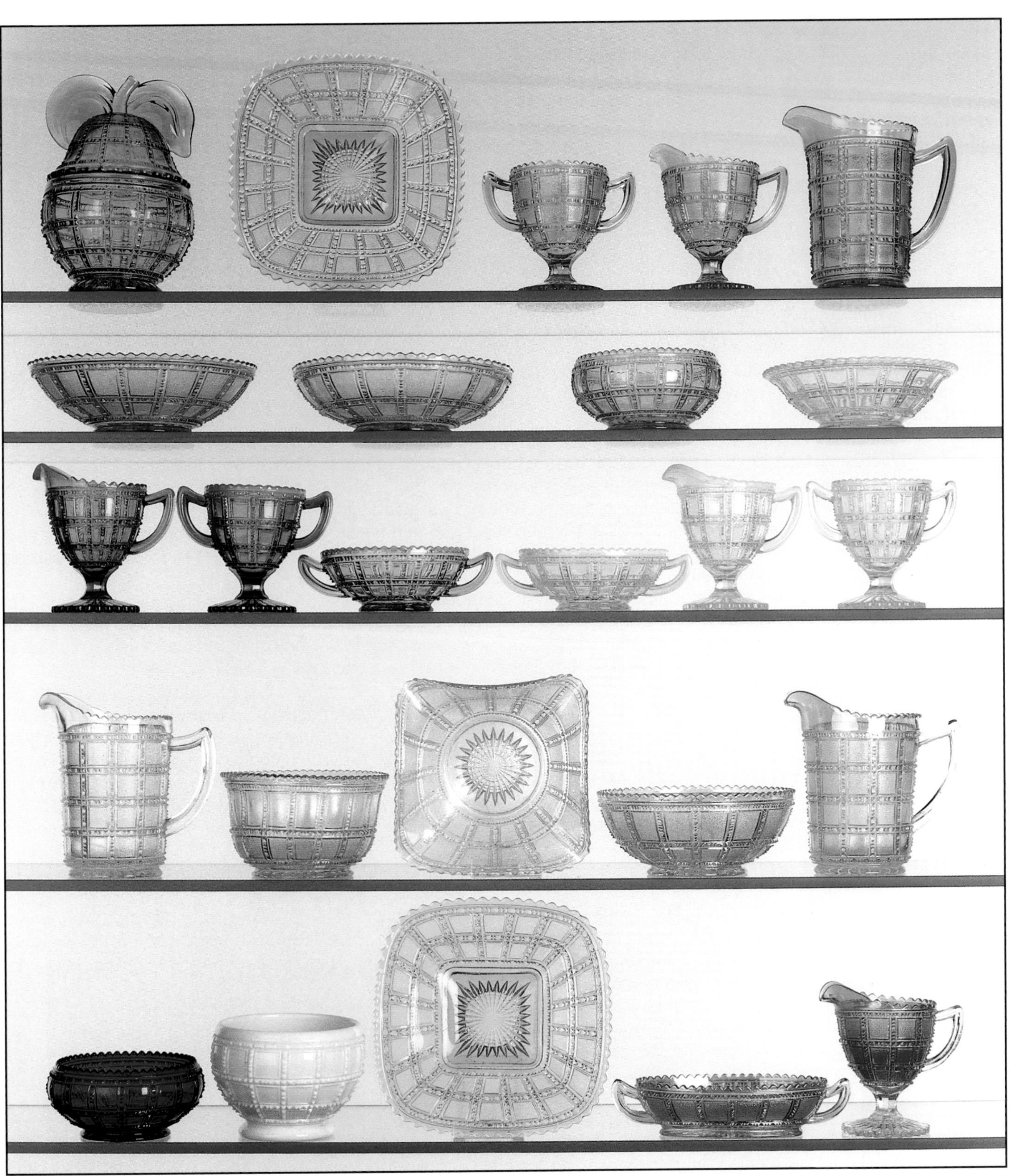

BLOCK OPTIC, "BLOCK" HOCKING GLASS COMPANY, 1929–1933

Colors: Green, pink, yellow, crystal, and some amber and blue.

Collectors (who thought they had completed sets) are now searching for a Block Optic console bowl, grill plates, and 3½" short wines. That short wine has finally been found in green after being seen in pink for years. These are like the elusive short Cameo wines and just as hard to find. The true Block Optic grill plate has the same rings and designed center as does the dinner plate. Some collectors have inadvertently bought Hazel Atlas grill plates instead of Anchor Hocking plates. The Hazel Atlas plates are plain centered, non-ringed grill plates; be aware of that when shopping for Block Optic.

Block Optic has always been a pattern chosen by many new collectors of Depression glass since it was broadly dispersed and a piece or two seems to have remained in everyone's family. When new collectors used to ask me to suggest a green or pink pattern, I would cite Block Optic because it was economically priced and a beginner could not only find it easily, but could also afford to buy it. Today, the cost is no longer so inexpensive as it once was! Of course, that goes for anything else we remember from the good old days. As far as collectibility goes, Block continues to be high on the list of collector demand. There is still an abundant supply of essential pieces; and occasionally found items are not completely priced "out of sight" as has happened in other Depression patterns.

The comport (mayonnaise) remains on many collectors' want lists. Pink comports are hard to find, but green ones are more sought; so, the price has almost doubled recently. Center-handled servers are another piece of Block Optic often unrecognized by collectors. A pink server is pictured at the bottom of page 22. Not all collectors want one in their sets. However, I'll pass along a comment I overheard in Texas in February. A collector was explaining to her friend that she used hers "all the time, for just about everything."

The 4¼" diameter bowl with a height of 1½" is difficult to find and appears to be made thicker than most Block Optic. The 7" salad bowl has become the high priced bowl in this set. It is rarely seen. A pricing error in one of my earlier books called attention to the piece and sent the price skyrocketing earlier; but, it continues its upward trend.

There are variations in handles and slight differences in style to make **a total of five *styles* of creamers and sugars** that can be collected in Block Optic. There are four basic **shapes** but five **styles.** In yellow, only the fancy handled, rounded type has been found. There are three styles of pink creamer/sugar sets, flat bottomed and two cone-shaped pairs. One of those cone styles has a base that is plain whereas the other has a rayed base. (This is true of many of Hocking's patterns. Some tumblers or stems also show variations of plain and ribbed bases.) In green creamers/sugars, there are two cone-shaped styles with one of these having pointed handles, the flat bottomed variety, and the rounded style with plain handles. I have never seen a green, fancy handled set like the yellow ones.

A reader sent some information about the green butter dish top. Over the years I have probably seen 15 or 20 green Block butter tops for every bottom. I had supposed that the heavy top had smashed many of the bottoms since it is somewhat difficult to hold as you lower it on the bottom. The **tops** were sold as a butter holder in old ice boxes. This **top slid into a metal holder** eliminating the need for a glass bottom! They must have sold well!

I get many letters concerning frosted or satinized Block Optic. Hocking, as well as other companies, satinized (frosted by using camphoric acid) many of their dinnerware lines. Evidently, these were special orders or promotions since many were hand decorated with flowers or fruit. For years, collectors shied away from these pieces; but lately, I've begun to notice more collectors buying satinized wares. Frosted items in Block Optic are beginning to command the price of their unfrosted counterparts. Until recently, these pieces sold 20 or 25 percent less if you could sell them at all. Even though these pieces are more scarce, lack of a **strong demand** has kept the price in line. That is one of the lessons beginners need to learn as soon as possible about collectibles. Rarity does not always determine price! **Demand** is the puissant determining factor of price!

A tumble-up set has been found explaining how they were marketed. A stopper in a bottle was marked "Bareé Fragrant Bath Salts Paris, New York." The tumbler was probably a measuring device for the salts.

Some green Block is found with a black foot or stem. As far as I can determine, it was a common occurrence in the early 1930s for glass companies to mix colors on a single piece. In fact, it was rather the "in" thing to do! Black, amber, blue, and pink feet (or tops) were often found on stems and other footed items. These, too, used to be ignored; but I have encountered collectors searching for these recently.

You may find Deco decorated pink candy dishes. I have seen more than one of these in my travels; thus, these candies may also have been a special order or promotional item at one time. Sixty-five years later, the paint tends to be worn on these; so, finding one in mint condition is a treasure. Many of the stems in this pattern have undergone significant price increases in the last few years. New collectors and the paucity of stems available have contributed to this. Be aware that many pink stems are light in color and do not match the normally found pink pieces very well. Not only are stems scarce, but how many pink serving pieces have you seen lately?

There is enough crystal Block Optic being found that you could put a basic set together if you wished to do so. You probably will have to inform dealers you are searching for crystal since many carry only colored Block Optic to shows. Presently, only the crystal butter dish has a premium value. Other crystal pieces sell for a little less than prices of green. Don't totally dismiss it. Crystal Block Optic could not only set a lovely table but might someday be as collectible as the colored ware because of its relative scarcity.

BLOCK OPTIC (cont.)

	Green	Yellow	Pink
Bowl, 4¼" diam., 1⅜" tall	9.00		12.00
Bowl, 4½" diam., 1½" tall	27.50		30.00
Bowl, 5¼" cereal	15.00		30.00
Bowl, 7¼" salad	175.00		
Bowl, 8½" large berry	30.00		35.00
* Bowl, 11¾" rolled-edge console	55.00		75.00
** Butter dish and cover, 3" x 5"	50.00		
Butter dish bottom	30.00		
Butter dish top	20.00		
*** Candlesticks, 1¾" pr.	120.00		80.00
Candy jar & cover, 2¼" tall	60.00	75.00	60.00
Candy jar & cover, 6¼" tall	60.00		150.00
Comport, 4" wide mayonnaise	90.00		90.00
Creamer, 3 styles: cone shaped, round, rayed-foot & flat (5 kinds)	13.00	13.00	13.00
Cup, four styles	7.00	8.00	7.00
Goblet, 3½" short wine	500.00		500.00
Goblet, 4" cocktail	40.00		40.00
Goblet, 4½" wine	40.00		40.00
Goblet, 5¾", 9 oz.	27.00		32.00
Goblet, 7¼", 9 oz. thin		40.00	
Ice bucket	42.00		75.00
Ice tub or butter tub, open	65.00		100.00
Mug	35.00		
Pitcher, 7⅝", 54 oz., bulbous	80.00		135.00
Pitcher, 8½", 54 oz.	60.00		50.00
Pitcher, 8", 80 oz.	100.00		130.00
Plate, 6" sherbet	3.00	3.00	3.00
Plate, 8" luncheon	7.00	8.00	7.00
Plate, 9" dinner	25.00	45.00	38.00
Plate, 9" grill	75.00	50.00	

	Green	Yellow	Pink
Plate, 10¼" sandwich	25.00		25.00
Plate, 12¾"	30.00	30.00	
Salt and pepper, ftd.	45.00	95.00	90.00
Salt and pepper, squatty	125.00		
Sandwich server, center handle	75.00		75.00
Saucer, 5¾", with cup ring	10.00		8.00
Saucer, 6⅛", with cup ring	10.00		8.00
Sherbet, non-stemmed (cone)	4.00		
Sherbet, 3¼", 5½ oz.	6.00	10.00	7.50
Sherbet, 4¾", 6 oz.	18.00	20.00	18.00
Sugar, 3 styles: as creamer	12.50	12.50	12.50
Tumbler, 3 oz., 2⅝"	25.00		28.00
Tumbler, 5 oz., 3½", flat	25.00		28.00
Tumbler, 9½ oz. flat, 3 13/16" flat	15.00		15.00
Tumbler, 10 or 11 oz., 5" flat	22.00		18.00
Tumbler, 12 oz., 4⅞" flat	28.00		28.00
Tumbler, 15 oz., flat, 5¼"	45.00		40.00
Tumbler, 3 oz., 3¼", ftd.	30.00		30.00
Tumbler, 9 oz. ftd.	18.00	22.00	17.00
Tumbler, 6", 10 oz. ftd.	35.00		35.00
Tumble-up night set	70.00		
Tumbler, 3" only	55.00		
Bottle only	15.00		
Vase, 5¾" blown	350.00		
Whiskey, 1⅝", 1 oz.	40.00		45.00
Whiskey, 2¼", 2 oz.	32.00		32.00

* Amber $45.00

** Green clambroth $250.00, blue $550.00, crystal $135.00

*** Amber $50.00

"BOWKNOT" MANUFACTURER UNKNOWN, PROBABLY LATE 1920S

Color: Green.

"Bowknot" is a minor Depression glass pattern that has captivated some persistent collectors! Their demand for "Bowknot" has caused price increases on bowls and tumblers because those items were already inadequately supplied. "Bowknot" remains a mystery pattern. Should you ever run across any documentation (magazine or catalog ads), please send it to me!

Only seven pieces of "Bowknot" are known, but I continue to receive letters from novice collectors who feel that they have found the first "Bowknot" creamer and sugar. Fostoria patterns "June" and "Romance" have a bow; but neither of these patterns were made in green. If you find a **green** "Bowknot" creamer or sugar or any green piece not listed in this pattern, give me a call or send a picture!

The critical detail to look for in "Bowknot" is inner rim roughness (irr) on bowls and sherbets. Add to that a cup with no saucer and two different style tumblers with no pitcher and you have a real enigma. That cup has driven collectors bananas for years trying to ascertain why there is only a cup and no saucer. My first meeting with John Davis, founder of the Peach State Depression Glass Club, was a discussion on that very problem. I sold him some cups for $3.00 each in 1973 and no saucer has yet appeared to our knowledge.

I had a troublesome time finding a cereal bowl without damage! The price has escalated on **perfect** pieces. Often dealers do not display some of the smaller patterns such as "Bowknot" at glass shows. After all, it takes up the same space to show popular cups such as Mayfair, as it does "Bowknot" cups. Space is valuable. I have found that "Bowknot" pieces sell. However, you may have to ask dealers if they have any in their inventory.

Item	Price
Bowl, 4½" berry	20.00
Bowl, 5½" cereal	35.00
Cup	9.00
Plate, 7" salad	15.00
Sherbet, low ftd.	20.00
Tumbler, 5", 10 oz.	25.00
Tumbler, 5", 10 oz. ftd.	25.00

CAMEO, "BALLERINA," or "DANCING GIRL" HOCKING GLASS COMPANY, 1930–1934

Colors: Green, yellow, pink, and crystal w/platinum rim. *(See Reproduction Section.)*

Cameo pattern was manufactured by Hocking Glass Company in the early 1930s, evidently incorporating a pattern design named "Springtime" from Monongah Glass Company (which had been bought by Hocking). Several of their patterns were altered or continued by Hocking. Monongah's glass was plate etched and made in crystal, and was usually gold trimmed. There are collectors now looking for "Springtime" and it is relatively scarce in comparison to Cameo.

The Cameo centered-handled sandwich server and short (3½") wines are still not turning up with any regularity. A couple of short pink wines have been found recently, but no green ones. I bought a center-handled server at the Heisey show last year. It had been purchased eight years earlier for $125 at an auction in Lancaster, Ohio, the home of Anchor Hocking. The owner and his brothers had been mould makers and had made many glassware moulds for Hocking. Sadly, two of the brothers have since died; but in talking with them, they shared some valuable information which I will try to impart where apropos.

I receive more letters and calls about Cameo saucers than any other piece of Cameo. The **real Cameo saucer has an *indented* cup ring.** Hocking made very few of these indented saucers. They ordinarily made a dual purpose saucer/sherbet plate for their patterns. The saucer has a distinct **indented** ring **(1¾" center).** I am now receiving calls about yellow saucers. I assume that should yellow Cameo saucers appear **(which have never yet been seen),** they would have the **same center measurement** as the green ones!

The yellow Cameo butter dish and milk pitcher are remarkably evasive. Yellow Cameo cups, saucer/sherbet plates, footed tumblers, grill, and dinner plates were heavily promoted by Hocking. These five pieces are abundant! Prices on commonly found yellow pieces have begun to climb. If you find it attractive, now may be the time to acquire a set!

Green Cameo is one of the most alluring Depression glass patterns. Most collectors cannot afford every piece made. Collecting six or eight of each stem and every tumbler can set you back several thousand dollars. Most purchase only one or two sizes of tumblers and stems. You can still assemble a large set of green Cameo without investing an enormous amount of money as long as you stay away from buying the rarer pieces. In other patterns, it is nearly impossible to amass a large set by avoiding rare items.

Cameo has two styles of grill plates. (A grill plate is a sectioned or divided plate that keeps the food separated. They were used mostly in restaurants and "grills" of that day; hence the name.) One has tab handles and one does not. Both styles are common in yellow. The green grill with the tab or closed handles is harder to find and priced accordingly. The 10½" rare, rimmed dinner or flat cake plate is like the heavy edged (no tabs) grill plate without the dividers! The regular dinner plate has a large center as opposed to the small centered sandwich plate. The less expensive sandwich plate is often priced as the more expensive dinner plate; be sure to avoid that trap!

The darker green bottles with Cameo design (shown below) are marked on the bottom "Whitehouse Vinegar." These were sold with vinegar — and a cork. Glass stoppers, however, are found atop water bottles. These stoppers do not have a Cameo pattern on them, but are plain, paneled stoppers with hollow centers.

All **miniature** pieces in Cameo are **new!** No small Cameo (children's) dishes were ever made during the Depression era. See the Reproduction Section in the back of the book for information on this. A new importer is making a sometimes weakly patterned shaker in pink, cobalt blue, and a darker shade of green than the original color. If new shaker tops are the first thing you notice — beware!

CAMEO (cont.)

	Green	Yellow	Pink	Crystal, Plat
Bowl, 4¼" sauce				6.00
Bowl, 4¾" cream soup	150.00			
Bowl, 5½" cereal	33.00	33.00	150.00	6.50
Bowl, 7¼" salad	60.00			
Bowl, 8¼" large berry	45.00		175.00	
Bowl, 9" rimmed soup	75.00		135.00	
Bowl, 10" oval vegetable	35.00	42.00		
Bowl, 11", 3-legged console	85.00	110.00	70.00	
Butter dish and cover	235.00	1,500.00		
Butter dish bottom	140.00	500.00		
Butter dish top	95.00	1,000.00		
Cake plate, 10", 3 legs	25.00			
Cake plate, 10½" flat	110.00		175.00	
Candlesticks, 4" pr.	110.00			
Candy jar, 4" low and cover	90.00	110.00	495.00	
Candy jar, 6½" tall and cover	185.00			
Cocktail shaker (metal lid) appears in crystal only			900.00	
Comport, 5" wide mayonnaise	40.00		195.00	
Cookie jar and cover	55.00			
Creamer, 3¼"	24.00	22.00		
Creamer, 4¼"	28.00		125.00	
Cup, 2 styles	15.00	7.50	85.00	5.50
Decanter, 10" with stopper	185.00			225.00
Decanter, 10" with stopper, frosted (stopper represents ⅓ value of decanter)	40.00			
Domino tray, 7" with 3" indentation	150.00			
Domino tray, 7" with no indentation			250.00	125.00
Goblet, 3½" wine	900.00		900.00	
Goblet, 4" wine	80.00		225.00	
Goblet, 6" water	60.00		175.00	
Ice bowl or open butter, 3" tall x 5½" wide	185.00		700.00	265.00

	Green	Yellow	Pink	Crystal, Plat
Jam jar, 2" and cover	185.00			160.00
Pitcher, 5¾", 20 oz. syrup or milk	250.00	2,000.00		
Pitcher, 6", 36 oz. juice	65.00			
Pitcher, 8½", 56 oz. water	60.00	1,500.00		500.00
Plate, 6" sherbet	5.00	2.50	90.00	2.00
Plate, 7" salad				3.50
Plate, 8" luncheon	12.00	11.00	33.00	4.00
Plate, 8½" square	50.00	250.00		
Plate, 9½" dinner	22.00	10.00	85.00	
Plate, 10" sandwich	20.00		55.00	
** Plate, 10½" rimmed dinner	110.00		175.00	
Plate, 10½" grill	12.00	8.00	50.00	
Plate, 10½" grill with closed handles	75.00	6.00		
Plate, 10½" with closed handles	12.00	12.00		
Platter, 12", closed handles	25.00	40.00		
Relish, 7½" ftd., 3 part	35.00			160.00
* Salt and pepper, ftd. pr.	70.00		900.00	
Sandwich server, center handle	6,500.00			
Saucer with cup ring	195.00			
Saucer, 6" (sherbet plate)	5.00	2.50	90.00	
Sherbet, 3⅛" molded	16.00	40.00	75.00	
Sherbet, 3⅛" blown	18.00		75.00	
Sherbet, 4⅞"	38.00	45.00	100.00	
Sugar, 3¼"	21.00	20.00		
Sugar, 4¼"	27.50		125.00	
Tumbler, 3¾", 5 oz. juice	33.00		90.00	
Tumbler, 4", 9 oz. water	30.00		80.00	9.00
Tumbler, 4¾", 10 oz. flat	30.00		95.00	
Tumbler, 5", 11 oz. flat	30.00	60.00	95.00	
Tumbler, 5¼", 15 oz.	80.00		135.00	
Tumbler, 3 oz. ftd. juice	65.00		135.00	
Tumbler, 5", 9 oz. ftd.	28.00	17.50	115.00	
Tumbler, 5¾", 11 oz. ftd.	70.00		135.00	
Tumbler, 6⅜", 15 oz. ftd.	500.00			
Vase, 5¾"	235.00			
Vase, 8"	40.00			
Water bottle (dark green) Whitehouse vinegar	25.00			

* Beware Reproductions

** Same as flat cake plate

CHERRYBERRY U.S. GLASS COMPANY, EARLY 1930s

Colors: Pink, green, crystal; some iridized.

Cherryberry collecting was begun by Strawberry collectors. There was little recognition of this pattern, except for those who were buying Strawberry and were constantly finding cherries instead of strawberries. Now, Cherryberry has become a credible Depression glass pattern with a few carnival glass supporters invading our territory to secure the iridescent pitchers, tumblers, and butter dishes, the most valuable pieces in both collectible areas. Not only do collectors of Cherryberry and carnival glass appreciate these, but collectors of butters and pitchers snare them, too.

Crystal is the rarest "color"; yet, there are few collectors seeking it. As with other U.S. Glass Company patterns, many pieces have rough mould seams.

Color inconstancies of green are causing an additional problem for Cherryberry collectors. The green can be found from a very yellow hue to a blue one. There is not as much color variance with the pink, but there are some pieces that are distinctly lighter than others. Some collectors worry about matching color hues; if you are one of these, this may not be the pattern for you.

This is another U.S. Glass pattern that has no cup or saucer and has a plain butter base. If all these U.S. Glass patterns are "sister" patterns, then Strawberry and Cherryberry are twins. You can only differentiate them by an inspection of the fruits.

	Crystal, Iridescent	Pink, Green
Bowl, 4" berry	6.50	12.00
Bowl, 6¼", 2" deep	50.00	125.00
Bowl, 6½" deep salad	20.00	25.00
Bowl, 7½" deep berry	20.00	28.00
Butter dish and cover	145.00	185.00
Butter dish bottom	77.50	100.00
Butter dish top	67.50	85.00
Comport, 5¾"	18.00	28.00
Creamer, small	12.00	22.50
Creamer, 4⅝" large	18.00	42.50

	Crystal, Iridescent	Pink, Green
Olive dish, 5" one-handled	9.00	22.00
Pickle dish, 8¼" oval	9.00	22.00
Pitcher, 7¾"	175.00	185.00
Plate, 6" sherbet	6.00	12.00
Plate, 7½" salad	8.00	20.00
Sherbet	6.50	11.00
Sugar, small open	12.00	22.50
Sugar, large	15.00	30.00
Sugar cover	30.00	65.00
Tumbler, 3⅝", 9 oz.	23.00	38.00

CHERRY BLOSSOM JEANNETTE GLASS COMPANY, 1930–1939

Colors: Pink, green, Delphite (opaque blue), crystal, Jadite (opaque green), and red. (See Reproduction Section.)

Time and education have now made collecting Cherry Blossom a credible choice again! In the early 1970s, collecting this Depression glass pattern was all the rage. Then, in 1973, reproductions occurred and scared people away. For a while, dealers were rejecting the acquisition of Cherry Blossom because it was not selling due to the reproductions in the market place. If you are a beginner, turn to the Reproduction section in the back of the book for your instruction on Cherry Blossom repros. (See page 230 – 231.) Almost all pieces in pink Cherry Blossom and most green pieces have increased in price over the last two years, indicating a flux of new buyers; but prices on basic dinnerware pieces have really pulled this pattern past the hiatus. It's delightful to see collectors enjoying it again.

Prices have inflated past pre-repro days except for the pink shakers that still have a long way to go. The dilemma with shakers is not only the large number of reproductions made, but that many collectors are willing to buy these to have a pair of shakers for their sets. I continue to get many calls and letters on pink Cherry shakers. The stories I've heard told at auctions and estate sales boggles the mind! Ask yourself, why would anyone offer you something worth more than a $1,000.00 for only a few hundred...or less? **Only two pairs of original pink Cherry Blossom shakers were ever documented;** so the possibility of your discovering another old pair at a bargain price is on par with winning the lottery. The odds are not on your side. I've learned never to say "never," however. People are still discovering scarce Depression glass, even today.

The 9" platter is the hardest piece to find (after genuine shakers). I have only seen **one** green 9" platter! (Measure this platter **outside edge to outside edge**.) Even with this explicit explanation I have calls for verification if I really mean outside edge. I **do!** The 11" platter measures 9" from the **inside to inside** rim and that common piece is not the rare 9" platter.

The only other problem in collecting Cherry Blossom aside from finding it, is the proclivity of inner rim chips, nicks, or those famous "chigger bites" as some auctioneers like to term them. Inner rim roughness (irr) was caused as much from stacking glass together as from using it. You can safely store dishes with proper sized paper plates between them. This is particularly true at glass shows where stacks of plates are often handled over and over. Why do customers look and handle every plate only to proclaim that they already have those?

Pieces of Cherry Blossom that are harder to acquire include the aforementioned 9" platter, mugs, flat iced teas, soup and cereal bowls, and the 10" green grill plate. That grill plate has never even been found in pink; yet, there are two sizes of grill plates in green. The 9" one can be found without much difficulty. Mint condition grill plates are a prize!

Crystal Cherry Blossom is sometimes spotted. Generally, it is the two-handled bowl that sells in the $20.00 to $25.00 range. It is scarce, but there is not enough crystal found to be collectible as a set. A few red pieces have been found, but the reproduction red wiped out most collectors' desire to own red.

The letters AOP in listings and advertisements stand for "all over pattern" on the footed tumblers and rounded pitcher. The large, footed tumblers and the AOP pitcher come in two styles. One style has a scalloped or indented foot while the other is merely round with no indentations. Sherbets are also found scalloped or with round bottoms. The letters PAT stands for "pattern at the top" illustrated by the flat bottomed tumblers and pitchers.

There are some known experimental pieces of Cherry such as a pink cookie jar, pink five-part relish dishes, orange with green trim slag bowls, and amber children's pieces. You can see most of these pieces in *Very Rare Glassware of the Depression Era* books. Pricing on experimental items is difficult to determine; but do not pass them up if the price is right—for you! There is always some market demand for rare items of Depression glassware. Just make sure the piece is old and not a modern day plaything from Taiwan!

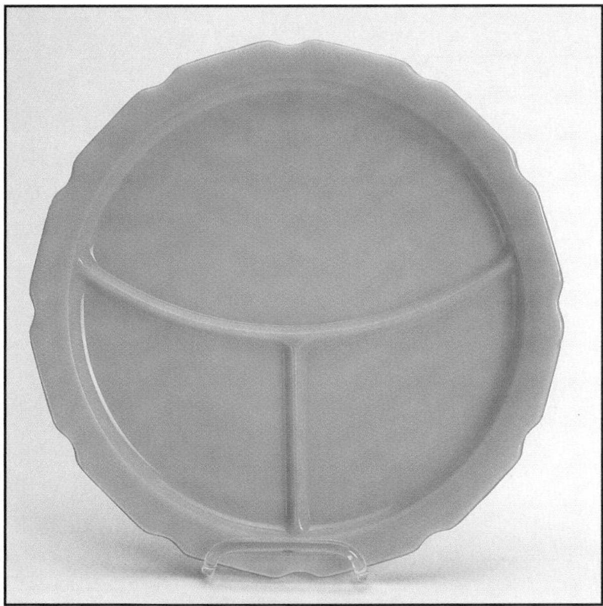

CHERRY BLOSSOM (cont.)

	Pink	Green	Delphite
Bowl, 4¾" berry	20.00	19.00	15.00
Bowl, 5¾" cereal	52.00	47.50	
Bowl, 7¾" flat soup	90.00	85.00	
* Bowl, 8½" round berry	50.00	50.00	50.00
Bowl, 9" oval vegetable	50.00	40.00	50.00
Bowl, 9" 2-handled	50.00	75.00	28.00
** Bowl, 10½", 3 leg fruit	100.00	100.00	
Butter dish and cover	90.00	110.00	
Butter dish bottom	20.00	25.00	
Butter dish top	70.00	85.00	
Cake plate (3 legs) 10¼"	35.00	40.00	
Coaster	14.00	14.00	
Creamer	23.00	22.00	20.00
Cup	23.00	23.00	20.00
Mug, 7 oz.	295.00	200.00	
*** Pitcher, 6¾" AOP, 36 oz.			
scalloped or round bottom	65.00	65.00	80.00
Pitcher, 8" PAT, 42 oz. flat	60.00	60.00	
Pitcher, 8" PAT, 36 oz.			
footed	60.00	60.00	
Plate, 6" sherbet	8.00	10.00	10.00
Plate, 7" salad	25.00	22.00	
**** Plate, 9" dinner	26.00	27.00	20.00
***** Plate, 9" grill	32.00	32.00	

	Pink	Green	Delphite
Plate, 10" grill		125.00	
Platter, 9" oval	950.00	1,100.00	
Platter, 11" oval	55.00	55.00	45.00
Platter, 13" and 13" divided	70.00	70.00	
Salt and pepper			
(scalloped bottom)	1,300.00	1,100.00	
Saucer	5.00	6.00	5.00
Sherbet	20.00	22.00	16.00
Sugar	14.50	17.50	18.00
Sugar cover	20.00	20.00	
Tray, 10½" sandwich	30.00	33.00	22.00
Tumbler, 3¾", 4 oz.			
footed AOP	20.00	22.00	22.00
Tumbler, 4½", 9 oz. round			
foot AOP	40.00	40.00	22.00
Tumbler, 4½", 8 oz.			
scalloped foot AOP	40.00	40.00	22.00
Tumbler, 3½", 4 oz.			
flat PAT	22.00	33.00	
Tumbler, 4¼", 9 oz.			
flat PAT	18.00	26.00	
Tumbler, 5", 12 oz.			
flat PAT	70.00	85.00	

* Yellow – $395.00
** Jadite – $325.00
*** Jadite – $325.00
**** Translucent green – $225.00
***** Jadite – $85.00

CHERRY BLOSSOM — CHILD'S JUNIOR DINNER SET

	Pink	Delphite
Creamer	50.00	50.00
Sugar	50.00	50.00
Plate, 6"	12.50	14.00 (design on bottom)
Cup	40.00	45.00
Saucer	6.50	7.25
14 Piece set	340.00	360.00

Original box sells for $35.00 extra with pink sets.

CHINEX CLASSIC MacBETH-EVANS DIVISION OF CORNING GLASS WORKS, LATE 1930s–EARLY 1940s

Colors: Ivory, ivory w/decal decoration.

Ivory tint Chinex Classic supporters are attempting to match all the different floral arrangements found on this and related Cremax ware. It is hard enough to find the scroll decorated Chinex Classic pattern; but spotting a piece you need only to have it adorned with a decal other than the one you want, is exasperating. Windsor castle decal items are the most fascinating decoration to collectors; darker blue trims seem to be more popular than the lighter blue or brown.

My personal preference leans to the blue trimmed Windsor castle decal decoration. I have found a butter bottom as you can see in the bottom photo. What I do not know is whether the top has a Windsor castle decal or just a blue trim. I suspected that it would have the Windsor castle decal; but I have had two reports from readers saying the top is plain on the ones they found. A reader was kind enough to set me up with a Chinex floral top. Unfortunately, I have not been able to find the bottom for that one. The floral decal on that top is like those pieces on the left of the photograph. If you have either of these butter parts to match mine that are missing in the photos, please let me know!

Chinex is found in the Pittsburgh area more than any other part of the country. Of course, MacBeth-Evans was just down the road and that has a great deal to do with this! However, a major portion of recent finds have been in Canada where Corning was a mainstay in glass production. Chinex was advertised as ware resistant to crazing and chipping which explains its relatively good condition when you find it today.

The plainer, undecorated ivory pieces are still awaiting collectors' notice. You will have limited competition in searching for Chinex Classic; that might be a determining factor for some new collectors! Prices are more reasonable than for many other patterns of this time period. If a limited amount of funds are available, you might consider looking here. Undecorated Chinex works wonderfully in the microwave according to several collectors. I must admit that I have never tried it; so remember to test it first by putting it in for a **short** time (a few seconds) and checking for hot spots just as you would any other dish not designed **specifically** for microwave usage. After removing the piece from the microwave, be sure to place it on a place mat or some surface that is not cold. A sudden temperature change may crack it. I speak from experience on Fire-King Ovenware that we used. Do not try this with decorated pieces of Chinex — just the unadorned!

Remember, butter bottoms look like Cremax pattern on the edge rather than Chinex. The butter tops have the scroll like design that distinguishes Chinex, but this scroll design is missing from the butter bottoms. The bottom has a plain "pie crust" edge. The floral or castle designs will be inside the base of the butter, and apparently surrounding the knob of the top if the top has a decoration.

	Browntone or Plain Ivory	Decal Decorated	Castle Decal
Bowl, 5¾" cereal	5.50	9.00	15.00
Bowl, 6¾" salad	12.00	20.00	40.00
Bowl, 7" vegetable	14.00	25.00	40.00
Bowl, 7¾" soup	12.50	22.00	40.00
Bowl, 9" vegetable	11.00	25.00	40.00
Bowl, 11"	17.00	35.00	45.00
Butter dish	55.00	75.00	150.00
Butter dish bottom	12.50	27.50	50.00
Butter dish top	42.50	47.50	100.00
Creamer	5.50	10.00	20.00
Cup	4.50	6.50	15.00
Plate, 6¼" sherbet	2.50	3.50	7.50
Plate, 9¾" dinner	4.50	8.50	22.00
Plate, 11½" sandwich or cake	7.50	13.50	28.00
Saucer	2.00	4.00	6.00
Sherbet, low ftd.	7.00	11.00	25.00
Sugar	6.00	10.00	20.00

CIRCLE HOCKING GLASS COMPANY, 1930s

Colors: Green, pink, and crystal.

Green Circle can be collected in sets with time and patience. It is reasonably priced, just not easily found. It will definitely take more than good luck to gather a pink set. As you can see by the lack of pink in the picture, I am not having much luck obtaining it either.

Two styles of cups add to the peculiarity of Circle. The flat bottomed style fits a saucer/sherbet plate while the rounded cup takes an indented saucer. I finally found an indented saucer for my round cup, but no saucer/sherbet plate for the flat one.

There have never been accounts of tumblers, pitchers, or bowls in pink. I presume only a pink luncheon set was made, but two styles of cups makes one wonder what else might be available. Notice, I have now separated the colors in the pricing. If you have a piece of pink not priced, let me know.

Green colored stems with crystal tops are more easily found than plain green stems. In many Elegant patterns, two-toned stems are often more expensive! This is not the case for Circle! Few collectors currently desire the crystal topped items. Due to that factor, you can usually buy these rather inexpensively. I prefer the two-toned variations!

Circle is often bought by collectors of kitchenware (particularly reamer collectors). The 80 oz. Circle pitcher with a reamer top is treasured by them! A predicament with the pitcher and reamer is that color dissimilarities on these pitchers make it difficult to obtain a reamer separately that correctly matches the green hue of the pitcher. That 80 oz. pitcher shown here is more yellow when contrasted with the other green pieces. The 60 oz. pitcher has made the biggest price leap by doubling since the last book. When have you seen one?

Both the 9⅜" and 5¼" green bowls pictured, have ground bottoms. At Hocking, ground bottoms usually indicated early production pieces. The 5" flared bowl is shown on the right front of the photograph. It is clearly a darker shade of green when compared with the other pieces.

	Green	Pink
Bowl, 4½"	8.00	
Bowl, 5¼"	10.00	
Bowl, 5" flared, 1¾" deep	14.00	
Bowl, 8"	18.00	
Bowl, 9⅜"	20.00	
Creamer	9.00	20.00
Cup (2 styles)	5.00	7.00
Decanter, handled	60.00	
Goblet, 4½" wine	15.00	
Goblet, 8 oz. water	11.00	
Pitcher, 60 oz.	75.00	
Pitcher, 80 oz.	35.00	
Plate, 6" sherbet/saucer	2.00	5.00
Plate, 8¼" luncheon	4.00	10.00
Plate, 9½"	12.00	
Plate, 10" sandwich	14.00	
Saucer w/cup ring	2.50	3.00
Sherbet, 3⅛"	4.00	10.00
Sherbet, 4¾"	6.00	
Sugar	7.00	20.00
Tumbler, 3½", 4 oz. juice	8.00	
Tumbler, 4", 8 oz. water	9.00	
Tumbler, 5", 10 oz. tea	18.00	
Tumbler, 15 oz. flat	25.00	

CLOVERLEAF HAZEL ATLAS GLASS COMPANY, 1930 – 1936

Colors: Pink, green, yellow, crystal, and black.

Cloverleaf is one Depression pattern that is readily recognized by the non-collecting public. Those shamrocks are symbols of good luck which is what you need in finding some of the rarer pieces. In show displays, I see green Cloverleaf commemorating St. Patrick's Day and black, Halloween! One combination of crystal and black with orange decorations made a dynamite Halloween display.

Pictured below are every piece of yellow Cloverleaf known. The grill plate (divided in three parts) must suffice as a dinner-sized plate. The candy dish, shakers, and bowls are all difficult to find in yellow. I have seen only five yellow bowls at all the glass shows I attended in the last year. You will be able to find the other pieces, but all yellow items are getting a little scarce and pricey!

There appear to be equal numbers of collectors for black, green, and yellow Cloverleaf. Few are latching onto pink or crystal since they are limited to only a luncheon set. Besides the traditional luncheon pieces in pink, a berry bowl and a flared, 10 oz. tumbler exist! That pink tumbler was quite sparsely distributed and has not been found in crystal at all. How many pink berry bowls have you seen? I've seen more yellow berry bowls than pink.

All Cloverleaf colors are selling well with green ruling. Every known piece of green is pictured on page 36. In green, the 8" bowl and tumblers are selling briskly. All the bowls, as well as grill plates and tumblers are becoming more difficult to round up. Of the three styles of tumblers pictured, it is the flat, straight sided one that is rarely found. Buy them if you get a chance — even if you do not collect them! There'll be someone who does!

Black Cloverleaf prices have slowed somewhat with the small ash trays being ignored while the larger ones are still selling — albeit slowly. The black sherbet plate and saucer are the same size. The saucer has no Cloverleaf design in the center, but the sherbet plate does! These sherbet plates still turn up in stacks of saucers occasionally; so keep your eyes open! Cloverleaf pattern comes on both the inside and outside of the pieces. That does not make a difference in value or collectibility. In order for the black to show the pattern, moulds had to be designed with the pattern on the visible side of pieces. On transparent pieces, the pattern could be on the bottom or the inside and it would still show. In black, the pattern on the bottom of a plate makes it look like a plain black plate. Over the years, transparent pieces also were made using the moulds designed for the black; so, you now find these pieces with designs on both sides.

CLOVERLEAF (Cont.)

	Pink	Green	Yellow	Black
Ash tray, 4", match holder in center				65.00
Ash tray, 5¾", match holder in center				90.00
Bowl, 4" dessert	35.00	35.00	35.00	
Bowl, 5" cereal		50.00	50.00	
Bowl, 7" deep salad		55.00	65.00	
Bowl, 8"		80.00		
Candy dish and cover		55.00	115.00	
Creamer, 3⅝" ftd.		10.00	20.00	20.00
Cup	9.00	9.00	11.00	20.00
Plate, 6" sherbet		5.00	8.00	40.00
Plate, 8" luncheon	11.00	8.00	14.00	15.00
Plate, 10¼" grill		25.00	28.00	
Salt and pepper, pr.		40.00	125.00	100.00
Saucer	3.00	3.00	4.00	6.00
Sherbet, 3" ftd.	9.00	12.00	14.00	22.00
Sugar, 3⅝" ftd.		10.00	20.00	20.00
Tumbler, 4", 9 oz. flat		60.00		
Tumbler, 3¾", 10 oz. flat flared	28.00	45.00		
Tumbler, 5¾", 10 oz. ftd.		28.00	38.00	

COLONIAL, "KNIFE AND FORK" HOCKING GLASS COMPANY, 1934–1936

Colors: Pink, green, crystal, and opaque white.

Green Colonial was strongly promoted! We know this because so much more green is found today than any other color. Hocking may have urged their buyers of pink wares toward the popular Mayfair or Miss America. Pink Colonial has several rarely found items that have kept a large number of collectors away from it. Were there to be a run toward pink Colonial, there is no telling where the prices would go!

My inventory of green Colonial has been wiped out at the last few shows, and I can't find enough crystal Colonial to make all the collectors wanting it happy. Color preferences in collecting have been cyclical for the nearly 30 years that I have been involved in Depression glass. Green is again preferred! No, wait it's pink! Dealers can never outguess collecting whims. Collectors have, recently, started to buy pink and crystal instead of the more expensive green. The problem in collecting anything other than green is limited availability.

Prices for crystal stems have risen! For years, these sold for about half the price of green because there were few collectors for them. The true scarcity of crystal stemware is now being discovered. No stems are found in pink. Some collectors are mixing crystal stems with their pink sets. Only footed tumblers are found in pink; do not mistake them for stems. You can see all three sizes of pink footed tumblers in the bottom photograph on page 38. (You should be able to distinguish the footed tumblers in the bottom photo from the green stems pictured in the top photo.) This has been something of a problem for beginning collectors; there are hundreds of these impassioned newcomers writing me for answers to their questions. You did know that collecting is contagious!

In the top photo on page 38 is the first beaded top green Colonial pitcher to appear. Notice that it is gold trimmed. A pink one was bought at an auction in the Cincinnati area in 1975. I bought the green one about 30 miles north of there almost twenty years later. To date, only one of each color has been spotted — though I doubt only one of each was made!

Colonial soup bowls (both cream and flat), cereals, mint shakers, and dinner plates are still difficult to obtain in all colors. The vertical ridges on Colonial have a tendency to chip; when examining a piece, look at those ridges first. Always take the top off of any shaker to check for damage. I once bought a shaker with a top I couldn't unloosen and when I soaked it free, I found it had been glued on to cover a large chip in the top edge. Cereal bowls in any color may be the most difficult to obtain in all of Depression glass.

Colonial mugs seldom are found today. However, you could find the next one for $5.00. It just takes work and a little luck to find these deals. I discover a few bargains in my travels, but I put a minimum of 45,000 miles on my vehicles every year. Also, I shopped over 450 different antique malls last year — many, several times! With enough looking, you are bound to spot a bargain once in a while.

The 11 ounce Colonial tumbler measures 2¾" across the top while the 12 ounce measures exactly 3". These two tumblers are repeatedly confused. It is easier to measure across the top than to measure the contents if you are out shopping! The spooner stands 5½" tall while the sugar without a lid is only 4½" high. That inch makes a big difference in price.

The cheese dish consists of a wooden board with an indented groove on which the glass lid rests. I showed a pink one in the thirteenth edition.

	Pink	Green	Crystal
Bowl, 3¾" berry	52.50		
Bowl, 4½" berry	18.00	20.00	10.00
Bowl, 5½" cereal	65.00	100.00	35.00
Bowl, 4½" cream soup	75.00	75.00	65.00
Bowl, 7" low soup	65.00	65.00	30.00
Bowl, 9" large berry	35.00	35.00	25.00
Bowl, 10" oval vegetable	35.00	40.00	22.00
Butter dish and cover	700.00	55.00	45.00
Butter dish bottom	450.00	32.50	30.00
Butter dish top	250.00	22.50	15.00
Cheese dish		225.00	
Cream/milk pitcher, 5", 16 oz.	65.00	25.00	20.00
Cup (white 8.00)	10.00	14.00	7.00
Mug, 4½", 12 oz.	500.00	800.00	
+ Pitcher, 7", 54 oz.	50.00	55.00	30.00
*+ Pitcher, 7¾", 68 oz.	70.00	80.00	40.00
Plate, 6" sherbet	6.00	9.00	3.00
Plate, 8½" luncheon	10.00	11.00	6.00
Plate, 10" dinner	55.00	65.00	30.00
Plate, 10" grill	25.00	25.00	15.00
Platter, 12" oval	35.00	25.00	20.00

	Pink	Green	Crystal
Salt and pepper, pr.	140.00	150.00	60.00
Saucer/sherbet plate (white 3.00)	6.00	9.00	3.00
Sherbet, 3"	25.00		
Sherbet, 3⅜"	12.00	15.00	8.00
Spoon holder or celery, 5½"	135.00	130.00	90.00
Stem, 3¾", 1 oz. cordial		30.00	20.00
Stem, 4", 3 oz. cocktail		25.00	17.00
Stem, 4½", 2½ oz. wine		28.00	17.00
Stem, 5¼", 4 oz. claret		25.00	20.00
Stem, 5¾", 8½ oz. water		35.00	25.00
Sugar, 4½"	25.00	15.00	10.00
Sugar cover	65.00	25.00	15.00
Tumbler, 3", 5 oz. juice	22.00	25.00	15.00
** Tumbler, 4", 9 oz. water	22.00	22.00	15.00
Tumbler, 5⅛" high, 11 oz.,	35.00	42.00	22.00
Tumbler, 12 oz. iced tea	52.00	52.00	24.00
Tumbler, 15 oz. lemonade	65.00	75.00	45.00
Tumbler, 3¼", 3 oz. ftd.	17.00	25.00	13.00
Tumbler, 4", 5 oz. ftd.	32.00	42.00	22.00
*** Tumbler, 5¼", 10 oz. ftd.	50.00	50.00	27.50
Whiskey, 2½", 1½ oz.	15.00	16.00	12.00

*Beaded top $1,100.00 **Royal ruby $110.00 ***Royal ruby $160.00 +With or without ice lip

COLONIAL

COLONIAL BLOCK HAZEL ATLAS GLASS COMPANY, EARLY 1930s

Colors: Green, crystal, black, pink, and rare in cobalt blue; white in 1950s.

Colonial Block is mostly collected in green. Some die-hard collectors are taking on the task of a pink set. You will spot an occasional crystal piece and white creamer and sugar sets. A few black and frosted green Colonial Block powder jars are being found. A cobalt blue Colonial Block creamer is shown in my *Very Rare Glassware of the Depression Years, Second Series.* So far, no sugar bowl has been found to match it. It's regrettable that more cobalt blue was not made!

Sets of green are possible to assemble, though **not very easily.** Both 4" and 7" bowls, butter tub, sherbets, and the pitcher are the pieces most often lacking in collections. You may now add to that the newly listed juice tumbler! You can check out one of these rare tumblers in *Very Rare Glassware of the Depression Years, Fifth Series.* How a small pattern like this can have so many hard to find pieces is difficult for new collectors to understand. To begin with, it probably was regionally distributed; and some of those hard to find pieces may have been premiums for something that did not sell well. Maybe the pattern was simply not accepted. Today, those are mysteries.

The goblet to the right of the green pitcher is Colonial Block and not Block Optic as it is often mislabeled. Some Block Optic collectors use these heavy goblets with their sets considering they are economical compared to those of Block Optic. The heavier Colonial Block goblets are unquestionably more durable when weighed against the thinner Block Optic. More green sherbets have been found recently! Sherbets went undiscovered for years until reported in this book.

Many pieces of Colonial Block are marked **HA**, but not all. The **H** is over top the **A** which confuses some inexperienced dealers and collectors who assume that this is the symbol for Anchor Hocking. The anchor is a symbol used by Anchor Hocking and that was not used until after the 1930s.

U.S. Glass made a pitcher similar to Colonial Block. There is little difference in them except most Hazel Atlas pitchers are marked. Collectors today are not as rigid in their collecting standards as they once were. Many collectors will buy either pitcher to go with their set. That is why items that are similar to a pattern, but not actually a part of it, are referred to as "go-with" or "look-alike" pieces. Usually, these items are more reasonably priced.

	Crystal	Pink, Green	White
Bowl, 4"	4.00	8.00	
Bowl, 7"	10.00	22.00	
Butter dish	25.00	45.00	
Butter dish bottom	5.00	12.50	
Butter dish top	20.00	32.50	
Butter tub	25.00	45.00	
Candy jar w/cover	22.00	40.00	
Creamer	6.00	12.00	7.00
Goblet	6.00	12.50	
Pitcher	22.00	45.00	
*Powder jar with lid	12.00	17.50	
Sherbet	4.00	6.00	
Sugar	6.00	9.00	5.50
Sugar lid	6.00	12.00	4.50
Tumbler, 5¼", 5 oz., ftd.		55.00	

*Black $22.50

COLONIAL FLUTED, "ROPE" FEDERAL GLASS COMPANY, 1928–1933

Colors: Green and crystal.

Colonial Fluted was a serviceable pattern that was relentlessly used; you will find most flat pieces with abrasions from heavy use, sharp knives, or tough meat. Knives scratch the surface of most glassware and this pattern testifies to that. Today, you need to choose your menus carefully, if you serve on your collection. I would not advocate a thick grilled steak. Colonial Fluted is normally priced moderately enough to use. Most guests recognize this old glass as antique and treat it with respect.

The "F" in a shield, usually found in the center of many Colonial Fluted pieces, is the symbol used by the Federal Glass Company. Not all pieces of Federal Glass are marked.

Colonial Fluted has been a starter set for many beginning collectors; but today quantities are so limited that a new collector might become discouraged looking for it. Some find it an ideal bridge set; but then, bridge parties are not as plentiful as they once were either. Actually, much of the original advertising for this pattern was for bridge parties. Crystal is seldom collected, except for decaled pieces with hearts, spades, diamonds, and clubs. We have a crystal set to photograph in the future, thanks to my wife's insistence that we needed to show them. (I passed them by as the price was not what I considered economical. I like to be able to, at least, break even on pieces I buy to photograph!)

Colonial Fluted can be mixed with other sets, too, which is a present trend with collectors. There is no dinner plate in the Colonial Fluted pattern. There is a dinner-sized plate made by Federal that goes very well with this which has the roping around the outside of the plate, but not the fluting. There is a grill plate that also goes well with the pattern. It has no roping either. Both of these pieces can expand the number of items in your set without looking out of place. Being made by Federal, they match color wise.

	Green
Bowl, 4" berry	11.00
Bowl, 6" cereal	15.00
Bowl, 6½", deep (2½") salad	35.00
Bowl, 7½" large berry	22.00
Creamer	10.00
Cup	8.00

	Green
Plate, 6" sherbet	3.00
Plate, 8" luncheon	7.00
Saucer	2.00
Sherbet	7.00
Sugar	10.00
Sugar cover	16.00

COLUMBIA FEDERAL GLASS COMPANY, 1938–1942

Colors: Crystal, some pink.

Pink Columbia sells extremely well for a pattern that has only four pieces! Prices continue to increase on crystal bowls, tumblers, and all pink items.

Columbia is another small Federal pattern that is not too plentiful, today. Tumblers in Columbia have always been a problem. Originally, it was finding them; but today, there are other problems. Two sizes of Columbia tumblers have now been corroborated, the 2⅞", 4 ounce juice and 9 ounce water. Both are pictured in the center. Nevertheless, a problem has recently transpired with "like" tumblers. Notice the two juice tumblers pictured in front. The one on the right is marked "France" on the bottom; so devotees of this glass need to be aware of this before paying big bucks for foreign-made glassware. I have had recurrent reports of other sizes of tumblers and have also had other tumblers shown to me at Depression glass shows. So far, these have all turned out to be Duncan and Miller Hobnail and not Columbia. You may find Columbia water tumblers with advertisements for dairy products printed on them. Cottage cheese seems to have been the product of choice.

The elusive snack tray (except in Colorado) is shown standing up in the back left. Many collectors have not known what to look for since it is an unusual piece and shaped differently from most Columbia. The pictures in recent editions have shown the tray so well that collectors are finding these to the point that supply is over running demand right now. These snack plates were found with Columbia cups in a boxed set over twenty-five years ago in northern Ohio. The box was labeled "Snack Sets" by Federal Glass Company. No mention was made of Columbia on the box. Snack trays are also being found with Federal cups **other than Columbia.** I have pictured a bowl and snack set that are designed like the Columbia snack tray in the right hand corner of the photo. They do not have the center design but do have the "winged" tab handles. These are being found in original boxes labeled "Homestead." They were manufactured by Federal, but you decide if you want to use them with your set.

You will find examples of Columbia butter dishes with various flashed colors and floral decal decorations. Some were even satinized (frosted) and others were flashed with color after the satinized finish was applied. Federal must have fervently promoted these since there are so many found today! The supply for this butter dish has always exceeded the demand.

Satinized, pastel-banded, and floral-decaled luncheon sets have been found. These sets are rare. In the past, they were difficult to sell, unless you found a complete set. It was too difficult to find matching pieces. However, lately, there's a movement toward ownership of these.

	Crystal	Pink
Bowl, 5" cereal	18.00	
Bowl, 8" low soup	22.00	
Bowl, 8½" salad	20.00	
Bowl, 10½" ruffled edge	20.00	
Butter dish and cover	20.00	
Ruby flashed (22.00)		
Other flashed (21.00)		
Butter dish bottom	7.50	
Butter dish top	12.50	

	Crystal	Pink
Cup	8.00	25.00
Plate, 6" bread & butter	3.00	15.00
Plate, 9½" luncheon	10.00	35.00
Plate, 11" chop	15.00	
Saucer	2.00	10.00
Snack plate	30.00	
Tumbler, 2⅞", 4 oz., juice	25.00	
Tumbler, 9 oz., water	30.00	

CORONATION, "BANDED RIB," "SAXON" HOCKING GLASS COMPANY, 1936–1940

Colors: Pink, green, crystal, and Royal Ruby.

Coronation pitchers are rarely seen in person, but you can enjoy two views of one on the next page! That pitcher is the one piece missing from most collections of Coronation. Most of these were bought long ago by collectors of pitchers and tumblers because Coronation collectors thought they were way too expensive! All other pieces of Coronation were less than $15.00 and no Coronation collector would shell out $200.00 for a pitcher. Now, avid Coronation collectors are willing to pay the price, but few pitchers are being marketed to satisfy their demands.

Coronation's tumblers are continuously confused with the rarely found Old Colony ("Lace Edge") tumblers. Even my wife blows this one on occasion. Look at the **fine ribs *above* the middle** of the Coronation tumbler. These ribs are missing there on an Old Colony footed tumbler. (Perhaps you can make a mental link between Coronation, a crowning *above* and Coronation ribs *above.)* They say to make the image stick you make it as ridiculous as possible. Maybe you could visualize a crown above ribs! Look at the bottom of page 151 to see the differences. Some collectors purposely buy Coronation tumblers to use with Old Colony since they cost a third as much. That one idea has doubled the price of Coronation tumblers in the last few years. Both are the same shape and color and both were made by Hocking. Just don't accidentally confuse the two since there is quite a price disparity! Of course, if you see Old Colony tumblers priced as Coronation, you had better make that purchase!

Notice that the handles on Royal Ruby Coronation bowls are open; handles on the pink are closed. Two newly discovered bowls in pink have been without handles! They measure 4¼" and 8" like the previously discovered green ones. The smaller pink berry is like the green one in the foreground of the top photo. The items in green Coronation at the bottom of page 43 are shown compliments of Anchor Hocking. They do not include the luncheon plate or small berry bowl, shown in the upper photo. That green crescent salad plate is a rather interesting item for Depression glass. That piece is more common to Elegant patterns. A couple of these have been spied in crystal.

The larger green tumbler in the lower photograph is 5 7/16" tall and holds 14¼ oz. This tumbler has never been seen outside the morgue. The morgue was so named since it contained examples of past (dead production) patterns made by the company. Unfortunately, this was not well kept. Many examples "walked" or were thrown out or given away over the years. It is now under lock! Who knew Depression glass was going to be so significant? Even movie producers are increasingly concerned to show correct dishes in their period movies! Several dealers in Canada have sold large sets of Depression glass to be used in movies being made there. I laughed at some of the prices one dealer in Montreal had on his glassware. Even with the currency exchange it was over fifty percent more than I could sell it for here. A prop buyer for a movie walked in, saw it, and said wrap it up. Who knows where some of our glassware will show up?

Novice dealers still stick big prices on those commonly found red, handled Coronation berry bowls. They have always been abundant! Some years ago a large accumulation was discovered in an old warehouse. They were still in the original boxes. Today, they are still hard to sell; yet, I regularly see them priced for four to five times their worth. Only today, I saw the large, two-handled berry priced for $65.00. It was marked "rare old pigeon blood." That "pigeon blood" term comes from old time collectors who used it to describe dark red glass (not made from the blood of dead birds). One dealer assured me that his Royal Ruby goblets were rare "old pigeon blood" pieces, and very valuable! He thought so — since they were priced at $30.00 each!

Royal Ruby Coronation cups were sold on crystal saucers. Those crystal saucer/sherbet plates are the only common crystal pieces found in Coronation. A few crystal pieces are beginning to turn up besides the crescent salad, but there is little demand for these at present. No Royal Ruby Coronation saucer/sherbet plates have ever been seen. I would not go so far as to say that red saucers do not exist. If I have learned anything in the last twenty-eight years, it is never to say some piece of glass was never made. Royal Ruby is the name of the **red glass that was made by Hocking** and only their red glassware can be called Royal Ruby.

	Pink	Royal Ruby	Green
Bowl, 4¼" berry, handled	7.00	7.00	
Bowl, 4¼", no handles	75.00		45.00
Bowl, 6½" nappy, handled	6.00	18.00	
Bowl, 8" large berry, handled	15.00	18.00	
Bowl, 8", no handles	175.00		175.00
* Cup	5.50	6.50	
Pitcher, 7¾", 68 oz.	550.00		
Plate, 6", sherbet	3.00		
Plate, 8½" luncheon	4.50		45.00
** Saucer (same as 6" plate)	3.00		
Sherbet	8.00		75.00
Tumbler, 5", 10 oz. ftd.	33.00		175.00

*Crystal $4.00 ** Crystal $.50

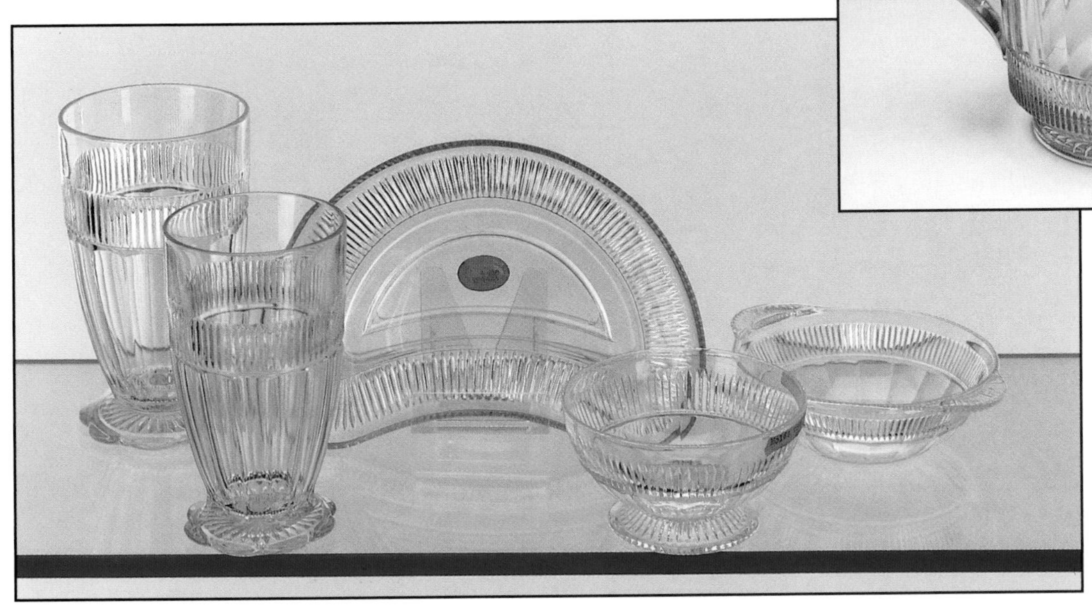

CREMAX MacBETH-EVANS DIVISION OF CORNING GLASS WORKS, LATE 1930s–EARLY 1940s

Colors: Cremax, Cremax with fired-on colored trim or decals.

Cremax is a broad term for several tableware patterns which were manufactured with the ivory glass coloring (called Cremax). These patterns also feature the color as part of the pattern name. For example, there was Cremax Bordette line, with pink, yellow, blue, and green borders; Cremax Rainbow line with pastel pink and green borders; the Cremax Windsor line, with Windsor brown, blue, and green castle decals; and a plain ware simply called Cremax pattern. There was, also, a six-sided center floral ware called Princess pattern and one with a floral spray known as Flora.

The blue Cremax added to the last book created quite a stir in the Cremax world. Although this is commonly seen in Canada and some of those states that border Canada, the Midwest and Southern collectors did not realize that there were so many pieces of this pattern to gather. I have been informed that the lighter robin's egg blue was distributed by Corning almost exclusively in Canada. That darker blue shade is not as common in Canada. Most of the pieces I have found have been in northern states. Notice the distinctly different hues of blue as well as the two shapes. The Delphite colored blue (shown below) has the same shapes as what we are familiar with, but the robin's egg blue has a flat sugar and creamer and a slightly smaller cup. At this time, price both shades of blue about the same as the pieces with decals. Assembling a set of the light blue will take time unless you live near the Canadian border, buy from northern dealers, or surf the Internet!

Cremax Bordette demitasse sets are being found in sets of eight. Some have been on a wire rack. The usual make-up of these sets has been two sets each of four colors: pink, yellow, blue, and green. I have finally obtained three of these to show you. Notice that the interior of these cups are plain.

The bottom to the butter dish in Chinex is often believed to be Cremax. The scalloped edges of the butter bottom are just like the edges on Cremax plates; however, the only butter tops ever found have the Chinex **scroll-like pattern.** Thus, if you find only the bottom of a butter, it is a Chinex bottom! There have been no Cremax butters found.

The green Windsor castle decal is the most difficult colored decal to find on Cremax. The one piece pictured in the top photo on page 45 is the only piece I have ever found! Besides collectors seeking the hexagonal red floral decorated Cremax called Princess (top page 45), there is not much activity in this pattern. Like Chinex, the undecorated ware should be usable in the microwave; but be sure to test it before putting it in for a long time. A Cremax set could be bought rather economically. It was advertised as resistant to chips and made to be in service for years. Most of what you find today is in good shape!

	Cremax	*Blue, Decal Decorated
Bowl, 5¾" cereal	3.50	10.00
Bowl, 7¾" soup	7.00	25.00
Bowl, 9" vegetable	8.00	18.00
Creamer	4.50	10.00
Cup	4.00	5.00
Cup, demitasse	15.00	25.00
Plate, 6¼" bread and butter	2.00	4.00
Plate, 9¾" dinner	4.50	12.00
Plate, 11½" sandwich	5.50	20.00
Saucer	2.00	3.50
Saucer, demitasse	5.00	10.00
Sugar, open	4.50	10.00

*Add 50% for castle decal

"CROW'S FOOT," Paden City Glass Company, Line 412 & Line 890, 1930s

Colors: Ritz blue, Ruby red, amber, amethyst, black, pink, crystal, white, and yellow.

"Crow's Foot" continues to attract new admirers. This new interest has made red and cobalt blue "Crow's Foot" difficult for dealers to keep in stock. "Crow's Foot" is the most frequently used mould blank for Paden City etchings. The squared shape is Line #412, and the round is Line #890. Collectors formerly buying Orchid or Peacock & Rose etched patterns are settling on the unadorned "Crow's Foot" blanks to fill in their gaps. Many new collectors are first attracted to the color and then the pattern! Some are buying only round or square items while others are mixing them. Few are buying amber, crystal, or yellow, but small sets are obtainable in any of those colors.

The red punch bowl has the telltale "Crow's Foot" pattern. One is pictured in the last edition. There are similar punch bowls without the "Crow's Foot" on them. Similar is not enough! If I had a dollar for every time I have heard, "It's just like that, except..." over the years, I would not have to write any more books! A blue punch set should exist; watch for it! Silver decorated designs on cobalt are attractive, and even non "Crow's Foot" collectors will buy them. I have seen several candleholders labeled Cambridge recently; be sure and notice Paden City candles are square based.

Many Paden City red pieces tend to run to amberina (especially tumblers). Some collectors will do without before they add a piece showing yellow color. Amberina is a collector's term for the yellowish tint in pieces that were supposed to be red. It was originally a not thoroughly heated glass mistake and not a color that glass manufacturers tried to make! Despite this, there are now collectors who pursue amberina colored wares!

	Red	Black/ Blue	Other Colors
Bowl, 4⅞", square	25.00	30.00	12.50
Bowl, 8¾" sq.	50.00	55.00	25.00
Bowl, 6"	40.00	35.00	15.00
Bowl, 6½", rd., 2½" high, 3½" base	45.00	50.00	22.50
Bowl, 8½", square, 2-hndl.	50.00	60.00	27.50
Bowl, 10" , ftd.	75.00	75.00	32.50
Bowl, 10", square, 2-hndl.	75.00	75.00	32.50
Bowl, 11", oval	35.00	42.50	17.50
Bowl, 11", square	60.00	70.00	30.00
Bowl, 11", square, rolled edge	65.00	75.00	32.50
Bowl, 11½", 3 ftd., round console	85.00	100.00	42.50
Bowl, 11½", console	75.00	85.00	37.50
Bowl, cream soup, ftd./flat	22.00	22.50	10.00
Bowl, Nasturtium, 3 ftd.	185.00	210.00	90.00
Bowl, whipped cream, 3 ftd.	55.00	65.00	27.50
Cake plate, sq., low pedestal ft.	85.00	95.00	42.50
Candle, round base, tall	75.00	85.00	37.50
Candle, square, mushroom	37.50	42.50	20.00
Candlestick, 5¾"	25.00	30.00	12.50
Candy w/cover, 6½", 3 part (2 styles)	65.00	75.00	25.00
Candy, 3 ftd., rd., 6⅛" wide, 3¼" high	150.00	185.00	75.00
Cheese stand, 5"	25.00	30.00	12.50
Comport, 3¼" tall, 6¼" wide	27.50	32.50	15.00
Comport 4¾" tall, 7⅜" wide	50.00	60.00	35.00
Comport, 6⅝" tall, 7" wide	60.00	75.00	30.00
Creamer, flat	12.50	15.00	6.50
Creamer, ftd.	12.50	15.00	6.50
Cup, ftd. or flat	10.00	12.50	5.00
Gravy boat, flat, 2 spout	85.00	100.00	40.00
Gravy boat, pedestal	135.00	150.00	65.00
Mayonnaise, 3 ftd.	45.00	55.00	22.50
Plate, 5¾"	2.25	3.50	1.25
Plate, 8", round	11.00	13.00	4.50
Plate, 8½", square	12.00	14.00	3.50
Plate, 9¼", round, small dinner	35.00	40.00	15.00
Plate, 9½", rd., 2-hndl.	65.00	75.00	32.50
Plate, 10⅜", rd., 2-hndl.	50.00	60.00	25.00
Plate, 10⅜", sq., 2-hndl.	40.00	50.00	20.00
Plate, 10½", dinner	90.00	100.00	40.00
Plate, 11", cracker	45.00	50.00	22.50
Platter, 12"	50.00	55.00	15.00
Relish, 11", 3 pt.	85.00	100.00	45.00
Sandwich server, rd., center-hndl.	65.00	75.00	32.50
Sandwich server, sq., center-hndl.	45.00	50.00	17.50
Saucer, 6", round	2.50	3.00	1.00
Saucer, 6", square	3.00	3.50	1.50
Sugar, flat	11.00	13.50	5.50
Sugar, ftd.	11.00	13.50	5.50
Tumbler, 4¼"	75.00	85.00	37.50
Vase, 4⅝" tall, 4⅛" wide	70.00	80.00	40.00
Vase, 10¼", cupped	100.00	129.00	45.00
Vase, 10¼", flared	95.00	115.00	32.50
Vase, 11¾", flared	150.00	195.00	65.00

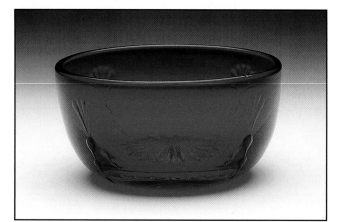

CUBE, "CUBIST" JEANNETTE GLASS COMPANY, 1929–1933

Colors: Pink, green, crystal, amber, white, Ultra Marine, canary yellow, and blue.

Cube is one Depression pattern that attracts the eye of non-collectors. It is commonly mixed up with Fostoria's American by novice collectors, especially the crystal Cube 2⅝" creamer and 2⁹⁄₁₆" sugar on the 7½" round tray. Very little Cube was made in crystal and very little Fostoria American was made in green. The very scarce original pink Fostoria American was really a lavender/pink; so those colors should be no problem. Cube is less vibrant and more wavy in appearance when compared to the brighter, clearer quality of Fostoria's American pattern.

If you locate a Cube-like pitcher shaped differently than the ones pictured on page 49, you probably are the owner of Indiana's Whitehall pattern that is in current production. I receive a lot of letters about these pitchers both as Cube or rare Fostoria! Other pieces of Cube-like pink Whitehall and a darker shade of green are also being made. Cube tumblers are **flat,** as pictured. If you see footed tumblers in any color, they are also Whitehall.

Green Cube is more bothersome to find than the pink, but there are more collectors for pink. The dilemma in collecting pink (after finding it), is locating it in the right tint. Pink Cube varies from a light pink to an orange-pink. You can see these different hues in the bottom photo on the next page. Pitchers always look darker due to thickness, but you can see other color discrepancies. This shows by example how difficult it was for glass factories in the Depression to mass produce **consistent quality** glassware. As glass tanks got hotter, the pink color got lighter. The orange-like shade of pink is troublesome to sell. However, I overheard one collector explain to a dealer that she didn't much care for the color — but now, she'd at least have a pitcher. As supplies dwindle, off colors are becoming more agreeable than they once were! There are two distinct shades of green. At present, the darker shade of green is not as alluring as the ordinarily found green. Both colors of Cube cause matching tint difficulties if ordering by mail or from the Internet. That is one reason it is preferable to attend Depression glass shows and see what you are buying! You might actually be willing to pay a little more for that convenience!

The green item on the left in the top photo is a topless candy. I would have preferred a topless sugar since the lids are interchangeable, and it would have not been as noticeable. Oft times I am lining up new photos or working on other problems at photo sessions and little things like this get by! Prices for pink Cube pitchers and tumblers are rising. Nearly all collectors are looking for four, six, or eight tumblers; as a result, it usually takes longer to find all these tumblers than the pitcher. Be sure to check the pointed sides of the tumblers and pitchers since they chipped on the sides long before the heavy rims did!

The Cube powder jar is three footed and shown in both colors. A few experimental colors have turned up. Canary yellow and two shades of blue have appeared in recent years. Occasionally, these jars are found with celluloid or plastic lids. Powder jars were not made with those lids at the factory. These may have been replacements when tops were broken. Another possibility is that powder bottoms were sold to someone who made non-glass lids to fit the bottoms. In any case, prices below are for intact, original glass lids. The powder jars with other types of lids sell for half or less. Most items from this era which require lids have left only bottoms as their legacy. Today, you sometimes have to buy the complete item to get only the lid. In any case, a celluloid lid is better than no lid at all!

	Pink	Green
Bowl, 4½" dessert	6.50	7.00
*Bowl, 4½" deep	8.00	
**Bowl, 6½" salad	10.00	15.00
Bowl, 7¼", pointed edge	16.00	18.00
Butter dish and cover	70.00	65.00
Butter dish bottom	20.00	20.00
Butter dish top	45.00	45.00
Candy jar and cover, 6½"	30.00	33.00
Coaster, 3¼"	9.00	9.00
***Creamer, 2⅝"	2.00	
Creamer, 3⁹⁄₁₆"	10.00	12.00
Cup	7.50	9.00
Pitcher, 8¾", 45 oz.	210.00	235.00
Plate, 6" sherbet	3.50	4.00
Plate, 8" luncheon	10.00	11.00
Powder jar and cover, 3 legs	30.00	33.00
Salt and pepper, pr.	35.00	35.00
Saucer	2.50	2.50
Sherbet, ftd.	10.00	11.00
***Sugar, 2⅜"	2.00	
Sugar, 3"	7.00	8.00
Sugar/candy cover	15.00	15.00
Tray for 3⁹⁄₁₆" creamer and sugar, 7½" (crystal only)	4.00	
Tumbler, 4", 9 oz.	72.50	75.00

*Ultra Marine – $40.00 **Ultra Marine – $80.00
***Amber or white – $3.00; crystal $1.00

"CUPID" PADEN CITY GLASS COMPANY, 1930s

Colors: Pink, green, light blue, peacock blue, black, canary yellow, amber, and crystal.

"Cupid" continues to surprise me. Cup and saucers have been found in Minnesota and Wisconsin. The owner of the saucers thought they were more valuable than the cups; so, the twain never met to my knowledge. I'm sure there will be others and I will be able to show them eventually. Only in rare instances are saucers harder to find than cups; but that takes years to determine. Collectors are not finding much etched Paden City glassware. Thus, the popular "Cupid" etched pieces have been sporting some serious prices. Most Paden City etchings have increased an average of twenty to thirty percent. All that searching every cubbyhole and crevice to find any piece of "Cupid" must be working since I have seen more pieces for sale in the last year than at any time in the past. I suspect more is being made available due to the prices being asked.

I previously mentioned that the bottom to a tumble up had been found, but no new reports of a tumbler or another bottom have been forthcoming. A 10" vase, in the style commonly found in Peacock & Rose, has been seen with "Cupid" etch; and several pink and green casseroles have been found. I previously pictured a casserole in black with a silver overlaid pattern.

Light blue "Cupid" pieces found include a 10½" plate, rolled edge candle, mayonnaise, and a 6¼" comport. I'd love to find a liner and spoon for that mayonnaise!

Samovars are rarely found, but are fetching big bucks when they are! I might point out that to be a "Cupid" samovar, the "Cupid" pattern has to be etched on it. Mould shape does not make the pattern; the etched pattern itself does!

Prices are the most difficult part of writing this book. Even with all the help from other dealers around the country, prices will never please everyone. If you own a piece, you want it to be highly priced; however, if you are wanting to buy the same piece and do not own it, you want the price to be low! Keep in mind that only one sale at a high price does not mean that everyone would be willing to pay that price. That is especially true of rare glass and Internet auctions. If two people want something and have more money than they know what to do with, then there may be a wild price paid. That does not mean that item will sell for that price the next time — or maybe ever again. Only you can determine whether a piece of glass is worth that price to you.

New discoveries in etched Paden City patterns are not unusual! Most pieces were shown in catalogs with no etchings; and until a piece shows up with a particular etching, there is no way to know if it exists in that pattern.

Those center-handled pieces were called sandwich trays and the odd, center-handled Paden City bowls were called candy trays.

No new information has been forthcoming regarding the "Cupid," "Made in Germany" silver overlay vases that have been found in cobalt and lavender in Arizona and Florida.

	Green/Pink
Bowl, 8½" oval-ftd.	275.00
Bowl, 9¼" ftd. fruit	295.00
Bowl, 9¼" center-handled	275.00
Bowl, 10¼", fruit	215.00
Bowl, 10½", rolled edge	200.00
Bowl, 11" console	200.00
Cake plate, 11¾"	200.00
Cake stand, 2" high, ftd.	215.00
* Candlestick, 5" wide, pr.	245.00
Candy w/lid, ftd., 5¼" high	395.00
Candy w/lid, 3 part	295.00
** Casserole, covered	495.00
*** Comport, 6¼"	195.00
Creamer, flat	175.00
Creamer, 4½" ftd.	150.00
Creamer, 5" ftd.	150.00
Cup	75.00
Ice bucket, 6"	325.00
Ice tub, 4¾"	325.00
**** Lamp, silver overlay	495.00
***** Mayonnaise, 6" diameter, fits on 8" plate, spoon, 3 pc.	210.00
****** Plate, 10½"	150.00
Samovar	995.00
Saucer	25.00
Sugar, flat	175.00
Sugar, 4¼" ftd.	150.00
Sugar, 5" ftd.	150.00
Tray, 10¾" center-handled	215.00
Tray, 10⅞" oval-ftd.	250.00
Vase, 8¼" elliptical	650.00
Vase, fan-shaped	450.00
Vase, 10"	315.00
Water bottle w/tumbler	500.00

*Blue $395.00
**Black (silver overlay) $600.00
*** Blue – $225.00
**** Possibly German
***** Blue – $295.00
****** Blue – $225.00

DELLA ROBBIA #1058 WESTMORELAND GLASS COMPANY, LATE 1920s – 1940s

Colors: Crystal, crystal w/applied lustre colors, milk glass, pink, and opaque blue.

This Della Robbia listing is truly only a start from the sparse catalog information that I own. Let me know of additional pieces or of other information to which you may have access. The popularity of Della Robbia is extending to new collectors and supplies of many pieces are beginning to be severely limited.

You will find Della Robbia in crystal, pink, opaque blue, milk glass, and crystal with applied lustre colors. Notice that the fruits on each piece are apples, pears, and grapes. There are a couple of other patterns similar to Della Robbia, but both include a banana in the design. I have pictured this design with banana on the bottom of page 54. This is not Della Robbia, but shown for comparison.

Two diverse color variations in the fruit decorations occur. All apples are red; pears, yellow; and grapes, purple; but the brightness of the colors applied is distinct. Look at the pictures on page 54 and compare them to the punch set at the bottom of page 53. The darker colored fruits on page 54 are the variation that is most in demand. The dilemma with this darker color is that the applied lustre scuffs easily. However, most collectors prefer not to mix the two.

If you have ever tried to carry around an 18" plate for that punch set, you will understand why you see so few of them for sale at shows. Special boxes have to be adapted to hold it. I was supposed to borrow a set of the lighter shade from one of my former customers in Kentucky, but my schedule didn't work out to go get it this time. Living in Florida does have some disadvantages for photography, but not enough to convince me to move back.

Note the two one-handled nappies on the second row of page 54. The one on the left is heart shaped and more desired. The bowl in the center of that row can also be found with the edge flatter than the one shown. Dinner plates now top $100.00, if you can find one. All serving pieces need to be **carefully examined** for wear. Remember the prices below are for **mint** condition pieces and not ones that are worn or scuffed.

The moulds of a Della Robbia pitcher and tumbler were used to make some carnival colored water sets. These were made for Levay just as were pieces of red English Hobnail. They were made in light blue and amethyst carnival and maybe other colors I have not seen. If you have more information than this, please share it!

Note that Della Robbia is pattern #1058. On page 56 at the bottom of the catalog reprint are candlesticks and a console bowl in pattern #1067. They are not priced in my listings and neither is the Zodiac plate on page 57 because they are not Della Robbia!

Item	Price
Basket, 9"	195.00
Basket, 12"	295.00
Bowl, 4½", nappy	27.50
Bowl, 5", finger	35.00
Bowl, 6", nappy, bell	35.00
Bowl, 6½", one hndl. nappy	35.00
Bowl, 7½", nappy	45.00
Bowl, 8", bell nappy	55.00
Bowl, 8", bell, hndl.	75.00
Bowl, 8", heart, hndl.	165.00
Bowl, 9", nappy	95.00
Bowl, 12", ftd.	135.00
Bowl, 13", rolled edge	135.00
Bowl, 14", oval, flange	250.00
Bowl, 14", punch	300.00
Bowl, 15", bell	225.00
Candle, 4"	35.00
Candle, 4", 2-lite	125.00
Candy jar w/cover, scalloped edge	100.00
Candy, round, flat, chocolate	95.00
Comport, 6½", 3⅝" high, mint, ftd.	30.00
Comport, 8", sweetmeat, bell	110.00
Comport, 12", ftd., bell	125.00
Comport, 13", flanged	125.00
Creamer, ftd.	18.00
Cup, coffee	18.00
Cup, punch	15.00
Pitcher, 32 oz.	250.00
Plate, 6", finger liner	12.00
Plate, 6⅛", bread & butter	10.00
Plate, 7¼", salad	22.00
Plate, 9", luncheon	35.00
Plate, 10½", dinner	100.00
*Plate, 14", torte	115.00
Plate, 18"	200.00
Plate, 18", upturned edge, punch bowl liner	200.00
Platter, 14", oval	165.00
Punch bowl set, 15 pc.	750.00
Salt and pepper, pr.	55.00
Salver, 14", ftd., cake	150.00
Saucer	10.00
Stem, 3 oz., wine	28.00
Stem, 3¼ oz., cocktail	25.00
Stem, 5 oz., 4¾", sherbet, high foot	25.00
Stem, 5 oz., sherbet, low foot	22.00
Stem, 6 oz., champagne	25.00
Stem, 8 oz., 6", water	30.00
Sugar, ftd.	18.00
Tumbler, 5 oz., ginger ale	25.00
Tumbler, 8 oz., ftd.	30.00
Tumbler, 8 oz., water	25.00
Tumbler 11 oz., iced tea, ftd.	35.00
Tumbler 12 oz., iced tea, bell	38.00
Tumbler 12 oz., iced tea, bell, ftd.	38.00
Tumbler 12 oz., 5³⁄₁₆", iced tea, straight	40.00

*Pink $135.00

DELLA ROBBIA

Westmoreland's Handmade,
Hand-Decorated Crystal

WESTMORELAND GLASS COMPANY

Handmade Glassware of Quality

GRAPEVILLE, PENNSYLVANIA

SINCE 1889

DELLA ROBBIA

"Della Robbia" Pattern in Crystal with Applied Lustre Colors.

"Della Robbia"

"Zodiac" Plate

TOP ROW: *1058/9"/L126. Plate, Luncheon. 1058/7½"/L126. Plate, Salad. 1058/8 oz./L126. Goblet. 1058/11 oz./L126. Ice Tea, Footed. 1058/8 oz./L126. Tumbler, Footed. 1058/L126/3¼ oz. Cocktail. 1058/L126. Sherbet, Low Foot.*

SECOND ROW: *1058/L126. Sugar and Cream Set, Individual.* "Della Robbia." *1058/L126. Salt, with Chrome Top. 1058/L126. Pepper, with Chrome Top. 1058/L126. Cup and Saucer. 1058/8 oz./L126. Tumbler. 1058/6½"/L126. Nappy, Cupped, Handled.*

THIRD ROW: *1058/6½"/L126. Mint, Footed. 1058/4"/L126. Candlestick. 1058/12"/L126. Bowl, Bell. 1058/½ lb./L126. Candy Jar and Cover. 1058/4½"/L126. Nappy, Round.*

BOTTOM ROW: *1058/14"/L126. Plate, Torte. 1058/8"/L126. Nappy, Heart Shape, Handled. 25/15"/L126. Plate,* "Zodiac." Pictures the twelve signs of the Zodiac. An attractive serving piece for sandwiches or canapes.

DIAMOND QUILTED, "FLAT DIAMOND" IMPERIAL GLASS COMPANY, LATE 1920s–EARLY 1930s

Colors: Pink, blue, green, crystal, black; some red and amber.

Diamond Quilted can only be collected in sets of pink, green, or blue. Pink and green have more pieces available than the other colors. Blue can be found, but it will take a stoke of luck in attaining very much. Not all pieces are found in the other colors. Red and amber Diamond Quilted are elusive, but there are few collectors of either color. Black Diamond Quilted can be found with searching, but it will take a long time to accumulate a luncheon set. There are some Fenton pieces (pictured in earlier editions) that can be mixed with this pattern quite well.

Diamond Quilted has no dinner-sized plate. Lack of a dinner plate stops a few admirers who plan on entertaining with their collection. I have always said that you should collect what you like. With some inventiveness, you can enjoy a less than perfect sized pattern. A willowy young lady told me she found the small size luncheon plates were a blessing to serve on since "The plate fills up faster; and you need less food!"

Hazel Atlas made a quilted diamond pitcher and tumbler set in pink, green, cobalt blue, and a light blue similar to the one shown here. They are often confused with Imperial's Diamond Quilted. The quilting on Hazel Atlas pieces ends in a **straight line** around the top of each piece. Notice **Imperial's** Diamond Quilted pattern ends **unevenly** in points. You may also notice that the diamond designs on Hazel Atlas pieces are flat as opposed to those Imperial ones that are curved. The Hazel Atlas pitcher is flat and shaped like the straight sided pitcher so commonly seen in Royal Lace.

Punch bowls are the creme de la creme of this pattern. The lady who bought both the pink **and** green Diamond Quilted punch bowl sets at the Chicago show a few years ago, dropped by my table to let me know she still enjoyed displaying them. I have only seen one set for sale since then.

Flat black pieces have the design on the bottom. Thus, the design on the plate can only be seen if it is turned over. Most black items have the pattern on the inside.

The candle shown in the catalog ad at the bottom of the page is occasionally confused with Windsor Diamond. Console sets at 65¢ and a dozen candy dishes in assorted colors for $6.95 would be quite a bargain today! No, **I do not have any for sale at that price.** This ad is from a 1930s catalog. I mention that since I continue to receive letters every year from people trying to order glass from these old catalog ads placed throughout the book! One arrived today asking that I send several sets. Nobody ever orders just **one** set. It has to be multiples! One individual said she understood if I had to add postal charges to the order. Considering the ad states the six sets weigh thirty pounds, she was being generous! One lady wrote three times! I am still not sure she ever understood that these were 69-year-old advertisements.

	Pink, Green	Blue, Black
Bowl, 4¾" cream soup	10.00	20.00
Bowl, 5" cereal	7.50	15.00
Bowl, 5½" one handle	7.50	22.00
Bowl, 7" crimped edge	9.00	22.00
Bowl, 7", straight	12.00	20.00
Bowl, 10½", rolled edge console	20.00	60.00
Cake salver, tall 10" diameter	60.00	
Candlesticks (2 styles), pr.	25.00	50.00
Candy jar and cover, ftd.	65.00	
Compote, 6" tall, 7¼" wide	45.00	
Compote and cover, 11½"	95.00	
Creamer	12.00	20.00
Cup	9.50	17.50
Goblet, 1 oz. cordial	12.00	
Goblet, 2 oz. wine	12.00	
Goblet, 3 oz. wine	12.00	
Goblet, 6", 9 oz. champagne	11.00	
Ice bucket	55.00	85.00
Mayonnaise set:		
ladle, plate, comport	36.00	56.00
Pitcher, 64 oz.	50.00	
Plate, 6" sherbet	4.00	7.00
Plate, 7" salad	6.00	11.00
Plate, 8" luncheon	9.00	14.00
Punch bowl and stand	450.00	
Plate, 14" sandwich	15.00	
Sandwich server, center handle	25.00	50.00
Saucer	4.00	6.00
Sherbet	9.00	16.00
Sugar	12.00	20.00
Tumbler, 9 oz. water	9.00	
Tumbler, 12 oz. iced tea	9.00	
Tumbler, 6 oz. ftd.	8.50	
Tumbler, 9 oz. ftd.	12.50	
Tumbler, 12 oz. ftd.	15.00	
Vase, fan, dolphin handles	55.00	75.00
Whiskey, 1½ oz.	8.00	

DIANA FEDERAL GLASS COMPANY, 1937–1941

Colors: Pink, amber, and crystal.

Pink Diana remains elusive but only the tumbler has had much of a price increase of late. Price advances are not as frenetic as they were five or six years ago when many new collectors started the pattern about the same time! Diana is not as available as it once was, and collectors have been paying more to finish sets that they started! Amber and crystal Diana are not as desirable to collectors as the pink; and it is probably a good thing! Were there to be a collecting rush on either color, the true scarcity would soon be revealed as it was with pink. Diana is one of the **used-to-be less expensive** patterns! I have seen pictures of one collector's rainbow Diana collection — a mixture of the colors. It was charming as she'd arranged it! Creativity is always a plus! Are these mixtures of colors the collecting trend of the future?

Collectors of crystal Diana have found out what collectors of other colors noticed years ago. There are a small number of tumblers available! Tumblers, demitasse sets, candy dishes, shakers, sherbets, and even platters are seldom found in any Diana colors. There are fewer demitasse sets being marketed than in the past. Sets in crystal are more plentiful, as are the sprayed-on cranberry pink or red sets. Flashed red demitasses are selling for $10.00 to $12.00 each. Pink demitasse cup and saucer sets are found occasionally, but you will have to search long and hard for an entire pink set of six on a rack!

The prices listed below are **actual selling** prices for Diana and **not advertised prices.** There is a **major difference** between an advertised price for an item and the price being accepted by both buyer and seller. Rarely have I heard of something selling for more than advertised, but often I have heard of less! Today, dealers coast to coast are sharing information on prices. That's been a tremendous help to me as I work to keep pricing current in these books! The Internet, though a new "tool" with pricing, has to be approached carefully and not taken too literally. I attend as many Depression glass shows as possible and spend many hours checking prices and talking to dealers about what is, and what is not selling — and for what price!

I have finally added the price for the amber 9" salad bowl that was inadvertently left out of earlier editions even though it was pictured. Sorry!

Frosted or satinized pieces of Diana that have shown up in crystal and pink have a few admirers. Some crystal frosted pieces have been trimmed in colors, predominantly red, but you might spot green, yellow, or blue. A set of crystal frosted items with different colored trims is not as bizarre looking as you might surmise! However, achieving any of these specialty sets is a major undertaking unless you spy a complete set to start.

Some new collectors tend to mistake Diana with other swirled patterns such as Swirl and Twisted Optic. The centers of Diana pieces are swirled where the centers of other swirled patterns are plain. That elusive and somewhat odd Diana sherbet is shown in amber and in pink. The spirals on this sherbet are often mistaken for Hocking's Spiral and it causes debate as to its authenticity; but it is shown in an original advertisement for Diana. As with many other patterns, pieces advertised along with a pattern are often accepted as that pattern. An excellent example is the Moderntone tumbler.

	Crystal	Pink	Amber
* Ash tray, 3½"	2.50	3.50	
Bowl, 5" cereal	6.00	10.00	14.00
Bowl, 5½" cream soup	10.00	25.00	20.00
Bowl, 9" salad	12.00	22.00	18.00
Bowl, 11" console fruit	15.00	42.50	18.00
Bowl, 12" scalloped edge	12.00	30.00	20.00
Candy jar and cover, round	16.00	50.00	40.00
Coaster, 3½"	2.50	8.00	10.00
Creamer, oval	8.00	12.00	9.00
Cup	6.00	20.00	9.00
Cup, 2 oz. demitasse and 4½" saucer set	13.00	45.00	
Plate, 6" bread & butter	2.00	5.00	2.00
Plate, 9½"	10.00	20.00	9.00
Plate, 11¾" sandwich	8.00	25.00	10.00
Platter, 12" oval	12.00	33.00	15.00
Salt and pepper, pr.	30.00	85.00	110.00
Saucer	1.50	5.00	2.00
Sherbet	3.00	12.00	10.00
Sugar, open oval	8.00	12.00	8.00
Tumbler, 4⅛", 9 oz.	30.00	50.00	30.00
Junior set: 6 demitasse cups & saucers with round rack	100.00	300.00	

* Green $3.00

DOGWOOD, "APPLE BLOSSOM," "WILD ROSE" MacBETH-EVANS GLASS COMPANY, 1929–1932

Colors: Pink, green, some crystal, Monax, Cremax, and yellow.

Dogwood commands attention as one of the more collected Depression patterns! Pink is the color in demand; and that is excellent, since green is found only sporadically. The large fruit bowl and platter are the nemesis of today's collectors. They were rarely found twenty years ago and now usually enter the market only through a collection being sold.

The reason the large fruit bowls are so difficult to find is that these were sold to someone who frosted the bowls, drilled a hole in the center, and made ceiling globes out of them. These globes sell in the $125.00 range. There is a growing trend among collectors to own Depression glass shades. It's a shame so many bowls were made into shades, but at least they can still be put to use! I irritated a dealer at a flea market when I commented that his pink shade would sell better — if it had not been made into a shade! He had $400.00 on it.

A sufficient supply of pitchers and most tumbler sizes in both colors can be found, but price may be an impediment for some collectors! Only the pink juice tumbler is rarely found; but the price has escalated so that few collectors buy more than one, if any!

Tumblers that have the same shape as the Dogwood tumblers, but are missing the Dogwood silk screening are **not** Dogwood! There are pitchers shaped like Dogwood that do not have the silk screen design of Dogwood. These are **not** Dogwood either! They are merely the blanks made by MacBeth-Evans to go with the plain, no design tumblers that they made and sold separately with various pink sets. The **pattern** (Dogwood) has to be silk screened onto the pitcher for it to be considered Dogwood and to command those prices shown below. Some collectors buy these blanks to use with their sets, and that's perfectly fine as long as they understand that they are not Dogwood. It is also easier on the pocketbook to replace a $8.00 or $10.00 tumbler than one that costs $50.00! However, I've gotten letters from irate collectors who've paid (Dogwood) prices for plain tumblers. **Don't!** I have said these are not Dogwood in every book; buyer beware!

A few pieces of yellow (cereal bowl and luncheon plates) are being found, but there is not much demand for it either. It is a rare color in Dogwood.

Cremax (beige) and Monax (white) are also rare colors of Dogwood that do not thrill many collectors. See a description and photo of these MacBeth-Evans colors under American Sweetheart. The Monax salver (12" plate) was once considered rare; but, over the years, it has turned out more common than thought and more of a novelty with collectors than a desired item. You can buy them for less, now, than you could 15 years ago. I used to sell them for twice the price of the pink one.

There is a rolled edge cereal bowl being found that is different from the regular cereal. The flattened edge turns outward making it not as tall nor would it hold as much as the normally found cereal. These are being priced in a wide range, but will sell for $10.00 to $15.00 more than the regular cereal. How rare these are is questionable. Most collectors never gave them much thought until a few dealers started pricing them higher than the regular cereal. It does give collectors a new piece to find.

The thick, footed style Dogwood sugar and creamer are illustrated in pink while the thin, flat style creamer and sugar are shown in green. Pink sets are found in both styles, but green is only found in the thin variety. Thin creamers were made by adding a spout to thin cups and some of these have very indefinite spouts. There are thick and thin pink cups, but saucers for both styles are the same. Green cups come only in thin.

Pink grill plates come in two styles. Some have the Dogwood pattern all over the plate as the pink one pictured does, and others have the pattern only around the rim of the plate. Sherbets, grill plates (rim pattern only), and the large fruit bowls are difficult to acquire in green Dogwood. (Shades were made from the large green bowl, also.)

Dogwood sherbets are found with a Dogwood blossom etched on the bottom or plain. It makes no difference in price since they are only from different moulds.

Very Rare Glassware of the Depression Years, Second Series has a picture of the only known Dogwood coaster. Can you be the lucky one to find another?

	Pink	Green	Monax Cremax
* Bowl, 5½" cereal	33.00	35.00	5.00
Bowl, 8½" berry	65.00	125.00	40.00
** Bowl, 10¼" fruit	525.00	275.00	110.00
Cake plate, 11" heavy solid foot	1,200.00		
Cake plate, 13" heavy solid foot	145.00	135.00	195.00
Coaster, 3¼"	550.00		
Creamer, 2½" thin, flat	20.00	47.50	
Creamer, 3¼" thick, footed	25.00		
Cup, thick	18.00		40.00
Cup, thin	16.00	40.00	
Pitcher, 8", 80 oz. decorated	250.00	525.00	
Pitcher, 8", 80 oz. (American Sweetheart Style)	625.00		
Plate, 6" bread and butter	9.00	11.00	21.00
* Plate, 8" luncheon	7.00	9.00	
Plate, 9¼" dinner	40.00		
Plate, 10½" grill AOP or border design only	25.00	25.00	
Plate, 12" salver	35.00		15.00
Platter, 12" oval (rare)	695.00		
Saucer	6.00	6.50	20.00
Sherbet, low footed	38.00	115.00	
Sugar, 2½" thin, flat	18.00	45.00	
Sugar, 3¼" thick, footed	16.00		
Tumbler, 3½", 5 oz. decorated	250.00		
Tumbler, 4", 10 oz. decorated	42.00	97.50	
Tumbler, 4¾", 11 oz. decorated	45.00	100.00	
Tumbler, 5", 12 oz. decorated	70.00	120.00	
Tumbler, moulded band	25.00		

* Yellow – $65.00

** Lampshade – $150.00

DORIC JEANNETTE GLASS COMPANY, 1935–1938

Colors: Pink, green, some Delphite, Ultra Marine, and yellow.

Collectors of green Doric have long been discouraged by the lack of pitchers and cream soups found. The green, 48 ounce pitcher, with or without the ice lip, is a nemesis for nearly everyone. Pitchers are only the tip of the iceberg; cereal bowls and all tumblers are only being spotted occasionally. Those pieces in pink are not commonly seen either, but they can all be found with persistent searching except for that cream soup which has never been located in pink. Cream soups, or consommés as some companies called them, are **two-handled.** Cereal bowls have no handles but are often advertised as cream soups. I'm never sure whether advertisers of these pieces can't read or hope someone is naive enough to pay $400 for a cereal and not know the difference. Someday, the cereal might be worth that; but not today!

Green Doric collecting is a pleasant chore many collectors relish, but it probably will not consume your checking account all at once since you may require years to finish a set. I have had many collectors tell me that they do not care how difficult a pattern is to find because it's the "hunt" that intrigues and enthralls them as much as the glass itself! "But when you find a piece," one said, "there's **nothing** like that feeling!" (I guess you call that a glass "high!") I have had that feeling hundreds of times when spotting something that has never been documented before.

Realize that mould seams are often rough on pieces of Doric, especially footed tumblers and cereals. This disheartens precise collectors who are looking for flawlessness. There are collectors who have never seen cereal bowls or footed tumblers! I, personally, would not let a little roughness stop me from owning these pieces if I saw them for sale. Depression glass was cheap, inexpensive, give-away glass and was never made for perfection. Mint condition is beneficial in glass collecting, but it can be carried to extremes. Magnifying glasses are usually confined to coin and stamp collecting; however, I have seen these being put to use in our collecting world! Even black (ultraviolet) lights are being used to show repairs on any glassware that is fluorescent. Pink or blue glass does not "glow," but green and yellow glass does!

I have noticed more green Doric in Florida than any place I have traveled. One obstacle in buying glass in Florida, however, is cloudy (or "sick") glass. Evidently, well water created mineral deposits that react with the glass. You could make a fortune if you could figure out a way to easily remove these deposits. I know I have heard of everything from Tidy Bowl to Efferdent! As far as I know, this cloudiness cannot be removed short of polishing it out over a period of time; and people are now doing that, but it is expensive. Do not be duped into buying cloudy glass unless it is inexpensive or you have that magic cure!

The yellow Doric pitcher is still the only one known! Large, footed Doric pitchers come with or without an ice lip as shown in pink. Candy and sugar lids in this pattern are **not interchangeable.** The candy lid is taller and more domed.

The sherbet and cloverleaf candy are commonly found in Delphite. All other Delphite pieces are rare in Doric. The price is still reasonable for so rare a color. Only the pitcher creates much of a pricing stir.

An iridescent, three-part candy was made in the 1970s and sold for 79¢ in our local dish barn. You will sometimes find this candy in Ultra Marine in a piece of hammered aluminum!

I have included a photo of a boxed set. Some collectors find boxed sets to their liking, but usually these old boxes are dirty and not very colorful. Whatever pleases you is what you should buy and they do lend a certain veracity to the product!

	Pink	Green	Delphite
Bowl, 4½" berry	11.00	11.00	50.00
Bowl, 5" cream soup		450.00	
Bowl, 5½" cereal	75.00	85.00	
Bowl, 8¼" large berry	30.00	32.00	135.00
Bowl, 9" 2-handled	20.00	25.00	
Bowl, 9" oval vegetable	40.00	45.00	
Butter dish and cover	70.00	85.00	
Butter dish bottom	25.00	32.50	
Butter dish top	45.00	52.50	
Cake plate, 10", 3 legs	27.00	30.00	
Candy dish and cover, 8"	38.00	42.00	
*Candy dish, 3-part	12.00	10.00	12.00
Coaster, 3"	18.00	18.00	
Creamer, 4"	16.00	14.00	
Cup	10.00	12.00	
Pitcher, 5½", 32 oz. flat	40.00	45.00	1,200.00
Pitcher, 7½", 48 oz.			
footed (yellow at $2,000.00)	700.00	1,150.00	

	Pink	Green	Delphite
Plate, 6" sherbet	6.00	7.00	
Plate, 7" salad	20.00	25.00	
Plate, 9" dinner			
(serrated 175.00)	18.00	19.00	
Plate, 9" grill	22.00	25.00	
Platter, 12" oval	30.00	35.00	
Relish tray, 4" x 4"	15.00	10.00	
Relish tray, 4" x 8"	22.00	18.00	
Salt and pepper, pr.	35.00	37.50	
Saucer	3.50	4.50	
Sherbet, footed	15.00	17.00	9.00
Sugar	14.00	15.00	
Sugar cover	20.00	30.00	
Tray, 10" handled	18.00	20.00	
Tray, 8" x 8" serving	25.00	28.00	
Tumbler, 4½", 9 oz.	75.00	110.00	
Tumbler, 4", 10 oz., footed	65.00	90.00	
Tumbler, 5", 12 oz., footed	80.00	125.00	

*Candy in metal holder – $40.00. Iridescent made recently. Ultra Marine $18.00.

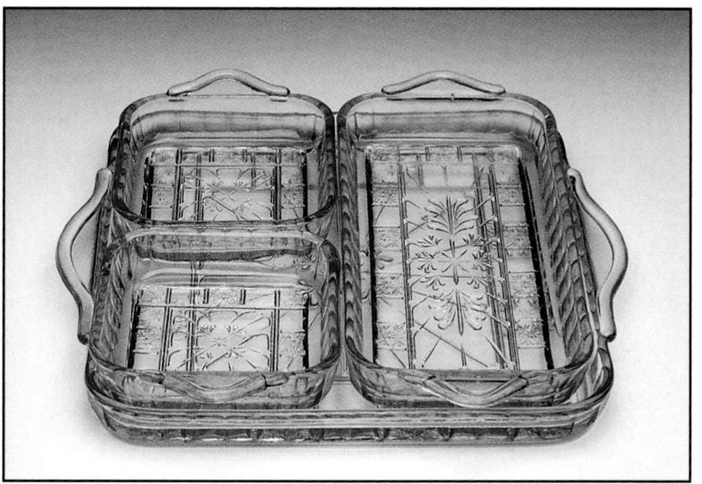

ONE 1200/4 RELISH SET
DORIC DESIGN
COLOR

DORIC AND PANSY JEANNETTE GLASS COMPANY, 1937–1938

Colors: Ultra Marine; some crystal and pink.

The supply of Ultra Marine Doric and Pansy keeps coming into America from English and Canadian suppliers! It is no wonder we thought Doric and Pansy was rare in the early collecting days. It is rare, but apparently only in the continental United States. Obviously, we were not looking outside our boundaries! The price of the butter dish remains steady, but you can not presently visit a glass show without seeing at least one for sale! (I had a contact for Depression glass in England, but lost it when I would not buy overpriced Fostoria and English made American.) I miss the Royal Lace I was buying, but not the quantities of Doric and Pansy I was receiving.

Although sugars, creamers, and shakers are usually found with those butter dishes, their price has not been as affected since they were not as highly priced as the butters. Tumblers and both sized berry bowls are not being found in the accumulations abroad. There are two tumblers pictured on the right. The ordinarily found tumbler is shaped like the flat Doric tumbler and is shown in front of the rarely found one. Only two of the 4¼", ten ounce tumblers have been observed. Peculiarly, there have been no reports of pink Doric and Pansy found abroad or discoveries of the children's sets in England or Canada — just pieces needed for serving "tea." Thus, we know how these Doric and Pansy items were marketed. A friend who visited England, said the only Depression glass he saw there was a pink Mayfair "tea set" which was what the luncheon set was called there.

Beware of weakly patterned shakers. These should be priced less (say twenty-five percent). If color and shape are the only clues to the shaker's pattern, then leave it alone unless it is seriously low-priced! Weak patterns and cloudiness befall many shakers shipped from England. Bear in mind, cloudy shakers are not worth mint prices! Cloudiness was caused by a chemical reaction between the glass and its contents. As a matter of fact, I have bought a sufficient number of shakers full of salt and pepper to observe that pepper causes as much cloudiness as salt! The cloudy salt container will frequently wash out, but not the pepper! Of course, salt does destroy metal shaker tops more than pepper.

Color variations face every collector who buys Ultra Marine in any Jeannette pattern. Some pieces have a distinct green hue instead of blue. You can spot the color differences in my picture. Few collectors presently buy the green shade of Ultra Marine. A matching group is easier to sell than a few pieces of differing colors. Usually, you can buy the greener tint at a lower price, and who is to know how it may be treasured down the road.

Berry bowls and children's sets are found in pink. Luncheon sets in crystal can be accumulated. Sugar and creamer sets in crystal are usually bought by collectors of sugar and creamers rather than Doric and Pansy collectors. Someday, these crystal pieces may be very appealing!

	Green, Teal	Pink, Crystal
Bowl, 4½" berry	22.00	12.00
Bowl, 8" large berry	85.00	30.00
Bowl, 9" handled	38.00	20.00
Butter dish and cover	450.00	
Butter dish bottom	70.00	
Butter dish top	380.00	
Cup	16.00	12.00
Creamer	115.00	85.00
Plate, 6" sherbet	10.00	7.50
Plate, 7" salad	40.00	
Plate, 9" dinner	38.00	15.00
Salt and pepper, pr.	400.00	
Saucer	5.00	4.00
Sugar, open	110.00	85.00
Tray, 10" handled	33.00	
Tumbler, 4½", 9 oz.	120.00	
Tumbler, 4¼", 10 oz.	595.00	

DORIC AND PANSY
"PRETTY POLLY PARTY DISHES"

	Teal	Pink
Cup	45.00	35.00
Saucer	8.00	7.00
Plate	10.75	8.00
Creamer	50.00	35.00
Sugar	50.00	35.00
14-Piece set	355.00	275.00

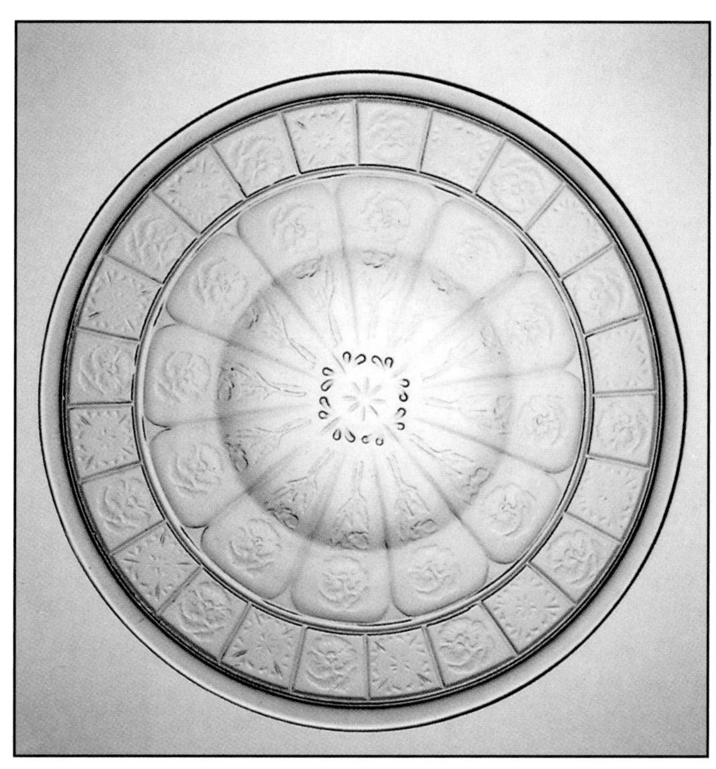

ENGLISH HOBNAIL WESTMORELAND GLASS COMPANY, 1920s–1940s; '70s

Colors: Pink, turquoise/ice blue, cobalt blue, green, black, and red.

English Hobnail was manufactured off and on for over fifty years. To offer some continuity, I have grouped crystal and amber into the *Collectible Glassware of the 40s, 50s, 60s…* and am including the rest of the colors in this book. It has taken several editions to determine what catalogued pieces exist in which colors. In the *Collectible Glassware of the 40s, 50s, 60s…* there are several catalog pages shown from the later years of Westmoreland's manufacture (when only amber and crystal were being regularly produced). Refer to that book for individual identification of pieces in English Hobnail.

There are two price arrangements. Pink and green make up one column and turquoise/ice blue make up the other. A piece in **cobalt blue or black will bring forty to fifty percent more** than the turquoise blue price listed. Very little cobalt English Hobnail is being unveiled and even fewer pieces in black. More collectors seek turquoise blue by virtue of its availability. I have been able to gather enough items for a decent blue photo on page 70. Bear in mind, that it took four years to accumulate what is shown, but I was picky! You can be patient and look for bargains or you can delve in and buy everything you see. The choice is yours.

Some pieces of turquoise were produced in the late 1970s. The later-made items seem to be of poorer quality and deeper color when compared to the older pieces. The two rounded stems in front of the plate are from this later production. Collectors use the term ice blue and turquoise blue interchangeably; do not become baffled on that topic. A few years ago, a large collection of turquoise English Hobnail was marketed at several shows. It was appealing and captivating to those who had never seen so much at one time. Several new collectors started with that set; I'm sure that everyone of them wishes they had bought the entire set, instead of trying to find it now.

Black English Hobnail pieces were found only a few years ago. You can see one of each of the four pieces that were found on the bottom of page 69. Note the flat, pink shaker in the same photograph. This is also a late discovery. Reports of a turquoise flat shaker never materialized, but I'm sure it's a possibility. Surprises still turn up in patterns that have been collected for years! That is part of the allure! What will turn up next?

Depending upon your inclination, large or small sets of pink or green English Hobnail can be assembled with time and perseverance. This pattern does have color inconsistencies. Pink is the simplest color to find, but it is found in two distinct shades. There are three different greens, from a light, yellow-green to a deep, dark green. Some collectors mix shades of color, but others aren't so inclined. This mixing is being called "rainbow collecting."

New collectors need to learn to distinguish English Hobnail from Miss America. The centers of English Hobnail pieces have rays of varying distances. Notice the upright pieces in the photographs for this six-point star effect. In Miss America, shown on page 126, the center rays all end equidistant from the center. The hobs on English Hobnail are more rounded and feel smoother to the touch; goblets flare and the hobs go directly into a plain rim area. Miss America's hobs are sharper to touch and the goblets do not flare at the rim. All goblets and tumblers of Miss America have three sets of rings above the hobs before entering a plain glass rim. If you have a candy jar that measures **more or less** than Miss America's 11½" including the cover, then it is probably English Hobnail which comes in several sizes.

	Pink/ Green	Turquoise/ *Ice Blue
Ash tray, 3"	20.00	
Ash tray, 4½"		22.50
Ash tray, 4½", sq.	25.00	
Bon bon, 6½", handled	25.00	40.00
Bottle, toilet, 5 oz.	25.00	50.00
Bowl, 3", cranberry	17.00	
Bowl, 4", rose	50.00	
Bowl, 4½", finger	15.00	
Bowl, 4½", round nappy	13.00	30.00
Bowl, 4½", sq. ftd., finger	15.00	35.00
Bowl, 5", round nappy	15.00	40.00
Bowl, 6", crimped dish	18.00	
Bowl, 6", round nappy	16.00	
Bowl, 6", square nappy	16.00	
Bowl, 6½", grapefruit	22.00	
Bowl, 6½", round nappy	20.00	
Bowl, 7", round nappy	22.00	
Bowl, 8", cupped, nappy	30.00	

	Pink/ Green	Turquoise/ *Ice Blue
Bowl, 8", ftd.	45.00	
Bowl, 8", hexagonal ftd., 2-handled	85.00	125.00
Bowl, 8", pickle	30.00	
Bowl, 8", round nappy	35.00	
Bowl, 9", celery	32.00	
Bowl, 10", flared	40.00	
Bowl, 11", rolled edge	45.00	80.00
Bowl, 12", celery	35.00	
Bowl, 12", flange or console	50.00	
Candlestick, 3½", rd. base	25.00	35.00
Candlestick, 9", rd. base	40.00	
Candy dish, 3 ftd.	55.00	
Candy, ½ lb. and cover, cone shaped	55.00	100.00
Cigarette box and cover, 4½" x 2½"	27.50	55.00
Cigarette jar w/cover, rd.	50.00	60.00
Compote, 5", round, ftd.	25.00	
Compote, 6", honey, rd. ftd.	30.00	
Compote, 8", ball stem, sweetmeat	60.00	

*Cobalt blue – 40 to 50 percent higher

ENGLISH HOBNAIL (Cont.)

	Pink/ Green	Turquoise/ *Ice Blue
Creamer, hexagonal, ftd.	22.50	45.00
Creamer, sq. ftd.	42.50	
Cup	18.00	25.00
Cup, demitasse	55.00	
Ice tub, 4"	47.50	90.00
Ice tub, 5½"	65.00	120.00
Lamp, 6¼", electric	65.00	
Lamp, 9¼", electric	135.00	
Marmalade w/cover	60.00	85.00
Mayonnaise, 6"	20.00	
Nut, individual, ftd.	18.00	
Pitcher, 23 oz., rounded	150.00	
Pitcher, 32 oz., straight side	185.00	
Pitcher, 38 oz., rounded	225.00	
Pitcher, 60 oz., rounded	295.00	
Pitcher, 64 oz., straight side	300.00	
Plate, 5½", rd.	9.50	
Plate, 6", sq. finger bowl liner	9.00	
Plate, 6½", rd.	10.00	
Plate, 6½, rd. finger bowl liner	9.50	
Plate, 8", rd.	12.50	
Plate, 8½", rd.	15.00	25.00
Plate, 10", rd.	45.00	85.00
Plate, 14", rd., torte	60.00	
Puff box, w/ cover, 6", rd.	45.00	77.50

*Cobalt blue – 40 to 50% higher

	Pink/ Green	Turquoise/ *Ice Blue
Saucer, demitasse, rd.	15.00	
Saucer, rd.	4.00	5.00
Shaker, pr., flat	150.00	250.00
Shaker, pr., rd. ftd.	77.50	
Stem, 2 oz., sq. ftd., wine	30.00	60.00
Stem, 3 oz., rd. ftd., cocktail	20.00	35.00
Stem, 5 oz., sq. ftd., oyster cocktail	16.00	
Stem, 8 oz., sq. ftd., water goblet	30.00	50.00
Stem, sherbet, rd. low foot		12.00
Stem, sherbet, sq. ftd., low	12.00	
Stem, sherbet, rd. high foot	1500	
Stem, sherbet, sq. ftd., high	15.00	35.00
Sugar, hexagonal, ftd.	22.50	45.00
Sugar, sq. ftd.	45.00	
Tid-bit, 2 tier	45.00	85.00
Tumbler, 5 oz., ginger ale	18.00	
Tumbler, 8 oz., water	22.00	
Tumbler, 10 oz., ice tea	25.00	
Tumbler, 12 oz., ice tea	30.00	
Urn, 11", w/cover (15")	395.00	
Vase, 7½", flip	75.00	
Vase, 7½", flip jar w/cover	125.00	
Vase, 8½", flared top	125.00	250.00
Vase, 10" (straw jar)	100.00	

FIRE-KING DINNERWARE "PHILBE" HOCKING GLASS COMPANY, 1937–1938

Colors: Blue, green, pink, and crystal.

Fire-King Dinnerware is attracting more admirers after its inclusion in my new book, *Anchor Hocking's Fire-King & More.* The most frequently asked question is where do I find a piece — any piece? If there were more available, then the price would be even higher due to the number of collectors wanting it. As it is, there is so little available that few actually are buying it. There are a number of collectors who want one piece from every pattern and Fire-King Dinnerware is still on almost everyone's list. I just received a wish list from a cup and saucer collector who needs only four or five sets to finish one of every pattern in my books. Topping the list is "Philbe" in any color.

I added the high sherbet/champagnes to our listing last time, and now I am adding a non-stemmed sherbet which is pictured in the Fire-King book mentioned above. Usually, Fire-King Dinnerware is found on Cameo shaped blanks; but some pieces, including footed tumblers, nine ounce water goblets, and the high sherbets are on a Mayfair shaped blank! Additional stems could be found. Watch for them!

Crystal cup and saucer sets were found in Michigan. The one pictured has a platinum band that was also on the blue set shown in a previous edition.

Has anyone found a green candy lid? I have owned two green candy bottoms and one complete blue, but I have never found the green top! I once had a lid brought to me that was supposed to fit the candy, but it turned out to be the lid for the cookie instead. The cookie lid is a tad larger — but only a tad.

The blue of Fire-King Dinnerware is very similar to Mayfair's blue. Many pieces have that platinum trim that can be seen in the photograph. All the platinum banded blue pieces in the picture, except the pitcher, turned up in 1975 at a flea market in Ohio. I have never seen blue Mayfair trimmed in platinum. This seems strange since these patterns were made about the same time. Mayfair was finishing up as Fire-King was being introduced. Maybe this was a special order production — which might account for its scarcity? As many different pieces as were made, there should be a supply just waiting to be retrieved.

Many pieces shown here are the only ones ever found! Of the four pitchers shown, only three other pitchers (two pink juice and a blue water without platinum band) have been unearthed. The easiest to find blue items (which are rare in other colors) are the footed tumblers; and the tea seems twice as available as the water.

Oval vegetable bowls and the 10½" salver are the only commonly found pieces of pink. That oval bowl is also available in green and crystal. I have only found three pieces since the last book was published two years ago. So "commonly found" may be a misnomer for this pattern.

Green grill plates or luncheon plates might end up in your collection with more ease than anything else in "Philbe" if you are searching for only a sample. Any color 6" saucer/sherbet plate is rarer than larger plates.

	Crystal	Pink, Green	Blue
Bowl, 5½" cereal	20.00	45.00	75.00
Bowl, 7¼" salad	50.00	80.00	115.00
Bowl, 10" oval vegetable	60.00	90.00	165.00
Candy jar, 4" low, with cover	215.00	725.00	795.00
Cookie jar with cover	600.00	950.00	1,500.00
Creamer, 3¼" ftd.	75.00	135.00	150.00
Cup	60.00	110.00	175.00
Goblet, 7¼", 9 oz. thin	95.00	185.00	235.00
Pitcher, 6", 36 oz. juice	295.00	625.00	895.00
Pitcher, 8½", 56 oz.	395.00	925.00	1,175.00
Plate, 6" sherbet	40.00	65.00	95.00
Plate, 8" luncheon	20.00	37.50	47.50
Plate, 10" heavy sandwich	32.50	75.00	100.00
Plate, 10½" salver	40.50	75.00	90.00
Plate, 10½" grill	40.00	75.00	95.00
Plate, 11⅝" salver	50.00	62.50	95.00
Platter, 12" closed handles	60.00	125.00	175.00
Saucer, 6" (same as sherbet plate)	40.00	65.00	95.00
Sherbet, 3¾," no stem	75.00		550.00
Sherbet, 4¾," stemmed		450.00	
Sugar, 3¼" ftd.	75.00	135.00	150.00
Tumbler, 4", 9 oz. flat water	40.00	105.00	130.00
Tumbler, 3½" ftd. juice	40.00	150.00	175.00
Tumbler, 5¼", 10 oz. ftd.	40.00	80.00	100.00
Tumbler, 6½", 15 oz. ftd. iced tea	50.00	85.00	90.00

FLORAL, "POINSETTIA" JEANNETTE GLASS COMPANY, 1931–1935

Colors: Pink, green, Delphite, Jadite, crystal, amber, red, black, custard, and yellow.

No letters this time from hemp smokers explaining the Floral design is obviously a hemp plant. With all the push from hemp growers, I expected one again. I assume the explanation from the botanist that this was a passion flower has settled all bets on this non-poinsettia pattern.

The newest discovery is a 6" pink Floral flat shaker with a rounded base instead of the normally found squared base style. You can see it pictured in the *Very Rare Glassware of the Depression Years, Sixth Edition.* Notice, on page 76, one of the first ruffled top pink Floral comports to be found. The normally found straight top comport is on the bottom row of page 74. Neither style is common. Pink comports are harder to find than green, but there are more collectors seeking green ones.

Some Green Floral pieces are rarely found in the United States but continue to be uncovered in England and Canada. As with Doric and Pansy, it is the **more unusual and previously thought to be rare pieces** that are being found. Many of these pieces have **only been found** in England! Some Floral discoveries were brought back to the United States by furniture dealers who filled space in container shipments with glassware. Today, these dealers have representatives in England hunting for American-made glassware as well as fine European antiques. Many of my books are being shipped to England as well as Australia and New Zealand. Yes, American Depression glass is being encountered "down under" — quite a bit of it, in fact!

Green Floral, flat bottomed pitchers and tumblers are specific pieces whose prices have remained steady for years. Color variations of green exist in items found in Canada and England; they are frequently a lighter green color, slightly paneled, and ground on the bottoms of flatware. Ground bottoms on Depression glass items ofttimes indicates an early production run of the pattern. Observe the oval vegetable bowl in the center of the picture which was placed there so you could see this paneled effect. The green cup without a saucer has a ground bottom and is slightly footed. The base of the cup is larger than the normally found saucer indentation! If you have relatives in England who didn't travel on the Mayflower, send them some of my books!

Northwestern dealers tell me that lemonade pitchers are disappearing from the market place in that area. For years, you could find either color you wanted in Oregon or Washington, but all good times come to an end. Pink lemonade pitchers substantially outnumber the green; that is one reason for price differences in these pitchers.

Two varieties of pink Floral platters exist. One has a normal flat edge as shown in the right of the photo; the other has a sharp inner rim like the platter in Cherry Blossom. Few collectors deem both necessary for their collections. The style similar to Cherry Blossom is rarer than the normally found platter, and therefore priced higher. This price keeps some Floral collectors from adding that to their pattern, settling for the more inexpensive one.

For a description of the lamp shown in the top row, be sure to read about a similarly made lamp in Adam pattern on page 6.

On a sour note, I must add that the smaller, footed Floral shakers have **now been reproduced** in pink, cobalt blue, red, and a very dark green color. Cobalt blue, red, and the dark green Floral shakers are of little concern since they were originally never made in these colors. The green is darker than the original green shown here and will not glow under a black (ultraviolet) light as will the old. The new pink shakers, however, are not only a very good pink, but they are also a reasonably good copy! There are many minor variations in design and leaf detail to someone who knows glassware well, but there is only one easy way to tell the Floral reproductions. Take off the top and look at the threads where the lid screws onto the shaker. On the old there are a **pair of parallel threads** on each side or at least a pair on one side that end right before the mould seams down each side. The new Floral has **one continuous line** thread that starts on one side and continues around the shaker until it ends above the beginning line on the other side. There is approximately one inch of overlapped thread making two lines for that inch; but the whole thread is **one continuous line** and not two separate ones as on the old. No other Floral reproductions have been made as of May 1999.

Floral is another of Jeannette's patterns in which the sugar and candy lids **are** interchangeable.

Unusual items in Floral (so far) include the following:

a) an entire set of **Delphite**
b) a **yellow** two-part relish dish
c) **amber** and **red** plate, cup, and saucer
d) green and crystal **juice pitchers** w/ground flat bottoms
e) ftd. **vases** in green and crystal, flared at the rim; some hold **flower frogs with the Floral pattern on the frogs**
f) **crystal** lemonade pitcher
g) **lamps**
h) green **grill** plate
i) an **octagonal** vase with patterned, octagonal foot
j) **ruffled edge** berry and master berry bowl
k) pink and green Floral **ice tubs**
l) oval vegetable with **cover**
m) **rose bowl** and **three ftd. vase**
n) two styles of **9" comports** in pink and green
o) 9 ounce **flat** tumblers in green
p) **3 ounce ftd.** tumblers in green
q) 8" round bowl in **beige** and **opaque red**
r) **caramel** colored dinner plate
s) **cream soups**
t) **beige** creamer and sugar
u) green **dresser set**
v) **beige,** 8½" bowl (like Cherry Blossom)
w) **black** footed water tumbler
x) round vegetable **w/o handles w/cover**
y) **round based 6" flat shaker**

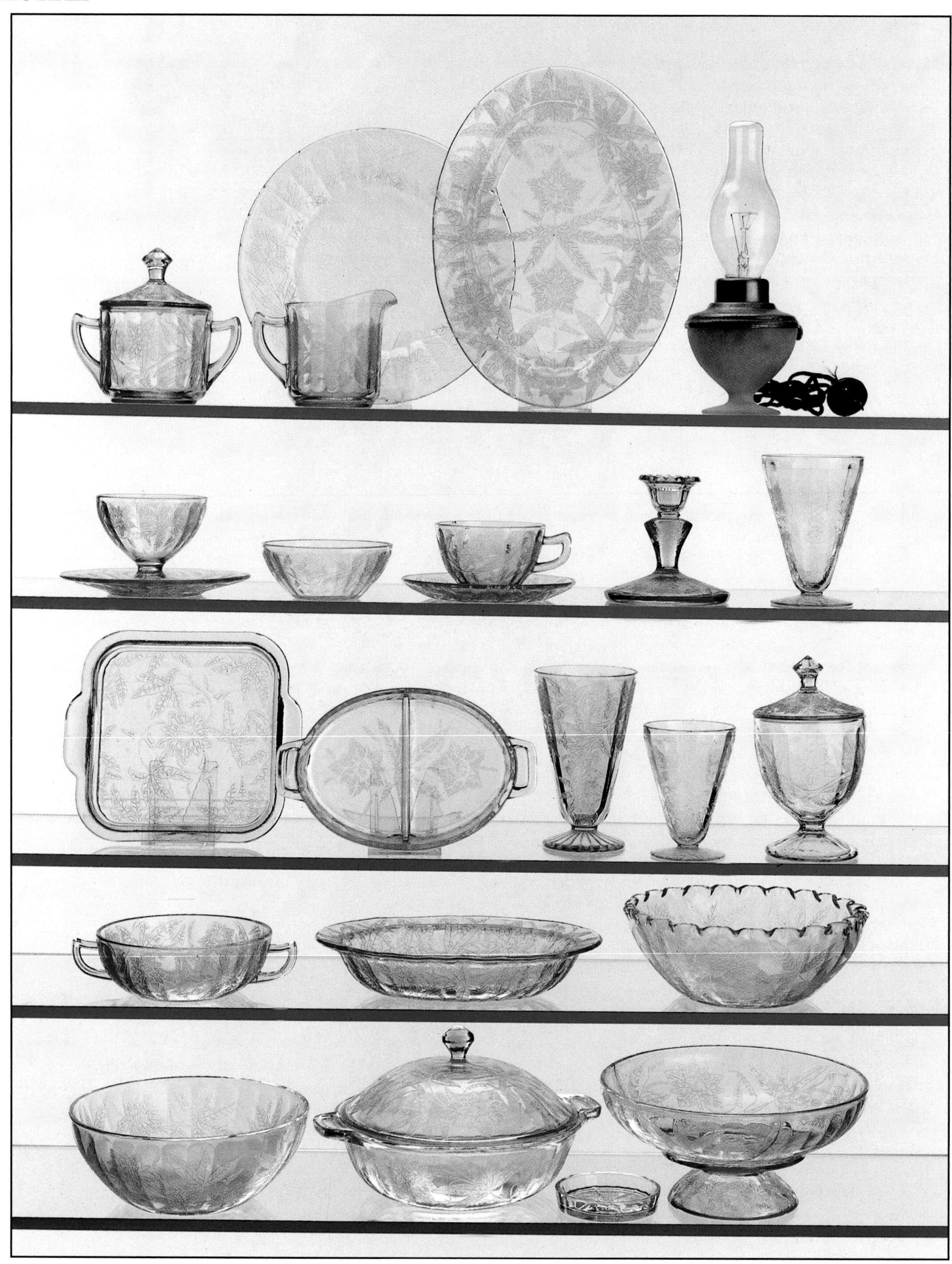

	Pink	Green	Delphite	Jadite
Bowl, 4" berry (ruffled $65.00)	20.00	22.00	50.00	
Bowl, 5½" cream soup	750.00	750.00		
* Bowl, 7½" salad (ruffled $150.00)	30.00	30.00	60.00	
Bowl, 8" covered vegetable	55.00	65.00	75.00 (no cover)	
Bowl, 9" oval vegetable	24.00	26.00		
Butter dish and cover	100.00	90.00		
Butter dish bottom	25.00	25.00		
Butter dish top	75.00	65.00		
Canister set: coffee, tea, cereal sugar, 5¼" tall, each				95.00
Candlesticks, 4" pr.	80.00	90.00		
Candy jar and cover	45.00	42.50		
Creamer, flat (Cremax $160.00)	18.00	20.00	77.50	
Coaster, 3¼"	15.00	14.00		
Comport, 9"	895.00	995.00		
*** Cup	14.00	14.00		
Dresser set		1,250.00		
Frog for vase (also crystal $500.00)		725.00		
Ice tub, 3½" high oval	850.00	895.00		
Lamp	250.00	275.00		
Pitcher, 5½", 23 or 24 oz.		550.00		
Pitcher, 8", 32 oz. ftd. cone	35.00	40.00		
Pitcher, 10¼", 48 oz. lemonade	245.00	265.00		
Plate, 6" sherbet	8.00	9.00		
Plate, 8" salad	14.00	16.00		
** Plate, 9" dinner	20.00	22.00	150.00	
Plate, 9" grill		295.00		
Platter, 10¾" oval	22.00	24.00	150.00	
Platter, 11" (like Cherry Blossom)	85.00			
Refrigerator dish and cover, 5" square		75.00	95.00	50.00
*** Relish dish, 2-part oval	22.00	24.00	160.00	
**** Salt and pepper, 4" ftd. pair	50.00	55.00		
Salt and pepper, 6" flat	55.00			
*** Saucer	12.00	12.00		
Sherbet	20.00	20.00	85.00	
Sugar (Cremax $160.00)	10.00	12.00	72.50 (open)	
Sugar/candy cover	15.00	20.00		
Tray, 6" square, closed handles	17.50	20.00		
Tray, 9¼", oval for dresser set		195.00		
Tumbler, 3½", 3 oz. ftd.		175.00		
Tumbler, 4", 5 oz. ftd. juice	18.00	25.00		
Tumbler, 4½", 9 oz. flat		185.00		
Tumbler, 4¾", 7 oz. ftd. water	22.00	24.00	195.00	
Tumbler, 5¼", 9 oz. ftd. lemonade	50.00	55.00		
Vase, 3 legged rose bowl		525.00		
Vase, 3 legged flared (also in crystal)		495.00		
Vase, 6⅞" tall (8 sided)		450.00		

* Cremax $125.00
** These have now been found in amber and red.
*** This has been found in yellow.
**** Beware reproductions!

FLORAL

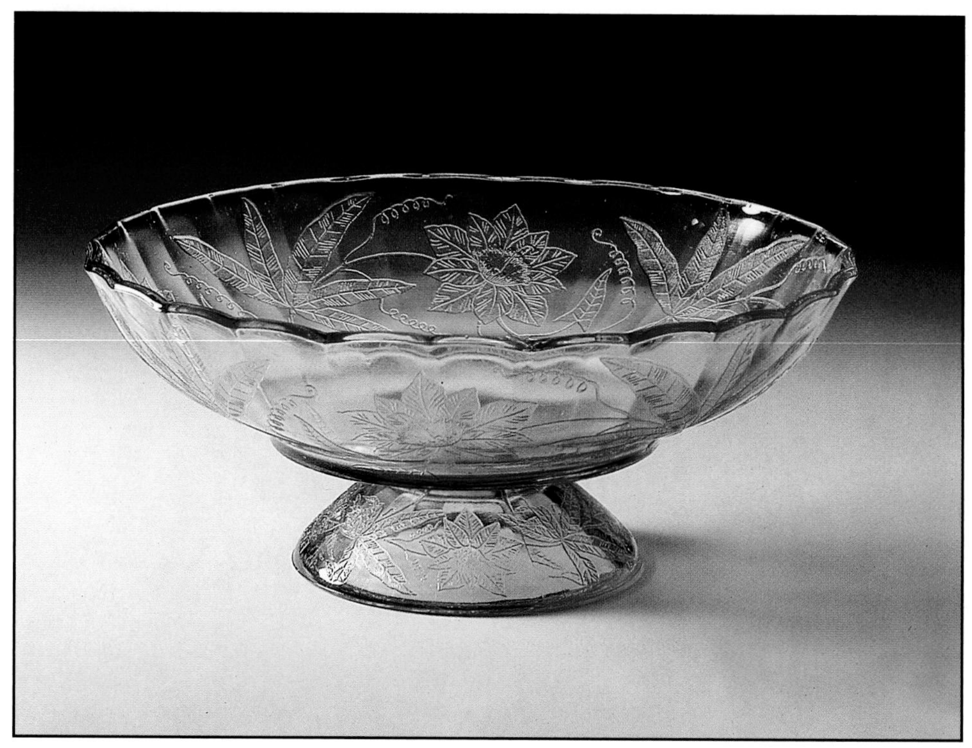

FLORAL AND DIAMOND BAND U.S. GLASS COMPANY, LATE 1920s

Colors: Pink, green; some iridescent, black, and crystal.

Floral and Diamond was shown in Sears catalogs in the late 1920s, but either it did not sell well or it was used to death as there is not enough available now to provide a great number of collectors with sets. Notice that half the ad for the berry set pictured below says **Diamond and Floral** and not vice versa. It was listed both ways in advertisements at the time. You cannot order these items shown in the old advertisement below! They were the prices for this pattern in the year 1928! Enjoy this piece of history while you can as it will be the last time I run this ad. Space is becoming too valuable to use it again.

Floral and Diamond luncheon plates, sugar lids, pitchers, and iced tea tumblers (in both pink and green) are hard to acquire. Many Floral and Diamond butter bottoms have been "borrowed" to be used on other U.S. Glass patterns such as Strawberry and Cherryberry. This has taken place because all U.S. Glass butter bottoms are plain and, thus, compatible, since the patterns are located on the top only. Floral and Diamond butter dishes used to be low priced in comparison to Strawberry and Cherryberry; so, collectors bought the bargain Floral and Diamond butter dishes to use the bottoms for those more costly patterns. These past collecting proclivities have now produced a dearth of butter bottoms for Floral and Diamond!

Rough mould lines on many Floral and Diamond pieces are typical of all U.S. Glass Company patterns of this era. This heavy seamed pattern was not finished as well as many of the later patterns. This is **normal** for Floral and Diamond and not considered an impairment by long-time collectors who have come to ignore some roughness. Another difficulty in gathering Floral and Diamond is the varying shades of green. Some of the green is blue tinted. You need to decide how flexible you are about color matching.

The small Floral and Diamond creamer and sugar have been found in black, but no other pieces have been spotted in that color. The small sugar and creamer are often found with a cut flower over the top of the customarily found moulded flower design. You can find this cut flower on other colors. My question is why cut a flower design over one already moulded into the glass?

Crystal pitchers and butter dishes are rare in Floral and Diamond! Notice the crystal pitcher on the right in the bottom photograph. It has a yellow hue which is one problem in collecting crystal. The biggest one is finding crystal at all!

Floral and Diamond pitchers with **exceptional** iridescent color bring premium prices from carnival glass collectors as a pattern called "Mayflower"! Unfortunately, these iridescent pitchers are regularly weakly colored and unacceptable to carnival glass collectors. Dealers who sell both Depression and carnival glass have been buying these pitchers at Depression glass shows and reselling them at carnival glass conventions and auctions for years. Sometimes glassware overlaps categories of collecting, as does Floral and Diamond; and, occasionally, it receives more respect from one group of collectors than it does the other.

	Pink	Green
Bowl, 4½" berry	10.00	12.00
Bowl, 5¾" handled nappy	15.00	15.00
Bowl, 8" large berry	20.00	20.00
* Butter dish and cover	140.00	130.00
Butter dish bottom	100.00	100.00
Butter dish top	40.00	30.00
Compote, 5½" tall	17.00	20.00
Creamer, small	10.00	12.00
Creamer, 4¾"	18.00	20.00
* Pitcher, 8", 42 oz.	115.00	125.00
Plate, 8" luncheon	45.00	45.00
Sherbet	7.00	8.00
Sugar, small	10.00	12.00
Sugar, 5¼"	18.00	18.00
Sugar lid	55.00	65.00
Tumbler, 4" water	25.00	25.00
Tumbler, 5" iced tea	40.00	50.00

* Iridescent – $275.00; Crystal – $125.00

Seven-Piece Berry Set

You'll really be most satisfied with the purchase of this set. It's very attractive, and affords a fitting and stylish addition to your present pieces. In green pressed glass, with diamond and floral design. Large bowl, 8 inches in diameter, and six sauce dishes to match, 4½ inches in diameter.
35N6838—Weight, packed, 7 pounds. Per set...... 68c

Seven-Piece Water Set

Made from green pressed glass, with a floral and diamond design. You'll find that the sparkling scintillating pitcher and glasses are a set you'll be mighty proud to own when serving cold drinks. 3-pint pitcher. Six 8-ounce tumblers.
35N6837—Weight, packed, 12 pounds. Per set. $1.18

FLORAL AND DIAMOND BAND

FLORENTINE NO. 1, OLD FLORENTINE, "POPPY NO. 1"

HAZEL ATLAS GLASS COMPANY, 1932–1935

Colors: Pink, green, crystal, yellow, and cobalt blue. See Reproduction Section.

Florentine No. 1 and Florentine No. 2 are regularly confused by new collectors. Just a couple of weeks ago I visited an antique mall a few miles from here and was greeted by one of the employees as just the person she wanted to see. A large set of crystal Depression glass had been brought in and they wanted it identified. It was a mixture of Florentine and it was giving them problems.

Notice the **outlines** of the pieces. The serrated edged pieces are hexagonal (six sided); this edging occurs on all flat pieces of Florentine No. 1. All footed pieces (such as tumblers, shakers, or pitchers) have the serrated edge on that foot. In Florentine No. 2, all pieces have a plain edge as can be seen in the photographs on page 82. Florentine No. 1 was once advertised as hexagonal and Florentine No. 2 was once advertised as round. Both Florentine patterns were advertised and sold together as proven by the mixed set in that antique mall. Today, some collectors are following that lead and blending the two patterns!

The 48 ounce, flat-bottomed pitcher was sold with both Florentine No. 1 and No. 2 sets. It was listed as 54 ounces in catalogs, but usually measures six ounces less. It depends upon the lip as to how many ounces it will hold before liquid runs out. My predisposition is to **only** list this pitcher with Florentine No. 1 using the handle shape as my criterion. In defiance of that logic, this pitcher is frequently found with flat-bottomed Florentine No. 2 tumblers, which forces me to list it with both Florentine patterns.

Many flat tumblers with paneled interiors are being found in sets with Florentine No. 1 pitchers. These paneled tumblers **should** be considered Florentine No. 1 rather than Florentine No. 2. That recommendation is for die-hard collectors only. Paneled flat tumblers are tough to find; but few collectors seem to make this a "must have" example. The paneled tumblers do not blend well with the non-paneled style; be conscious of that!

Pink Florentine No. 1 is the most difficult color in which to complete a set. The pink footed tumblers, covered oval vegetable bowl, and ruffled creamer and sugar are all but unavailable at any price. Sets can be collected in green, crystal, or yellow with time and effort. Those irregular edges are easily damaged; that is the first place you should look when you pick up a piece to buy. Be sure to check underneath those edges and not just on the top side.

Fired-on colors are materializing in luncheon sets, but there is little collector fervor for these at the moment. You can find all sorts of colors and colored bands on crystal if that strikes your fancy. There are even some banded designs found on colors besides crystal. A primary disadvantage to these banded colors is finding enough to put a set together.

Many 5½" yellow ash trays have VFW (Veterans of Foreign Wars) embossed in the bottom. I have seen more with this imprint than without it. I have not seen an embossed design on any color other than yellow!

Florentine No. 1 shakers have been reproduced in pink and cobalt blue. Other colors normally follow. No original cobalt blue Florentine No. 1 shakers have ever been found; so those are easy to spot.

The reproduction pink shaker is somewhat more difficult to differentiate. When comparing a reproduction shaker to several old pairs from my inventory, the old shakers have a major open flower on each side. There is a top circle on this blossom with three smaller circles down each side. The **seven circles form the outside** of the blossom. The new blossom looks more like a strawberry with **no circles** forming the outside of the blossom. Do not use the threading test mentioned under Floral for the Florentine No. 1 shakers, however. It will not work for Florentine although these are made by the same importing company out of Georgia. The threads are correct on this reproduction pattern. The reproductions I have seen have been badly moulded, but that is not to say that it will not be corrected. As of May 1999, it has not been!

	Crystal, Green	Yellow	Pink	Cobalt Blue
Ash tray, 5½"	22.00	30.00	30.00	
Bowl, 5" berry	12.00	15.00	15.00	20.00
Bowl, 5", cream				
soup or ruffled nut	25.00		20.00	60.00
Bowl, 6" cereal	25.00	30.00	30.00	
Bowl, 8½" large berry	25.00	35.00	35.00	
Bowl, 9½" oval vegetable				
and cover	55.00	75.00	75.00	
Butter dish and cover	125.00	160.00	160.00	
Butter dish bottom	50.00	85.00	85.00	
Butter dish top	75.00	95.00	75.00	
Coaster/ash tray, 3¾"	18.00	20.00	28.00	
Comport, 3½", ruffled	*40.00		18.00	65.00
Creamer	9.50	18.00	20.00	
Creamer, ruffled	45.00		37.50	65.00
Cup	9.00	10.00	12.00	85.00
Pitcher, 6½", 36 oz., ftd.	40.00	45.00	45.00	850.00
Pitcher, 7½", 48 oz.				
flat, ice lip or none	75.00	195.00	135.00	
Plate, 6" sherbet	6.00	7.00	6.00	

	Crystal, Green	Yellow	Pink	Cobalt Blue
Plate, 8½" salad	8.00	12.00	11.00	
Plate, 10" dinner	18.00	25.00	25.00	
Plate, 10" grill	12.00	15.00	20.00	
Platter, 11½" oval	20.00	25.00	25.00	
**Salt and pepper, ftd.	37.50	55.00	55.00	
Saucer	3.00	4.00	4.00	17.00
Sherbet, 3 oz., ftd.	11.00	14.00	12.00	
Sugar	9.50	12.00	12.00	
Sugar cover	18.00	30.00	30.00	
Sugar, ruffled	40.00		40.00	60.00
Tumbler, 3¼", 4 oz., ftd.	16.00			
Tumbler, 3¾", 5 oz.				
ftd. juice	16.00	25.00	25.00	
Tumbler, 4", 9 oz., ribbed	16.00		22.00	
Tumbler, 4¾", 10 oz.				
ftd. water	22.00	24.00	24.00	
Tumbler, 5¼", 12 oz.				
ftd. iced tea	28.00	30.00	30.00	
Tumbler, 5¼", 9 oz.				
lemonade (like Floral)			125.00	

*Crystal $15.00 ** Beware reproductions

FLORENTINE NO. 1

FLORENTINE NO. 2, "POPPY NO. 2" HAZEL ATLAS GLASS COMPANY 1932–1935

Colors: Pink, green, crystal, some cobalt, amber, and ice blue. See Reproduction Section.

Read about the differences between the two Florentines in the first paragraph on page 79 (under Florentine No. 1). If you are a new or advanced collector running out of pieces to find, why not try mixing the Florentines together. You can stick with the same color or branch out and blend some colors together. Pieces of both patterns have been found in boxed sets over the years; so, the factory mixed them as well. In the top photograph is a green ruffled nut or cream soup to the back and left of the regularly found cream soup. This piece qualifies as Florentine No. 1 because it matches the other ruffled pieces (comport, creamer, and sugar) in that pattern, not found in Florentine No. 2. The frustration here is the shape of the handles on the bowl which only match items in Florentine No. 2. Thus, we have an overlapping piece that can be used with either pattern. A pink one is pictured with Florentine No. 1.

The seldom found 6¼", twenty-four ounce, footed, cone-shaped pitcher is shown on the right in the top photograph. The more frequently found footed pitcher stands 7½" tall and is shown on the left. These pitchers have been confused for years because of ounce capacities that often fluctuate due to the hand-produced spout and inaccurate measuring abilities. When you measure capacity, fill the object to the point where liquid runs out of the container being measured, and not to the point you think it looks full. Measure height from the base to the top of the spout. There is over an inch difference and this will not vary as greatly as ounce capacities. There is a vast price difference in these pitchers; so, get it right.

That 7½" pitcher and footed water tumbler have been reproduced in cobalt blue, pink, and a dark green. This pitcher was never originally made in those colors; therefore, no one should assume these reproductions to be old. See page 232 for information.

Custard cups or jello molds remain the most elusive piece in Florentine No. 2; you can see a crystal one pictured on a yellow indented plate in the lower photograph of page 82. The custard is similar to a small, flared bowl and fits a 6¼" indented plate. I have bought these plates mistakenly labeled as saucers. The saucer curves up on the edges while the custard plate is flat with a larger indentation.

The bulbous, 76 oz. pitcher eludes many collectors, particularly in yellow. The 10" relish dish comes in three styles. There are two divided styles and one undivided. The most commonly found "Y" style is pictured in green and yellow. The different style has two curved, separate divisions, one on each side. So far, there are no price distinctions on these relish dishes; the undivided is the most difficult to acquire if you want all three types.

Grill plates with a round indent for the cream soup have been found in green and crystal but have yet to be witnessed in yellow. Inasmuch as they are a recent discovery, it is reasonable to deem they are not abundant.

Green Florentine is more requested than crystal, but crystal is hardly found; hence, prices are similar. Amber, shown in earlier editions, is the rarest Florentine color; but not enough is available to begin to collect a set. Most sizes of flat tumblers have been found in amber, but no pitcher.

Both lids to the butter dishes and the oval vegetables are compatible in the two Florentine patterns. Candy lids and butter lids are similar in size. The candy lid measures 4¾" in diameter, but the butter dish lid measures 5" exactly. Those measurements are from **outside edge to outside edge!**

Fired-on colors such as the red saucer in the top photo are not common in Florentine. Luncheon sets of red, orange, green, and blue have been reported. The fired-on colors are sprayed over crystal. Once it has been fired-on (baked, so to speak), the colors will not strip off even with paint removers as some collectors have learned.

	Crystal, Green	Pink	Yellow	Cobalt Blue
Bowl, 4½" berry	14.00	17.00	22.00	
Bowl, 4¾" cream soup	16.00	16.00	22.00	
Bowl, 5½"	33.00		42.00	
Bowl, 6" cereal	33.00		42.00	
Bowl, 7½" shallow			95.00	
Bowl, 8" large berry	28.00	32.00	38.00	
Bowl, 9" oval vegetable and cover	65.00		85.00	
Bowl, 9" flat	27.50			
Butter dish and cover	110.00		160.00	
Butter dish bottom	25.00		70.00	
Butter dish top	75.00		80.00	
Candlesticks, 2¾" pr.	50.00		70.00	
Candy dish and cover	100.00	145.00	155.00	
Coaster, 3¼"	14.00	16.00	22.00	
Coaster/ash tray, 3¾"	17.50		30.00	
Coaster/ash tray, 5½"	17.50		38.00	
* Comport, 3½", ruffled	40.00	15.00		65.00
Creamer	8.00		10.00	
Cup (amber 50.00)	8.00		10.00	
Custard cup or jello	60.00		85.00	
Gravy boat			60.00	
Pitcher, 6¼", 24 oz., cone-ftd.			175.00	
** Pitcher, 7½", 28 oz., cone-ftd.	35.00		35.00	
Pitcher, 7½", 48 oz.	75.00	135.00	195.00	
Pitcher, 8¼", 76 oz.	110.00	225.00	450.00	

	Crystal, Green	Pink	Yellow	Cobalt Blue
Plate, 6" sherbet	4.00		6.00	
Plate, 6¼" with indent	20.00		30.00	
Plate, 8½" salad	8.50	8.50	9.00	
Plate, 10" dinner	16.00		16.00	
Plate, 10¼" grill	14.00		18.00	
Plate, 10¼", grill w/cream soup ring	40.00			
Platter, 11" oval	16.00	16.00	22.50	
Platter, 11½" for gravy boat			45.00	
Relish dish, 10", 3-part or plain	22.00	28.00	32.00	
*** Salt and pepper, pr.	42.50		50.00	
Saucer (amber $15.00)	4.00		5.00	
Sherbet, ftd. (amber $40.00)	12.00		13.00	
Sugar	10.00		12.00	
Sugar cover	15.00		28.00	
Tray, rnd., condiment for shakers, creamer/sugar			80.00	
Tumbler, 3⅜", 5 oz. juice	14.00	12.00	21.00	
Tumbler, 3$\frac{9}{16}$", 6 oz., blown	18.00			
**** Tumbler, 4", 9 oz. water	13.00	16.00	21.00	70.00
Tumbler, 5", 12 oz., blown	20.00			
**** Tumbler, 5", 12 oz., tea	35.00		55.00	
Tumbler, 3¼", 5 oz., ftd.	15.00		17.50	
Tumbler, 4", 5 oz., ftd.	15.00		17.00	
Tumbler, 4½", 9 oz., ftd.	30.00		35.00	
Vase or parfait, 6"	33.00		65.00	

*Crystal – $15.00 ** Ice Blue – $500.00 *** Fired-on Red, Orange, or Blue, Pr. – $42.50 **** Amber – $75.00

FLORENTINE NO. 2

FLOWER GARDEN WITH BUTTERFLIES, "BUTTERFLIES AND ROSES"

U.S. GLASS COMPANY, LATE 1920s

Colors: Pink, green, blue-green, canary yellow, crystal, amber, and black.

Flower Garden with Butterflies was one pattern we enjoyed collecting for 20 years! After letting it go, I have had a troublesome time buying enough to photograph for the book! I should have kept more pieces; but hindsight is always 20-20, so I've been told. This pattern is found so rarely that few new collectors are buying it. Over the years, collections have been assembled and today, some patterns only appear on the market when these sets are sold.

I recently was shown a black candlestick that only had the end of a butterfly antenna on it. You really had to search to find that little piece of butterfly. The other candlestick of the pair had half a butterfly. Maybe other pieces will turn up where the butterfly flew away. So far, I have not seen one.

The crystal cologne with black stopper turned up after I had previously shown a black cologne sans stopper. To my chagrin I didn't find this cologne while I had access to the topless one. Be sure to check out the dauber in the perfumes. Many of them are broken off or ground down to hide the broken end. Daubers are much harder to find than the bottles themselves; take that into consideration if buying only the bottle. That goes for any perfume or cologne in any pattern. The piece handled most often is the piece that was damaged or broken and tossed away.

The green, heart-shaped candy is shown in front of a box. This box held the heart-shaped candy Valentine's Day gift for someone special. I am amazed that the box was kept all those years.

Flower Garden with Butterflies has three styles of powder jars, which probably explains why so many oval and rectangular dresser trays are found! Dresser trays and luncheon plates are the only routinely found items in this pattern. Indubitably, more powder jars than trays were broken through years of use. Two different footed powders exist with the smaller, 6¼", shown in amber and green. The taller, not shown, stands 7½" high. Thankfully, the lids for these footed powders are the same. The flat powder jar has a 3½" diameter. We never found a blue, flat powder in the time we collected this pattern.

I have already discussed the so-called "Shari" perfume or cologne set in earlier books, but I frequently get letters about it as an unlisted piece of Flower Garden. It's a semi-circular, footed glass dresser box that holds five wedge (pie shaped) bottles. This container is often confused with Flower Garden because it has flower designs on it. Labels found intact on bottles promoted the New York/Paris affiliation of "Charme Volupte" but nowhere was the word "Shari" mentioned on the labels. One bottle had contained cold cream, another vanishing cream, and three others once held "parfumes." There are dancing girls at either end of the box, and flowers abound on the semi-circle. There are no dancing girls on Flower Garden. Other not-to-be-mistaken-for Flower Garden pieces include the 7" and 10" trivets with flowers all over them made by U.S. Glass. They were mixing bowl covers and they do not have butterflies.

	Amber Crystal	Pink Green Blue-Green	Blue Canary Yellow
Ash tray, match-pack holders	165.00	185.00	195.00
Candlesticks, 4" pr.	42.50	55.00	95.00
Candlesticks, 8" pr.	77.50	135.00	130.00
Candy w/cover, 6", flat	130.00	155.00	
Candy w/cover, 7½", cone-shaped	80.00	130.00	175.00
Candy w/cover, heart-shaped		1,250.00	1,300.00
* Cologne bottle w/stopper, 7½"		210.00	350.00
Comport, 2⅞" h.		23.00	28.00
Comport, 3" h., fits 10" plate	20.00	23.00	28.00
Comport, 4¼" h. x 4¾" w.			50.00
Comport, 4¾" h. x 10¼" w.	48.00	65.00	85.00
Comport, 5⅞" h. x 11" w.	55.00		95.00
Comport, 7¼" h. x 8¼" w.	60.00	80.00	
Creamer		75.00	
Cup		70.00	

	Amber Crystal	Pink Green Blue-Green	Blue Canary Yellow
Mayonnaise, ftd., 4¾" h. x 6¼" w., w/7" plate & spoon	70.00	90.00	135.00
Plate, 7"	16.00	21.00	30.00
Plate, 8", two styles	15.00	17.50	25.00
Plate, 10"		42.50	48.00
Plate, 10", indent for 3" comport	32.00	40.00	45.00
Powder jar, 3½", flat		80.00	
Powder jar, ftd., 6¼" h.	75.00	135.00	175.00
Powder jar, ftd., 7½" h.	80.00	145.00	195.00
Sandwich server, center handle	60.00	75.00	110.00
Saucer		25.00	
Sugar		75.00	
Tray, 5½" x 10", oval	55.00	60.00	
Tray, 11¾" x 7¾", rectangular	50.00	65.00	85.00
Tumbler, 7½" oz.	175.00		
Vase, 6¼"	70.00	95.00	160.00
Vase, 10½"		125.00	225.00

* Stopper, if not broken off, ½ price of bottle

FLOWER GARDEN WITH BUTTERFLIES

PRICE LIST FOR BLACK ITEMS ONLY

Item	Price
Bon bon w/cover, 6⅝" diameter	250.00
Bowl, 7¼", w/cover, "flying saucer"	375.00
Bowl, 8½", console, w/base	150.00
Bowl, 9", rolled edge, w/base	200.00
Bowl, 11", ftd. orange	225.00
Bowl, 12", rolled edge console w/base	200.00
Candlestick 6" w/6½" candle, pr.	425.00
Candlestick, 8", pr.	325.00
Cheese and cracker, ftd., 5⅜" h. x 10" w.	325.00
Comport and cover, 2¾" h. (fits 10" indented plate)	200.00
Cigarette box & cover, 4⅜" long	150.00
Comport, tureen, 4¼" h. x 10" w.	250.00
Comport, ftd., 5⅝" h. x 10" w.	225.00
Comport, ftd., 7" h.	175.00
Plate, 10", indented	100.00
Sandwich server, center-handled	135.00
Vase, 6¼", Dahlia, cupped	145.00
Vase, 8", Dahlia, cupped	200.00
Vase, 9", wall hanging	350.00
Vase, 10", 2-handled	225.00
Vase, 10½", Dahlia, cupped	265.00

FORTUNE HOCKING GLASS COMPANY, 1937–1938

Colors: Pink and crystal.

Fortune is a small pattern where luncheon plates are costly and you customarily find them only one at a time. Increased prices greet collectors on nearly all pieces of this small set. This attests to there being collectors who are discovering and treasuring Fortune. In the past, both Fortune tumblers have been bought by collectors of Queen Mary and Old Colony to use with those sets because they were inexpensive and looked fine! Now the prices of Fortune tumblers have come into their own and it is not as feasible to use them with other sets. A little expenditure of time and a little fortune can assemble a set.

A few pitchers whose patterns are similar to Fortune are turning up and some collectors are buying them for use with their sets. These "go-with" pitchers are selling in the $25.00 to $30.00 range. So far, no actual Fortune pitcher has turned up; but never say never!

That covered candy makes a great gift for new collectors or whomever!

	Pink, Crystal
Bowl, 4" berry	8.00
Bowl, 4½" dessert	10.00
Bowl, 4½", handled	10.00
Bowl, 5¼", rolled edge	18.00
Bowl, 7¾" salad or large berry	22.00
Candy dish and cover, flat	25.00

	Pink, Crystal
Cup	10.00
Plate, 6" sherbet	5.00
Plate, 8" luncheon	25.00
Saucer	3.00
Tumbler, 3½", 5 oz. juice	10.00
Tumbler, 4", 9 oz. water	12.00

FRUITS HAZEL ATLAS AND OTHER GLASS COMPANIES, 1931–1935

Colors: Pink, green, some crystal, and iridized.

Fruits collectors have several pieces that are almost impossible to find in this very small pattern. The 3½" (5 ounce) juice and 5" (12 ounce) ice tea tumblers have replaced the large and small berry bowls as the pieces to own. Few of the berry bowls are being found, but even fewer tumblers. I own one ice tea, but two juice tumblers promised to me turned out to be Cherry Blossom. Fruits tumblers have only cherries and no cherry blossoms.

Fruits patterned water tumblers (4") in all colors are the pieces usually seen. Iridescent "Pears" tumblers are abundant. These iridescent tumblers may have been made by Federal Glass Company while they were making iridescent Normandie and a few pieces in Madrid. These are not carnival glass as they are often designated. These tumblers were made over 20 years after the carnival glass era ended. Tumblers with cherries or other fruits are regularly found in pink, but finding any green tumbler is more of a problem.

Since so many collectors are searching for tumblers and bowls, their prices continue upward. I have never seen pink juice or tea tumblers; I am removing them from the listing until someone can prove their existence. Originally, there was only one price listed for all Fruits colors. As more collectors bought the green, the price of green rose faster than that of pink and I split them into two listings, not realizing the nonexistence of pink was hidden under that "all colors" label. Most collectors pursue green water tumblers to go with the pitcher. There are pink water tumblers, but never a pitcher — so far.

Fruits berry bowls in both sizes are among the hardest to obtain in all Depression glass patterns. Since this is not one of the major collected patterns and does not have thousands of admirers, the paucity of both sizes of bowls is only just dawning.

Fruits pitchers have only cherries in the pattern. Sometimes they are mistaken for Cherry Blossom flat bottomed pitchers. Notice that the handle is shaped like that of flat Florentine pitchers (Hazel Atlas Company) and not like Cherry Blossom (Jeannette Glass Company) flat pitchers. Crystal Fruits pitchers sell for less than half the price of green, if they sell at all. Crystal pieces are hardly collected, but tumblers are available should you like an economically priced beverage set!

	Green	Pink
Bowl, 5" berry	32.00	25.00
Bowl, 8" berry	85.00	45.00
Cup	8.00	7.00
Pitcher, 7", flat bottom	90.00	
Plate, 8" luncheon	10.00	10.00
Saucer	5.50	4.00

	Green	Pink
Sherbet	12.00	10.00
Tumbler, 3½" juice	60.00	
* Tumbler, 4" (1 fruit)	20.00	18.00
Tumbler, 4" (combination of fruits)	28.00	22.00
Tumbler, 5", 12 oz.	150.00	

* Iridized $7.50

GEORGIAN, "LOVEBIRDS" FEDERAL GLASS COMPANY, 1931–1936

Colors: Green, crystal, and amber.

Georgian was christened "lovebirds" by early collectors because of those two birds perched side by side on most pieces. Pieces without the birds include both sizes of tumblers, the hot plate, and a few dinner plates. Few collectors seek dinner plates without birds; that style plate sells for less. Baskets customarily alternate with birds in the design on all other pieces. The tumblers only have baskets; you can sometimes find a bargain on tumblers if the seller does not know about the missing birds. A reader informed me that those birds are parakeets. I never gave it much thought since it was being called "lovebirds" when I first learned about Depression glass.

Has anyone else wondered why Federal Glass Company created two bird patterns at the same time. Parrot was the other pattern (early 1930s) made predominately in the same green color. Parrot was also made in amber; and coming full circle, **amber** Georgian 6" sherbet plates are turning up! Birds were very popular designs for glassware in the late 1920s and early 1930s.

Georgian tumblers are difficult to find. Several boxed sets of water tumblers have been found in the Chicago area. These boxes have 36 tumblers still packed in them. I have learned that a Chicago paper gave the tumblers away to subscribers in the 1930s and was told that these were found stored in Al Capone's vault. Geraldo missed them! Prices for iced teas have more than doubled the price of water tumblers. I have owned at least a dozen Georgian waters for every iced tea to give you an idea of how difficult teas are to find. Now, they have gotten so expensive that new collectors are beginning to only buy waters — if they buy tumblers at all.

A few Georgian pieces are easily found. Berry bowls, cups, saucers, sherbets, sherbet plates, and luncheon plates can be readily accumulated. You will have to search hard for other pieces. There are not as many collectors buying this pattern, today, as there were in the mid-1970s when a set was donated to the Smithsonian by the Peach State Depression Glass Club in the name of then President Jimmy Carter. Those particular pieces were engraved and numbered. The extras were sold or given as prizes. If you run into such a prize, cherish it!

Many of the Georgian serving pieces were heavily utilized; so be wary of pieces that are scratched and worn from usage. You **pay a premium for condition!** Remember that all prices listed in this book are for **mint condition** pieces. Damaged or scratched and worn pieces **should go for less** depending upon the extent of damage and wear. If you are gathering this glass to use, some imperfections may not make as much difference as collecting for eventual selling. Mint condition glass will sell more readily and for a much better price if you ever decide to part with your collection. I know you may not plan to ever sell it; but sometimes the best laid plans....

Georgian Lazy Susans (cold cuts servers) are more rarely seen than the Madrid ones that turn up, sporadically, at best! You can see one pictured on page 88. A walnut tray turned up in Ohio with an original decal label that read "Kalter Aufschain Cold Cuts Server Schirmer Cincy." Most of these servers have been found in Kentucky and southern Ohio. These wooden Lazy Susans are made of walnut and are 18½" across with seven 5" openings for holding the so called hot plates. Somehow, I believe these 5" hot plates are mislabeled since they are found on a cold cuts server! These cold cuts (hot) plates also have only the center motif design.

Reports of a Georgian mug have been greatly exaggerated. Someone found a creamer without a spout and labeled it a mug. There are other patterns known that have creamers or pitchers without a spout; and one other Federal pattern, Sharon, has at least one two-spouted creamer known! Spouts were applied by hand at most glass factories using a wooden tool. Quality control of this glass was not as demanding as today.

	Green
Bowl, 4½" berry	10.00
Bowl, 5¾" cereal	25.00
Bowl, 6½" deep	68.00
Bowl, 7½" large berry	62.00
Bowl, 9" oval vegetable	62.00
Butter dish and cover	85.00
Butter dish bottom	50.00
Butter dish top	35.00
Cold cuts server, 18½", wood with seven 5" openings for 5" coasters	900.00
Creamer, 3", ftd.	12.00
Creamer, 4", ftd.	17.00
Cup	10.00
* Hot Plate, 5", center design	50.00
** Plate, 6" sherbet	7.00
Plate, 8" luncheon	12.00
Plate, 9¼" dinner	25.00
Plate, 9¼", center design only	22.00
Platter, 11½", closed-handled	68.00
Saucer	3.00
Sherbet	12.00
Sugar, 3", ftd.	10.00
Sugar, 4", ftd.	12.00
Sugar cover for 3"	45.00
Sugar cover for 4"	165.00
Tumbler, 4", 9 oz., flat	65.00
Tumbler, 5¼", 12 oz., flat	135.00

* Crystal – $20.00

** Amber – $40.00.

GEORGIAN

GOTHIC GARDEN PADEN CITY GLASS COMPANY, 1930s

Colors: Pink, green, black, yellow, and crystal

Gothic Garden is found mostly on Paden City's Line #411 (square shapes with the corners cut off), but you could find it on any Paden City blank. They put their etched lines on whatever blank looked good with the pattern. You may find other colors than those I have listed; let me know if you do, so I can add to the listing. Notice that each etching medallion has two birds, one on each side, looking outward. Pieces may vary up to an inch due to the turned up edges on bowls; so, do not take these measurements as gospel.

I just bought a black bowl like the one pictured in pink at a outdoor antique show last weekend and I saw a flat, yellow candy like the one pictured in "Peacock Reverse" on page 163. It was prized more highly by the owner than by me and he still owns it.

Gothic Garden does have a creamer and sugar which lends credence to the thought that there may be a luncheon set available; lack of cups and saucers hasn't hurt the collecting of other Paden City patterns. All cup and saucers are rare in all etched patterns of this company. Did the etching department not like to work on smaller pieces? For the time being I will only list one price; add 25 percent for black and subtract 25 percent for crystal. What little crystal I have seen has been gold trimmed and will fetch the price of colored ware.

	All colors
Bowl, 9", tab hndl.	45.00
Bowl, 10", ftd.	85.00
Bowl, 10⅛", hndl.	95.00
Bowl, 10½", oval, hndl.	100.00
Cake plate, 10½", ftd.	75.00
Candy, flat	100.00
Comport, tall, deep top	65.00
Creamer	45.00
Plate, 11", tab hndl.	60.00
Server, 9¾", center handled	85.00
Sugar	45.00
Vase, 6½"	125.00
Vase, 8"	145.00
Vase, 9½"	100.00

HEX OPTIC, "HONEYCOMB" JEANNETTE GLASS COMPANY, 1928–1932

Colors: Pink, green, Ultra Marine, and iridescent in 1950s.

Hex Optic pitchers with flat bottoms have been discovered in green. Note the plural. I have had five or six letters telling me they are being found in Minnesota and Wisconsin. For years, no one noticed these pitchers; but once it was illustrated, they seemed to "rain" for a while! The footed pitcher is hardly seen. The flat pitcher is 8" tall and holds 70 ounces. Notice that the Hex Optic pitcher is thick! There are other "honeycomb" impostors out there that are thin. These thin pitchers are not Jeannette and are not rare! Many companies made patterns with a honeycomb design, but this book only covers Jeannette's Hex Optic!

Hex Optic is more noticed by kitchenware clientele than all other patterns of Depression glass because kitchenware pieces were made in Hex Optic. Sugar shakers, bucket reamers, mixing bowls, stacking sets, and butter dishes are desired in green and pink. In fact, were it not for kitchenware collectors becoming addicted to Hex Optic, it might still be inconspicuous and unnoticed.

Iridescent oil lamps, pitchers, and tumblers were all made during Jeannette's iridized craze of the 1950s. I have never been able to verify when the company made the Ultra Marine tumblers. My guess would be in the late 1930s when the company was making Doric and Pansy, but that is only conjecture. You can also find that flat bottomed pitcher iridized. On a recent trip to an antique mall in Kentucky, I spotted three of the iridescent pitchers in different booths. They must have been sold or given away in that area. I had only seen one before then; now that my curiosity is aroused, I will go back in a couple of months and see if they changed hands.

	Pink, Green
Bowl, 4¼" ruffled berry	7.00
Bowl, 7½" large berry	10.00
Bowl, 7¼" mixing	12.00
Bowl, 8¼" mixing	17.50
Bowl, 9" mixing	22.00
Bowl, 10" mixing	25.00
Bucket reamer	55.00
Butter dish and cover, rectangular 1 lb. size	90.00
Creamer, 2 style handles	5.50
Cup, 2 style handles	4.50
Ice bucket, metal handle	20.00
Pitcher, 5", 32 oz., sunflower motif in bottom	22.00
Pitcher, 9", 48 oz., ftd.	50.00
Pitcher, 8", 70 oz., flat	225.00
Plate, 6" sherbet	2.50

	Pink, Green
Plate, 8" luncheon	5.50
Platter, 11" round	15.00
Refrigerator dish, 4" x 4"	12.00
Refrigerator stack set, 4 pc.	65.00
Salt and pepper, pr.	27.50
Saucer	2.50
Sugar, 2 styles of handles	5.50
Sugar shaker	225.00
Sherbet, 5 oz., ftd.	4.50
Tumbler, 3¾", 9 oz.	4.50
Tumbler, 5", 12 oz.	7.00
Tumbler, 4¾", 7 oz., ftd.	7.50
Tumbler, 5¾" ftd.	10.00
Tumbler, 7" ftd.	12.00
Whiskey, 2", 1 oz.	8.00

HOBNAIL HOCKING GLASS COMPANY, 1934–1936

Colors: Crystal, crystal w/red trim, and pink.

Hobnail patterns were made by most Depression era glass companies, but Hocking's Hobnail is easier to recognize because its pieces are shaped like those found in Miss America or Moonstone. In fact, the 1940s Moonstone pattern is actually Hocking's Hobnail design with an added white accent to the hobs and edges. Hobnail serving pieces are difficult to find, but beverage sets are abundant.

Did the picture below stop you as you turned through the book? The light amethyst color pictured below was Lilac according to Anchor Hocking labels on most of the pieces shown. The other color is Ivory which was made mostly for ovenware usage. I believe the Lilac would have sold well, but who could guess why it was never marketed? These pieces are shown compliments of Anchor Hocking. They have been extremely helpful in allowing me to show you pieces that you would never get a chance to view otherwise.

Notice how red-trimmed crystal Hobnail stands out on page 92! Collectors have been captivated by this red trim which is found primarily on the West Coast. The decanter and footed juices are the only red-trimmed pieces I see with any regularity in my travels of the South and Midwest. I bought some additional pieces other than those pictured. They rapidly sold at the first glass show we attended!

Footed juice tumblers were sold along with the decanter as a wine set; thus, it was also a wine glass unless the preacher stopped by. Wine glasses during this era customarily held three ounces. Today, people think water goblets from the Depression era are wine goblets; today's wine connoisseurs need a bigger glass. Dealers should check with customers when they ask for wines since they may really want water goblets!

Only four pieces were made by Hocking in pink. Another pink Hobnail pattern, such as one made by MacBeth-Evans, can coexist with Hocking's; that way, you add a pitcher and tumbler set, something unavailable in Hocking ware. Most other companies' Hobnail patterns will blend with Hocking's Hobnail.

	Pink	*Crystal
Bowl, 5½" cereal		4.00
Bowl, 7" salad		4.50
Cup	6.00	4.50
Creamer, ftd.		3.50
Decanter and stopper, 32 oz.		30.00
Goblet, 10 oz. water		8.00
Goblet, 13 oz. iced tea		10.00
Pitcher, 18 oz. milk		20.00
Pitcher, 67 oz.		25.00
Plate, 6" sherbet	2.50	1.50
Plate, 8½" luncheon	7.50	3.50
Saucer/sherbet plate	2.50	1.50
Sherbet	3.50	3.00
Sugar, ftd.		4.00
Tumbler, 5 oz. juice		4.00
Tumbler, 9 oz., 10 oz. water		5.50
Tumbler, 15 oz. iced tea		15.00
Tumbler, 3 oz. ftd. wine/juice		6.50
Tumbler, 5 oz. ftd. cordial		6.00
Whiskey, 1½ oz.		6.00

*Add 20 – 25% for red trimmed pieces

HOMESPUN, "FINE RIB" JEANNETTE GLASS COMPANY, 1939–1949

Colors: Pink and crystal.

I show all nine Homespun tumblers below. If nothing else, this pattern had tumblers. Unfortunately, there is no pitcher to go with them. Banded top tumblers are hard to find; but most collectors seek the ribbed variety.

Pictured on the right are the 13½ ounce (band at top) tea and the 12½ ounce (no band) tea. In front of them is the 9 ounce (band above ribs, waffle bottomed) tumbler. These are easily distinguished, but confusion reigns with the three tumblers in the middle. There is little difference in height; but the 7 ounce (ribs to top, straight, concentric ring bottom) is on the left, next to the 9 ounce (ribs to top, straight, waffle bottomed). Even though there is a two ounce difference in capacity, there is only 3/16" difference in height. Notice the small 8 ounce (ribs to top, flared, plain bottomed) tumbler on the right. This style is difficult to find. The two footed teas are often confused because they both hold 15 ounces and there is only ⅛" difference in height. Collectors sometimes refer to them as skinny and fat bottomed. There is a slight stem on the taller one and no stem on the other. It only makes a difference when ordering by mail or off the Internet. If you can see them first, you need to remember what you want.

The Homespun cereal bowl has tab handles; but they are difficult to find without inner rim chips! Actually, all three bowls and sherbets suffer from the malady of inner rim roughness (irr). Sherbets do an admirable job of hiding! I haven't seen one at the last few shows I've attended.

Children's Homespun sets are still in demand. There is no child's teapot in crystal and there are no sugar and creamers in this tea set. The teapot looks like a creamer with a sugar lid. You can see the teapot in the center below.

There is no Homespun sugar lid! The lid sometimes found on the sugar is a Fine Rib powder jar top (added by mistake or purposely because it looked right).

	Pink, Crystal
Bowl, 4½", closed handles	15.00
Bowl, 5" cereal, closed handles	27.50
Bowl, 8¼" large berry	24.00
Butter dish and cover	60.00
Coaster/ash tray	6.50
Creamer, ftd.	12.50
Cup	11.00
Plate, 6" sherbet	6.00
Plate, 9¼" dinner	22.00
Platter, 13", closed handles	20.00
Saucer	4.00
Sherbet, low flat	17.50
Sugar, ftd.	12.50
Tumbler, 3⅞", 7 oz., straight	22.00
Tumbler, 4⅛", 8 oz. water, flared top	22.00
Tumbler, 4¼", 9 oz., band at top	22.00
Tumbler, 4 5/16", 9 oz., no band	22.00
Tumbler, 5⅜", 12½ oz. iced tea	33.00
Tumbler, 5⅞", 13½ oz. iced tea, banded at top	33.00
Tumbler, 4", 5 oz., ftd.	7.00
Tumbler, 6¼", 15 oz., ftd.	33.00
Tumbler, 6⅜", 15 oz., ftd.	33.00

HOMESPUN CHILD'S TEA SET

	Pink	Crystal
Cup	35.00	25.00
Saucer	11.00	8.00
Plate	14.00	10.00
Teapot	55.00	
Teapot cover	80.00	
Set: 14-pieces	375.00	
Set: 12-pieces		175.00

INDIANA CUSTARD, "FLOWER AND LEAF BAND" INDIANA GLASS COMPANY 1930s; 1950s

Colors: Ivory or custard, early 1930s; white, 1950s.

Indiana Custard enchants new collectors each year, but few are able to find much of it unless they live in the area of the country near Indiana. Quantities of this pattern have been seen in Ohio and Indiana in the past, but even those areas are beginning to be depleted. This is the region to visit if you are earnestly searching for any Indiana glassware pattern! Collecting Indiana Custard will take time and luck, but it can be done! Most collectors never get a chance to see it in quantity. Once a large group is assembled, you will understand its attraction since it displays much better in a group setting. There is not a appreciable supply of Indiana Custard left to maintain extensive collecting demand; if you like it, better get started gathering it while you can.

Indiana Custard is the only Depression era pattern where cups and sherbets are the most exasperating items to find! Some collectors consider the sherbet overvalued; but those who have searched for years without owning one, would contradict that point! In all honesty, they are probably a good buy at today's price. Cups have been more difficult for me to find than the sherbets, but I usually have found the sherbets in groups of six or eight and the cups one or two at a time. Both sell promptly; there is demand for them even at the expensive prices! One minor problem is consistent color. Some pieces have a whiter cast than the normally found beige color. Speaking of white, Indiana did make this pattern in white in the 1950s under the name Orange Blossom. So far, there is minor demand for that color.

I have been unable to establish if there is a full set available of yellow floral decorated pieces like the plate pictured on the left below. I have seen a set of Indiana Custard decorated like the saucer with the colored flowers standing behind the oval vegetable. After 60 years, a primary problem to collecting this set would be that the decorations flake. Too, after all these years, obtaining an entire set a piece or two at a time is a formidable task! However, most people enjoy the chase! One collector told me that he deliberately chose a infrequently seen pattern so he could have greater satisfaction in finding just one piece!

	French Ivory
Bowl, 5½" berry	12.00
Bowl, 6½" cereal	27.00
Bowl, 7½" flat soup	35.00
Bowl, 9", 1¾" deep, large berry	35.00
Bowl, 9½" oval vegetable	33.00
Butter dish and cover	63.00
Cup	37.50
Creamer	16.00
Plate, 5¾" bread and butter	6.50

	French Ivory
Plate, 7½" salad	18.00
Plate, 8⅞" luncheon	18.00
Plate, 9¾" dinner	30.00
Platter, 11½" oval	38.00
Saucer	8.00
Sherbet	100.00
Sugar	12.00
Sugar cover	25.00

IRIS, "IRIS AND HERRINGBONE" JEANNETTE GLASS COMPANY, 1928–1932; 1950s; 1970s

Colors: Crystal, iridescent; some pink and green; recently bi-colored red/yellow and blue/green combinations, and white.

Crystal production for Iris began in 1928. However, some crystal was made in the late 1940s and into the 1950s, with candy bottoms and vases appearing as late as the early 1970s. Iridescent Iris belongs entirely within the time structure of *Collectible Glassware from the 40s, 50s, 60s....* I settled on including both colors in both books so as to not frustrate collectors.

Prices for crystal Iris have finally stabilized; but for a while, fanatic collectors helped boost prices by buying harder-to-find pieces no matter what the expense. There was already a short supply of several Iris pieces because of heavy demand. That short supply became even shorter for a while. However, as prices increased, collectors who already had sets saw the prices and began to sell their sets; thus rare items again began to appear for sale. Had you bought an eight or twelve place setting a few years ago, you could have made a tidy profit even if you sold it to a dealer. Now, some dealers are stocked with hard-to-find cereals, soups, coasters, and demitasse sets that are not selling well in the new price zone.

Collectors often have affected prices by refusing to buy when they deem items too expensive. Unfortunately, this can boomerang! Pieces can totally disappear into collections while collectors dither. I've heard some lamenting that they had an opportunity to buy such and so previously, but thought it too highly priced. Now, they can't find any for sale! Iris is one of those patterns where this has happened.

Iris used to be a plentiful pattern; now, there is so much sitting in collections that only a few pieces are plentiful. There are enough pitchers, water tumblers, butter dishes, ruffled bowls, and wines to satisfy demands for them! Demitasse **cups** are available; saucers are not. Many of these cups were originally sold on copper saucers instead of glass. The 11" flat fruit bowl is turning up in several variations with pronounced or slightly rolled edges.

Iridescent candy bottoms are a product of the 1970s when Jeannette made crystal bottoms and flashed them with two-tone colors such as red/yellow or blue/green. Many of these were sold as vases; and, over time, the colors have peeled off or been purposely stripped to make them, again, crystal candy bottoms. **These later pieces can be distinguished by the lack of rays on the foot of the dish.** Similarly, white vases were made and sprayed outside in green, red, and blue. White vases sell in the area of $12.50–15.00. Yes, the colors can be removed. **These are not rare!** I saw a pink over white vase in an antique mall yesterday for $90.00 marked "rare pink Iris." I hope that no one believes that! The rare vase is **transparent** pink! Good pink color in transparent Iris vases will bring the price below, but weakly colored pink will not!

The decorated red and gold Iris that keeps turning up was called "Corsage" and "styled by Century" in 1946. This information was on a card attached to a 1946 wedding gift of this ware.

The 8 ounce water goblet; 5¾", 4 ounce goblet; 4" sherbet; and the demitasse cup and saucer are the most difficult pieces to find in iridescent. The 5¾", 4 ounce goblet is shown in the *Very Rare Glassware of the Depression Era, 4th Series.* Three iridescent 4" sherbets were found in Texas.

Published reports on **"new"** Iris iced teas and berry bowls were premature and erroneous. These tea tumblers turned out to be a years-old stash of originally issued Iris packaged in original Jeannette boxes and not scare-touted reproductions.

	Crystal	Iridescent	Transparent Green/ Pink
*** Bowl, 4½", berry, beaded edge	45.00	10.00	
Bowl, 5", ruffled, sauce	9.00	28.00	
Bowl, 5" cereal	125.00		
Bowl, 7½" soup	165.00	60.00	
Bowl, 8" berry, beaded edge	85.00	25.00	
Bowl, 9½", ruffled, salad	12.50	13.00	150.00
Bowl, 11½", ruffled, fruit	15.00	14.00	
Bowl, 11" fruit, straight edge	65.00		
Butter dish and cover	47.50	45.00	
Butter dish bottom	12.50	12.50	
Butter dish top	35.00	32.50	
Candlesticks, pr.	45.00	48.00	
Candy jar and cover	175.00		
Coaster	110.00		
Creamer, ftd.	12.00	12.00	150.00
Cup	15.00	14.00	
* Demitasse cup	35.00	150.00	
* Demitasse saucer	145.00	250.00	
Fruit or nut set	110.00	150.00	
Goblet, 4" wine		30.00	

	Crystal	Iridescent	Transparent Green/ Pink
Goblet, 4½", 4 oz. cocktail	27.50		
Goblet, 4½", 3 oz. wine	17.00		
Goblet, 5½", 4 oz.	28.00	225.00	
Goblet, 5½", 8 oz.	26.00	225.00	
** Lamp shade, 11½"	95.00		
Pitcher, 9½", ftd.	40.00	42.50	
Plate, 5½" sherbet	15.00	14.00	
Plate, 8" luncheon	110.00		
Plate, 9" dinner	55.00	48.00	
Plate, 11¾" sandwich	33.00	33.00	
Saucer	12.00	11.00	
Sherbet, 2½", ftd.	28.00	15.00	
Sherbet, 4", ftd.	28.00	225.00	
Sugar	11.00	11.00	150.00
Sugar cover	12.00	12.00	
Tumbler, 4", flat	150.00		
Tumbler, 6", ftd.	18.00	16.00	
*** Tumbler, 6½", ftd.	35.00		
Vase, 9"	27.50	25.00	195.00

* Ruby, Blue, Amethyst priced as iridescent
** Colors, $85.00
*** Has not been reproduced

JUBILEE LANCASTER GLASS COMPANY, EARLY 1930s

Colors: Yellow, crystal, and pink.

A definition of Jubilee accepted by more and more dealers and collectors is that if the piece has a 12 or 16 petaled open centered flower, then it is Jubilee, regardless of the blank on which it is cut. A pink 12" vase, previously listed only in yellow, has now been discovered. It has a 4" top, 3½" base, and a bulbous 6" middle.

A predicament in buying Jubilee is all the look-alike items as well as all the items with the same cutting on different mould blanks. Some Jubilee collectors exasperate dealers with their nit-picking over what is (and what isn't) Jubilee, while others are just happy to discover any similar flower cuttings on Lancaster blanks! The four pink pieces pictured below all have the Jubilee cutting, but are on a different mould blank that is not considered to be Jubilee by purists. There are, also, other Lancaster look-alike patterns that have 16 petals or 12 petals with a smaller petal in between the larger ones. Most of my customers delight in buying look-alike items for less!

Reports continue to come in about 11½", three-footed, scalloped, flattened bowls to go with the curved up 11½" bowl customarily called a rose bowl. The 3", eight ounce, non-stemmed sherbet has 11 petals as does the three-footed covered candy. You can see that sherbet and the oyster cocktail in the *Very Rare Glassware of the Depression Years, Fourth Series.* Having only 11 petals on the candy and sherbet apparently came from cutting problems experienced when using the standard 6" cutting wheel. The foot of the sherbet and the knob on the candy were in the way when a petal of the design was cut directly up and down. The glass cutter had to move over to the side in order to cut a petal. Because of this placement, only an 11 petal flower resulted on these pieces. Yes! Those two 11 petal pieces are Jubilee and both are hard to find. Those two exceptions nit-pickers have had to accept.

According to the catalog number, the liner plate to the mayonnaise is the same piece as the 8¾" plate. There is no indented plate for the mayonnaise shown in the catalogs. However, some plates found under the mayonnaise have an indent. Most mayonnaise sets have 16 petals! As I mentioned above, most Jubilee should have 12 petals and an open-centered flower, but there are exceptions! The catalog sheets that show the mayonnaise picture one with 16 petals!

Groups of Jubilee luncheon pieces consisting of cups, saucers, creamer, sugar, footed tumblers, and luncheon plates are available. In fact, the seeming plethora of these items for sale has prices for those on a slight downward trend. However, there is a problem finding any other pieces of Jubilee. New collectors **can** obtain a gorgeous luncheon set in Jubilee reasonably; but prices on the seldom found items are high! Fortunately, you can choose whatever pieces you wish to own.

I have found Jubilee mostly in Ohio in the past; but I've come to believe that it must have been distributed in Florida. For example, I attended a show here just this morning and saw three sets of Jubilee for sale — and reasonably priced!

Crystal pieces are turning up in small batches and I have shown a few in the top photograph. It's attractive; but, for me, it hasn't the attraction of the yellow!

	Pink	Yellow
Bowl, 8", 3-ftd., 5⅛" high	250.00	200.00
Bowl, 9" handled fruit		125.00
Bowl, 11½", flat fruit	195.00	160.00
Bowl, 11½", 3-ftd.	250.00	250.00
Bowl, 11½", 3-ftd., curved in		225.00
Bowl, 13", 3-ftd.	250.00	225.00
Candlestick, pr.	185.00	185.00
Candy jar, w/lid, 3-ftd.	325.00	325.00
Cheese & cracker set	255.00	265.00
Creamer	35.00	18.00
Cup	40.00	13.00
Mayonnaise & plate	295.00	250.00
w/original ladle	310.00	265.00
Plate, 7" salad	22.50	14.00
Plate, 8¾" luncheon	27.50	12.00
Plate, 13½" sandwich, handled	85.00	50.00
Plate, 14", 3-ftd.		200.00
Saucer, two styles	12.00	4.00
Sherbet, 3", 8 oz.		70.00
Stem, 4", 1 oz. cordial		250.00
Stem, 4¾", 4 oz. oyster cocktail		75.00
Stem, 4⅞", 3 oz. cocktail		150.00
Stem, 5½", 7 oz. sherbet/champagne		95.00
Stem, 7½", 11 oz.		165.00
Sugar	35.00	18.00
Tray, 11", 2-handled cake	65.00	45.00
Tumbler, 5", 6 oz. ftd. juice		95.00
Tumbler, 6", 10 oz. water	75.00	33.00
Tumbler, 6⅛", 12½ oz. iced tea		150.00
Tray, 11", center-handled sandwich	195.00	210.00
Vase, 12"	350.00	350.00

LACED EDGE, "KATY BLUE" IMPERIAL GLASS COMPANY, EARLY 1930s

Colors: Blue w/opalescent edge and green w/opalescent edge.

Pieces of Imperial's Laced Edge pattern were manufactured in a prodigious display of colors; only **opalescent** blue and green are being dealt with in this book. Most of the colors without the white edge were made into the 1950s and later; so, they creep out of the time setting (pre 1940) for this book! Imperial called this white edging "Sea Foam." Some Sea Foam treatment barely covers the edge of pieces while others have a ½" of prominent, opalescent edging.

The opalescent blue is frequently called "Katy Blue" by its long-time collectors, but I have never heard the green called "Katy Green." Blue and green pieces without the white edge sell for about half of the prices listed. There does not appear to be much demand for crystal. I have never seen crystal pieces with Sea Foam. Have you?

Some collectors do not accept the 12" cake plate (luncheon plate in Imperial catalog) or the 9" vegetable bowl (salad in ad) as Laced Edge because the edges are more open than those of the other items. Thanks go to a Laced Edge collector from Illinois for sharing an original ad (page 100) showing an inflated retail price along with the cost in coupons for Laced Edge pieces. **Notice the bowl and cake plate are shown with this pattern!** Originally, you could obtain six tumblers for fewer coupons than the platter or divided, oval bowl!

The rarely encountered, undivided, oval vegetable bowl is missing from this ad and most collections today!

Creamers have several different styles of lips because their spouts were individually made. Cereal bowls vary from 4⅞" to 5⅝", soup bowls from 6⅞" to 7¼", and berry bowls from 4⅜" to 4¾". Size differences were caused by turning out the edge of the bowl. Some edges go straight up while others are flattened. Collectors will accept differences in order to have enough bowls!

	Opalescent
Basket bowl	225.00
Bowl, 4⅜"–4¾" fruit	30.00
Bowl, 5"	37.50
Bowl, 5½"	37.50
Bowl, 5⅞"	37.50
Bowl, 7" soup	85.00
Bowl, 9" vegetable	100.00
Bowl, 11" divided oval	115.00
Bowl, 11" oval	150.00
Candlestick, double, pr.	175.00
Cup	35.00
Creamer	40.00
Mayonnaise, 3-piece	135.00
Plate, 6½" bread & butter	18.00
Plate, 8" salad	35.00
Plate, 10" dinner	85.00
Plate, 12" luncheon (per catalog description)	80.00
Platter, 13"	175.00
Saucer	15.00
Sugar	42.50
Tidbit, 2-tiered, 8" & 10" plates	100.00
Tumbler, 9 oz.	55.00

LACED EDGE

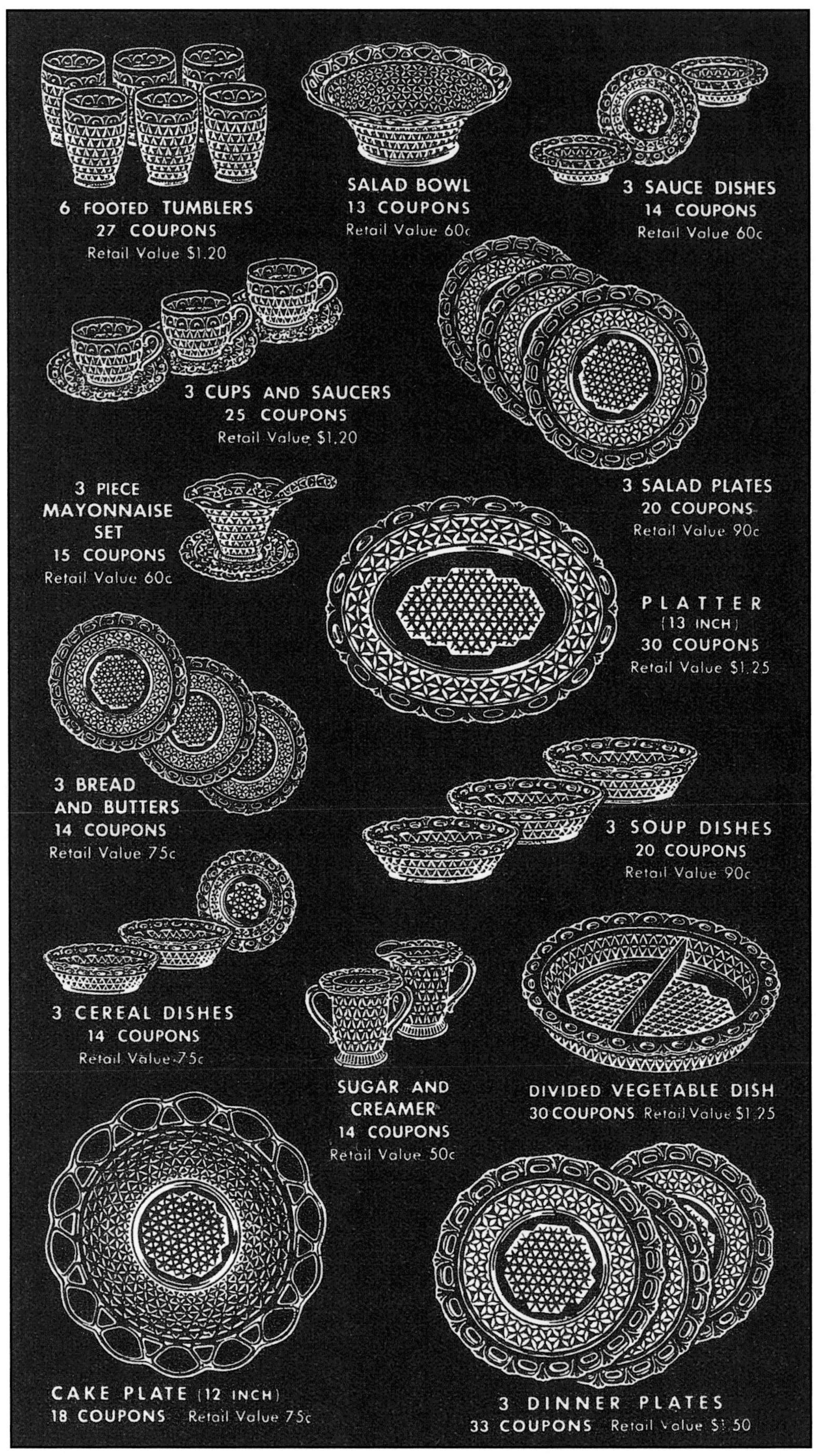
6 FOOTED TUMBLERS
27 COUPONS
Retail Value $1.20
SALAD BOWL
13 COUPONS
Retail Value 60c
3 SAUCE DISHES
14 COUPONS
Retail Value 60c
3 CUPS AND SAUCERS
25 COUPONS
Retail Value $1.20
3 SALAD PLATES
20 COUPONS
Retail Value 90c
3 PIECE
MAYONNAISE
SET
15 COUPONS
Retail Value 60c
PLATTER
(13 INCH)
30 COUPONS
Retail Value $1.25
3 BREAD
AND BUTTERS
14 COUPONS
Retail Value 75c
3 SOUP DISHES
20 COUPONS
Retail Value 90c
3 CEREAL DISHES
14 COUPONS
Retail Value 75c
SUGAR AND
CREAMER
14 COUPONS
Retail Value 50c
DIVIDED VEGETABLE DISH
30 COUPONS Retail Value $1.25
CAKE PLATE (12 INCH)
18 COUPONS Retail Value 75c
3 DINNER PLATES
33 COUPONS Retail Value $1.50

LAKE COMO HOCKING GLASS COMPANY, 1934–1937

Color: White with blue scene.

You can find only thirteen different pieces of Lake Como and each of these are pictured below. However, only the sugar, creamer, and shakers are found regularly. Other pieces are seen occasionally; they are usually worn or badly faded from use. The prices below are for **mint** condition Lake Como (full bright pattern). You should be able to buy worn Lake Como at 50% to 80% of the prices listed depending upon the amount of wear.

Lake Como is an elusive pattern that some collectors say they never see when looking for glass. I find it sporadically, but some pieces in all the sets I have acquired have been worn. One collector informed me that he had decided to buy less than mint glass in order to have some of the harder-to-find pieces. When exhibited for sale, "like new" Lake Como sells very quickly!

The cereal bowl is pictured standing up next to the sugar so you can see the pattern. It is not a smaller plate that is unlisted.

The flat soup is standing up on the right of the middle row. The floral decoration on the edge is embossed (like the normally found Vitrock soup) instead of painted in blue. You will find platters and vegetable bowls are almost as difficult to find as soup bowls; but most collectors are looking for several soups, which creates a greater problem than finding only one platter or bowl. Finding either style cup will be a headache. That collector who only needed six more cup and saucer sets to have one of every pattern in the book still had Lake Como to find. Part of the charm of collecting is in the **hunt!**

Item	Price
Bowl, 6" cereal	27.50
Bowl, 9¾" vegetable	55.00
Bowl, flat soup	100.00
Creamer, ftd.	32.50
Cup, regular	30.00
Cup, St. Denis	30.00
Plate, 7¼" salad	20.00
Plate, 9¼" dinner	35.00
Platter, 11"	75.00
Salt & pepper, pr.	45.00
Saucer	12.00
Saucer, St. Denis	12.00
Sugar, ftd.	32.50

LARGO LINE #220 and MAYA LINE #221 PADEN CITY GLASS COMPANY, 1930s

Colors: Amber, cobalt blue, crystal, crystal w/ruby flash, light blue, red.

Paden City's Largo (#220) and Maya (#221) are most often noticed by Cambridge collectors due to the propensity of dealers mislabeling the light blue color as Cambridge. These small patterns were not as widely distributed as was Cambridge glass, but there are collectors now who wish they had been. We have been buying them piece by painstaking piece for several years in order to put them in the book; and from that experience of buying, I can tell you that the cheese dish and candy are both relatively scarce, if not rare. If you bump into those pieces, you'd better latch onto them.

The elegant, four-footed sugar and creamer are also prized by sugar and creamer collectors. Those item collectors can put a dent in the meager supply for Largo/Maya seekers. Etched patterns can be found on both light blue and crystal. (See the blue Largo plate standing in the back of the top picture.) I have never seen etches on red or cobalt blue. Unfortunately, we sold some cobalt items before Cathy talked me into looking for these patterns for the book; and we didn't find any pieces in that color to replace them. Please note that Maya pieces can be distinguished from Largo by the thistle (ball) design. Perhaps we can find enough pieces of each to separate the two patterns in future editions.

You have to be observant to notice the Largo pattern line on the candle. I glanced right over one at a show recently; fortunately, Cathy noticed it and we have a red one to show you next time! Actually, she even found a blue one just yesterday.

Since these are new patterns to the book, I would greatly appreciate your sharing any further information you might have regarding them!

	Crystal	Colors
Bowl, 6", deep	18.00	35.00
Bowl, 7½"	20.00	37.50
Bowl, 7", flared rim	18.00	35.00
Bowl, 9", tab-handled	25.00	65.00
Bowl, 11⅝", 3½" deep, tri-ftd., flared rim	30.00	70.00
Bowl, 12¾", 4¾" deep, tri-ftd., flat rim	30.00	70.00
Cake plate, pedestal	35.00	75.00
Candleholder	25.00	50.00
Candy, flat w/lid, 3-part	30.00	95.00
Cheese dish w/lid	65.00	150.00
Comport, cracker	15.00	25.00
Comport, fluted rim, pedestal	35.00	75.00

	Crystal	Colors
Comport, 6½" x 10", plain rim, pedestal	32.50	70.00
Creamer, ftd.	22.00	45.00
Cup	15.00	25.00
Mayonnaise, tri-ftd.	15.00	30.00
Plate, 6⅝"	8.00	15.00
Plate, 7", mayo	10.00	20.00
Plate, 8"	10.00	20.00
Plate, 10¾", cheese w/indent	20.00	40.00
Saucer	5.00	10.00
Sugar, ftd.	22.00	45.00
Tray, 13¾", tri-ftd., serving	20.00	60.00
Tray, 14", five-part, relish	27.50	75.00
Tray, tab-handled	20.00	50.00

LARGO

LAUREL McKEE GLASS COMPANY, 1930s

Colors: French Ivory, Jade Green, White Opal, and Poudre Blue.

McKee's Poudre Blue Laurel has traditionally been the color most desired by collectors. However, the demand for Jade-ite collectibles has spilled over into the Jade Green Laurel and rapidly raised prices in that color. Most collectors (incorrectly) refer to McKee's Jade Green by the Hocking name, Jade-ite. Jade Green is the Laurel color most often found followed closely by French Ivory (beige) and then Poudre Blue, usually called Delphite by collectors. I mentioned that some collectors were beginning to search for Jade Green Laurel two years ago. Little did I know what was about to happen with the pattern when I wrote that. Jade-ite's popularity has certainly been a boon for Jade Green Laurel. It had been pretty much ignored by collectors for years. There may be some portent in that regarding other overlooked Depression wares!

A soup bowl in blue has recently been found. You can see it pictured in *Very Rare Glassware of the Depression Years, Fifth Series.* French Ivory (beige) excites few collectors; so, prices there have remained stable for several years. Now might be the time to consider a set in that color before other collectors get that idea! Ivory colored ware may be the next big color acquisition. I'm noticing some of that trend in Fire-King already.

Serving pieces in all colors are insufficient. Some collectors of Depression glass are sending photos showing how they have **combined several colors in one or more patterns** to achieve ample serving capabilities. Sparseness of pieces in a single color is giving birth to some pleasingly creative settings!

Children's Laurel tea sets are rarely seen today. The Scottie dog decorated sets are the most desired children's sets in Depression glass in both Jade Green and French Ivory! Collectors of Scottie dog items have pushed the prices of these sets to double what they were selling for only a few years ago! Add to that all the collectors of children's dishes and there is not enough of this scarce set to accommodate all collecting fields! One collector told me she'd be happy just to own *one* piece, let alone the entire set!

In limited quantities, Laurel children's sets are also found with border trims of red, green, or orange. Orange borders are the most difficult to discover. Watch for wear on these colored trims; it appears many children did, in fact, play with these dishes!

Laurel shakers are hard to find with **bold** patterns. Many Laurel shaker designs are vague and indistinct. Definitely, it's better to own a patterned Laurel shaker than one that has only the right shape! Doric and Pansy shakers are the only other Depression pattern to have this same problem! Jade Green Laurel shakers are quite rare. There are enough collectors buying Jade, today, to expose this scarcity.

	White Opal, Jade Green	French Ivory	Poudre Blue
Bowl, 4¾" berry	14.00	9.00	15.00
Bowl, 6" cereal	20.00	12.00	28.00
Bowl, 6", three legs	20.00	15.00	
Bowl, 7⅞" soup	38.00	35.00	85.00
Bowl, 9" large berry	32.00	28.00	55.00
Bowl, 9¾" oval vegetable	45.00	28.00	55.00
Bowl, 10½", three legs	50.00	38.00	70.00
Bowl, 11"	50.00	40.00	85.00
Candlestick, 4" pr.	60.00	40.00	
Candlestick, 3 ftd.	60.00		
Cheese dish and cover	75.00	58.00	
Creamer, short	20.00	10.00	
Creamer, tall	22.00	15.00	40.00
Cup	12.00	9.00	22.00

	White Opal, Jade Green	French Ivory	Poudre Blue
Plate, 6" sherbet	12.00	5.00	10.00
Plate, 7½" salad	15.00	10.00	16.00
Plate, 9⅛" dinner	17.00	15.00	30.00
Plate, 9⅛" grill, round or scalloped	20.00	15.00	
Platter, 10¾" oval	33.00	30.00	50.00
Salt and pepper	75.00	45.00	
Saucer	3.50	3.00	7.50
Sherbet	18.00	12.00	
Sherbet/champagne, 5"	60.00	50.00	
Sugar, short	20.00	10.00	
Sugar, tall	22.00	11.00	35.00
Tumbler, 4½", 9 oz., flat	60.00	40.00	
Tumbler, 5", 12 oz., flat		55.00	

CHILDREN'S LAUREL TEA SET

	Plain	Green or Decorated Rims	Scottie Dog Green	Scottie Dog Ivory
Creamer	25.00	50.00	150.00	100.00
Cup	20.00	35.00	80.00	50.00
Plate	10.00	16.00	55.00	35.00
Saucer	8.00	10.00	55.00	25.00
Sugar	25.00	50.00	150.00	100.00
14-piece set	205.00	335.00	1,075.00	650.00

LAUREL

LINCOLN INN FENTON GLASS COMPANY, LATE 1920s

Colors: Red, cobalt, light blue, amethyst, black, green, green opalescent, pink, crystal, amber, and jade (opaque).

Evidently, Fenton's Lincoln Inn stems were bought to go with china patterns. They abound! Today, you might be able to collect an entire setting in crystal, but any other color will be a battle, although tableware was advertised in at least eight of the above listed colors in 1929. Red and the several shades of blue remain the most alluring colors for collectors. The good news is that those are the colors that are most often found! Depicted are some of the sundry colors you could collect if you are willing to buy a piece or two at a time. This pattern fits the rainbow collecting scheme that is beginning to mushroom in glass collecting circles.

The most plentiful stems are the champagne/sherbets in all colors. You can also find tumblers and stems with little difficulty; but acquiring a pitcher or serving pieces in **any** color is a chore. Bear in mind that Fenton remade an iridized, dark carnival colored pitcher in the 1980s! Any other **iridescent** piece you might see in this pattern is of recent vintage! All light blue pitchers have been found in the south; so watch for them!

A 1930s catalog shows Lincoln Inn plates with a fruit design in the center. I have a crystal one pictured in the bottom photo, and I saw a 9" crystal bowl with the fruit center at an antique mall in Florida. Also, a collector reported owning several 8" pink plates with this (fruits) intaglio design.

Shakers in Lincoln Inn continue to be troublesome to find in all colors. Collectors who only search for shakers tell me these may not be the highest priced in the book, but they are among the most difficult to find. Red and black shakers are the favored colors; but do not pass **any** color in your travels — even crystal. I once found a red pair sitting with Royal Ruby in a dark corner of a shop. They were a bargain! You need to check in every nook and cranny in shops that do not specifically admire Depression glass as we do.

Many red Lincoln Inn pieces are more amberina in color. For novices, amberina is red glass that has some yellow tint to it. Older red glass was made by reheating glass that first came from the furnace as yellow glass. The glass was then reheated to change it to red; irregular heating caused some parts of it to remain yellow. Some dealers have told collectors this is a rare color in order to sell it. In a certain sense, that may have an element of truth. Actually, it was a mistake; and the differing amounts of yellow on each piece make it hard to match colors. Some old timers in glass collecting refuse amberina pieces for their collections. However, there is a growing body of followers for amberina glass! That may have something to do with the growing fascination I'm beginning to see for any two-toned glassware.

	Cobalt Blue, Red	**All Other Colors
Ash tray	17.50	12.00
Bon bon, handled square	15.00	12.00
Bon bon, handled oval	16.00	12.00
Bowl, 5" fruit	11.50	8.50
Bowl, 6" cereal	15.00	9.00
Bowl, 6", crimped	15.00	8.50
Bowl, handled olive	15.00	9.50
Bowl, finger	20.00	12.50
Bowl, 9", shallow		23.00
Bowl, 9¼", ftd.	75.00	30.00
Bowl, 10½", ftd.	75.00	35.00
Candy dish, ftd. oval	45.00	20.00
Comport	30.00	14.50
Creamer	22.50	14.50
Cup	20.00	10.00
Goblet, water	27.00	15.50
Goblet, wine	30.00	16.50
Nut dish, ftd.	25.00	12.00
Pitcher, 7¼", 46 oz.	800.00	700.00
Plate, 6"	7.50	4.50
Plate, 8"	12.50	10.00
Plate, 9¼"	35.00	11.50
Plate, 12"	40.00	15.50
* Salt/pepper, pr.	275.00	175.00
Sandwich server, center hndl.	175.00	100.00
Saucer	5.00	3.50
Sherbet, 4½", cone shape	17.00	11.50
Sherbet, 4¾"	20.00	12.50
Sugar	20.00	14.00
Tumbler, 4 oz. flat juice	30.00	9.50
Tumbler, 9 oz. flat water		19.50
Tumbler, 5 oz., ftd.	30.00	11.00
Tumbler, 9 oz., ftd.	30.00	14.00
Tumbler, 12 oz., ftd.	45.00	19.00
Vase, 9¾"	150.00	85.00
Vase, 12", ftd.	195.00	100.00

*Black $300.00 ** w/fruits, add 20 – 25%

LINCOLN INN

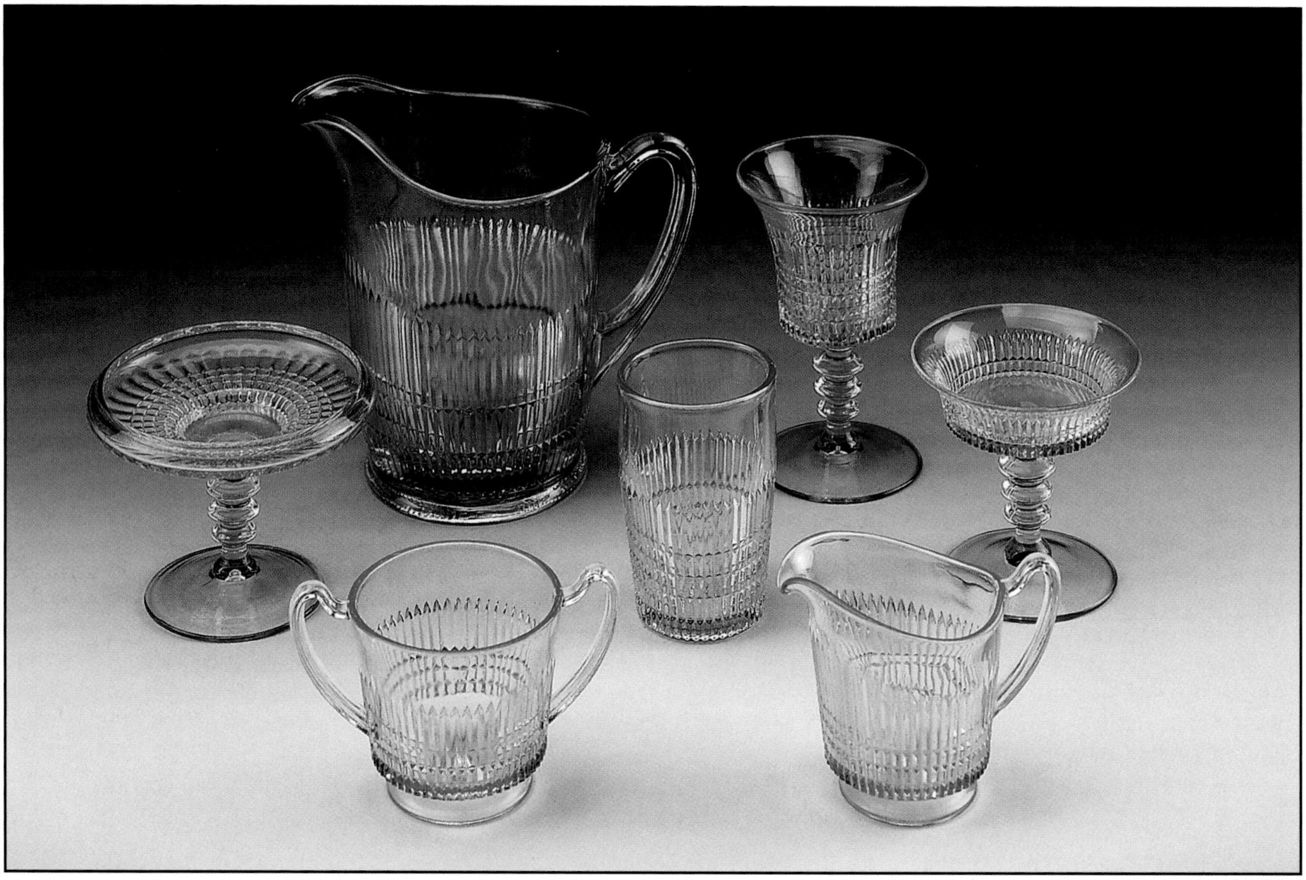

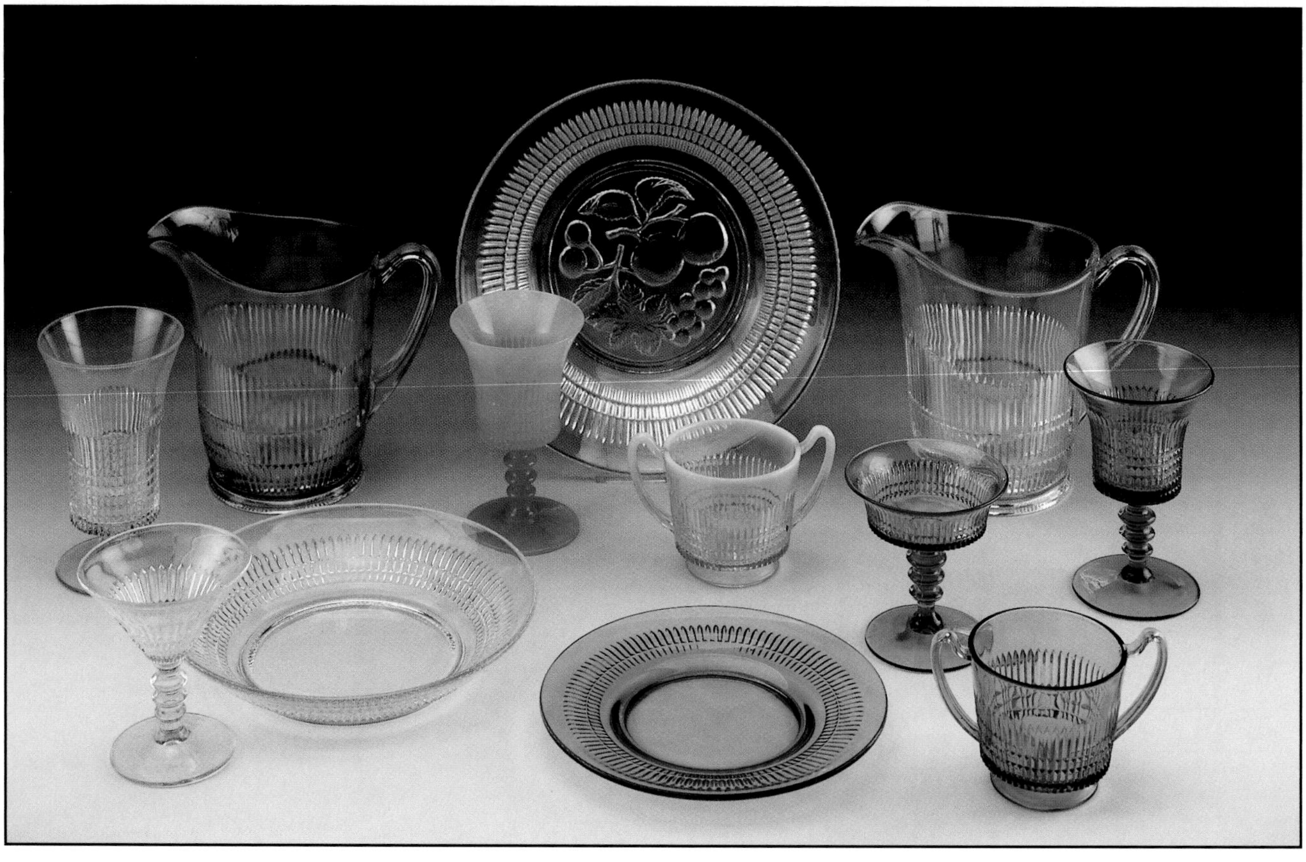

"LITTLE JEWEL" Line #330 DIAMOND BLOCK IMPERIAL GLASS COMPANY, LATE 1920s–EARLY 1930s

Colors: Black, crystal, green, iridescent, pink, white, yellow.

"Little Jewel" is a wee Imperial pattern that is beginning to attract a few collectors by its appealing design. Rarely do people even know what pattern they are buying. They are only purchasing it because it looks pleasing to the eye. Colored items are admired the most, but little color is being found. I did buy a green sugar and creamer last week which will add to the next book's picture.

The blue handled jelly on the second row almost disappeared in the dark blue background, but that color is found in small quantities. I suggest if you find items in blue, buy them!

You will find mostly crystal, which will stand on its own merit due to the strong design. This "Little Jewel" won't cause you sticker shock and I think you'll enjoy having it in your home!

	Crystal	Colors
Bowl, 5½", square, honey dish	10.00	15.00
Bowl, 5", lily	10.00	12.00
Bowl, 6½"	10.00	15.00
Bowl, 7½", berry	15.00	18.00
Celery, 8½", tray	18.00	22.50
Creamer	8.00	15.00

	Crystal	Colors
Jelly, 4½", hndl.	8.00	12.00
Jelly, 5", ftd.	10.00	15.00
Jug, pint tankard	22.50	45.00
Pickle dish, 6½"	12.50	20.00
Sugar	8.00	15.00
Vase, 6", bouquet	12.00	18.00

LORAIN, "BASKET," No. 615 INDIANA GLASS COMPANY, 1929–1932

Colors: Green, yellow, and some crystal.

Lorain's only problem for collectors, other than its scarcity, is a bit of mould roughness on the seams. If you are obstinate about absolutely **mint** condition glassware, then you should concentrate on some other pattern.

After buying and selling various collections of Lorain and discussing ideas with collectors who have hunted Lorain for years, I have reached several conclusions. Buy any cereal bowls you can find! Check the inner rims closely; they damage easily. The 8" deep berry is the most difficult piece to ferret out. A majority of collectors only want one of these; that is not as big an impediment as finding four or more cereals. Dinner plates are almost as scarce as cereals. Watch for scratching on the plates since they can be concealed by the pattern if you do not inspect them closely! Oval vegetable bowls are sporadically found in both colors. Saucers are harder to encounter than cups because of mould roughness and wear and tear on them over the years. Collecting has reversed. Dealers used to refuse to buy saucers unless there were cups with them. Today, many of these once spurned saucers are enthusiastically bought whether there are cups or not! There are at least a dozen or more patterns of Depression glass where saucers are more difficult to find than cups. Since Lorain is scarce, you might be tempted to buy pieces that are less than mint when you find them; just try to do so at less than the **mint prices** below!

Rarer pieces of Lorain display the tendency to surge in price occasionally. Usually that means several collectors are all needing the same piece at about the same time. Collectors are starting to buy green Lorain because of price and availability. Green is less expensive and more easily found. A few pieces are found in crystal, but I'm not sure a set could be found in crystal. A few items could complement your colored sets, however.

Some crystal is found with colored borders of red, yellow, green, and blue. For those who have written to ask about the snack tray, one with yellow trim is pictured in the top photograph. It was made from the platter mould that had an indent added for a cup rest. Crystal cups are sometimes found trimmed in the four colors to match the snack trays; frequently, they are only crystal. To date, these snack trays have only been found in crystal or crystal with trims.

New collectors, please note that the white and green avocado colored sherbets (which have an open lace border) are a mid-1950s (or later) issue made by Anchor Hocking. They were used regularly by florists for small floral arrangements and many are found with a tacky, clay-like substance in the bottom that was used to secure flowers. Not long ago, they were acclaimed as an Indiana product; but several have been found with Anchor Hocking stickers. I have not been able to find these in catalogs, but Anchor Hocking did affix labels in the late 1950s and early 1960s.

I've had a couple of letters regarding goblets with a basket design like that of Lorain. These are an early Tiffin product. If you want to use them with Lorain, do so!

	Crystal, Green	Yellow
Bowl, 6" cereal	47.50	67.50
Bowl, 7¼" salad	47.50	67.50
Bowl, 8" deep berry	110.00	175.00
Bowl, 9¾" oval vegetable	50.00	65.00
Creamer, ftd.	20.00	27.50
Cup	11.00	15.00
Plate, 5½" sherbet	10.00	12.50
Plate, 7¾" salad	10.00	15.00
Plate, 8⅜" luncheon	20.00	30.00
Plate, 10¼" dinner	48.00	63.00
Platter, 11½"	30.00	45.00
Relish, 8", 4-part	20.00	38.00
Saucer	4.50	6.00
Sherbet, ftd.	25.00	35.00
Snack tray, crystal/trim	22.50	
Sugar, ftd.	20.00	27.50
Tumbler, 4¾", 9 oz. ftd.	25.00	35.00

LOTUS PATTERN #1921 WESTMORELAND GLASS COMPANY, 1921 – 1970

Colors: Amber, amethyst, black, blue, crystal, green, milk, pink, red, and various satinized applied colors; cased colors.

Lotus was a very long lived Westmoreland pattern which (thanks to Chas West Wilson's *Westmoreland Glass* book) we know to have been designed by Gustav Horn. We began buying Lotus because my allergic wife loves flowers but can't be around the real ones. So, she compensates with glass or silk varieties. Her first encounter with Lotus (instant delight) was with the green, petal bottomed candles which immediately decorated our dining room table. Then came the tall, twist stem compote which joined the candles as a centerpiece. Next, I noticed little mayo bowls clustered about like water lilies on a pond. I got the message; I began to pick up a piece every so often to her delight. Pictured are various items we've accumulated over the years. Indeed, when we decided to include this pattern in the book, she had to go throughout the house dismantling arrangements from mantles and tabletops. In the satinized items pictured below, the green on the right and the domed blue candle are later issues.

Atop page 113 are transparent colors. The amethyst and the domed amber candle are later colors as is the red candle. Notice the flattened foot on the green candle in front. This mashed version indicates it is from an older mould. That green candy in the back needs a lid, which is flat, not domed, and nestles below the petal rim. The bottom photo on 113 illustrates some of the cased colors found. My wife is partial to the yellow with amethyst tipped overlay, but I prefer the blue. I bought a large grouping of the two-toned yellow (Cathy's "sunshine bowls") labeled as Hocking. The dealer thought it was like the petal bowl and liner in Fire-King which have delighted everyone for 60 years past their manufacture.

There are several rare pieces of Lotus including a lamp, tumbler, cologne bottle, and puff box, although most colognes found are of later manufacture. They are still desirable. You can be assured they are old if they have cased colors. The elusive tumbler is crystal with a green petal foot. All opalescent edged Lotus was made near the end of Westmoreland's production.

	Amber Crystal White	Blue, Green Pink	*Satinized Colors
Bowl, 6", lily (flat mayonnaise)	15.00	25.00	40.00
Bowl, 9", cupped	55.00	85.00	110.00
Bowl, 11", belled	65.00	95.00	125.00
Bowl, oval vegetable	55.00	85.00	110.00
Candle, 4", single	20.00	35.00	40.00
Candle, 9" high, twist stem	40.00	65.00	85.00
Candy jar w/lid, ½ lb.	65.00	95.00	125.00
Coaster	12.00	15.00	20.00
Cologne, ½ oz.	75.00	100.00	125.00
Comport, 2½", mint, twist stem	35.00		
Comport, 6½" honey	18.00	25.00	45.00
Comport, 5" high	30.00	40.00	50.00
Comport, 8½" high, twist stem	50.00	85.00	110.00
Creamer	22.00	28.00	35.00
Lamp	150.00	200.00	
Mayonnaise, 4", ftd., flared rim	15.00	20.00	30.00
Mayonnaise, 5", ftd., bell rim	27.50	52.50	72.50
Plate, 6" mayonnaise	8.00	12.00	15.00
Plate, 8½" salad	10.00	35.00	40.00
Plate, 8¾" mayonnaise	12.50	17.50	22.50
Plate, 13", flared	35.00	50.00	65.00
Puff box, 5", w/cover	85.00	110.00	
Salt, individual	9.00	15.00	20.00
Shaker	25.00	35.00	
Sherbet, tulip bell	20.00	30.00	35.00
Sugar	22.00	28.00	35.00
Tray, lemon, 6", hndl.	22.50	30.00	40.00
Tumbler, 10 oz.		25.00	

* Add ⅓ for cased colors

MADRID FEDERAL GLASS COMPANY, 1932–1939; INDIANA GLASS COMPANY, 1980s

Colors: Green, pink, amber, crystal, and "Madonna" blue. (See Reproduction Section.)

An about-to-be collector at a recent show looked at an amber Madrid, thin tumbler and remarked, "Isn't this exquisite!" It reminded me that much glass made during this period is just that! Madrid has been subject of controversy since 1976 when the Federal Glass Company remanufactured this pattern for the Bicentennial under a new name, "Recollection" glassware. Each piece was embossed '76 in the design; but it was remade in an amber color comparable to the original which caused concern with collectors of the older amber Madrid. (This resurrecting older patterns under new headings and colors has been a standard practice by the more enduring glass companies over the years.) Because collectors were informed about the product and many presumed it would someday be collectible as a Bicentennial product, if nothing else, many purchased these sets. Unhappily, Indiana Glass bought the Madrid moulds when Federal went out of business, removed the '76 date and made crystal. The older crystal butter was selling for several hundred dollars and the new one sold for $2.99. Prices nose-dived! Next, they made pink; and even though it was a lighter pink than the original, prices dipped in the collectibles market for the old pink. Later, Indiana made blue; it is a brighter, harsher blue than the beautiful, soft blue of the original Madrid; still, it had a devastating effect on the prices of the 1930s blue. All pieces made in pink have now been made in blue. Any blue piece found without a price below is new! After blue came teal, finally, a color not made in the 1930s! Remarkably, today, that is all water under the bridge and knowledgeable collectors are, once again, seeking the beautiful Madrid with aplomb.

I keep spotting the later-made pink Madrid sugar and creamers with high prices at flea markets and antique malls. Originally, there were no pink sugar and creamers made. Check my list below for pieces made in pink. If no price is listed, then it was not made in the 1930s. (See the new pink in the Reproduction Section in the back.)

The rarely seen Madrid gravy boats and platters have almost always been found in Iowa. I am betting it was a premium for some item used by rural folks — seed or chicken feed! At an auction recently, a gravy boat and platter brought $2,700.00. The lady who bought it came by to talk to me in Chicago. I couldn't help but wonder if the back bidder would like to buy mine, pictured in the top photo. Strangely enough, platters for this boat are being found less than the gravy itself. I have priced these two pieces separately, but with a serious price increase! Rare Depression glass is beginning to command higher and higher prices. I do not expect this trend to stop as more and more collectors enter the field and the rare pieces become even more scarce than they already are!

Mint condition sugar lids in any color Madrid are a treasure. Footed tumblers are harder to find than flat ones. Amber footed shakers are harder to find than flat ones. Footed shakers are the only style you can find in blue. Any heavy, flat ones you spot are new!

Collectors of green Madrid have turned out to be almost as sparse as the pattern! Green is possibly as rare as blue, but with fewer collectors.

A wooden Lazy Susan is pictured in *Very Rare Glassware of the Depression Years, Second Series.* It is like the Georgian one pictured on page 88.

	Amber	Pink	Green	Blue
Ash tray, 6" square	225.00		195.00	
Bowl, 4¾" cream soup	18.00			
Bowl, 5" sauce	6.00	8.00	7.00	30.00
Bowl, 7" soup	13.00		16.00	
Bowl, 8" salad	14.00		17.50	50.00
Bowl, 9⅜" lg. berry	20.00	20.00		
Bowl, 9½" deep salad	30.00			
Bowl, 10" oval veg.	15.00	15.00	22.50	40.00
* Bowl, 11" low console	14.00	11.00		
Butter dish w/lid	70.00		90.00	
Butter dish bottom	27.50		40.00	
Butter dish top	37.50		50.00	
* Candlesticks, pr., 2¼"	22.00	20.00		
Cookie jar w/lid	45.00	30.00		
Creamer, ftd.	7.00		12.50	20.00
Cup	5.00	7.50	8.50	16.00
Gravy boat	1,000.00			
Gravy platter	1,000.00			
Hot dish coaster	50.00		50.00	
Hot dish coaster w/Indent	55.00		55.00	
Jam dish, 7"	25.00		20.00	40.00
Jello mold, 2⅛" T	12.00			
Pitcher, 5½" 36 oz. juice	40.00			
** Pitcher, 8", sq., 60 oz.	50.00	35.00	145.00	160.00
Pitcher, 8½", 80 oz.	60.00		200.00	
Pitcher, 8½", 80 oz., ice lip	60.00		225.00	
Plate, 6" sherbet	4.00	3.50	4.00	8.00
Plate, 7½" salad	10.00	9.00	9.00	20.00
Plate, 8⅞" luncheon	7.00	7.00	9.00	18.00
Plate, 10½" dinner	55.00		45.00	75.00
Plate, 10½" grill	9.50		18.00	
Plate, 10¼" relish	15.00	12.50	16.00	
Plate, 11¼" rd. cake	20.00	10.00		
Platter, 11½" oval	15.00	14.00	16.00	24.00
Salt/pepper, 3½", ftd., pr.	135.00		110.00	165.00
Salt/pepper, 3½", flat, pr.	45.00		64.00	
Saucer	3.00	5.00	5.00	10.00
Sherbet, two styles	7.00		12.00	17.50
Sugar	6.00		12.00	15.00
Sugar cover	50.00		60.00	225.00
Tumbler, 3⅞", 5 oz.	13.00		32.00	40.00
Tumbler, 4¼", 9 oz.	14.00	15.00	20.00	32.50
Tumbler, 5½", 12 oz., 2 styles	22.00		30.00	40.00
Tumbler, 4", 5 oz., ftd.	28.00		40.00	
Tumbler, 5½", 10 oz., ftd.	30.00		45.00	
Wooden Lazy Susan, cold cuts coasters	895.00			

* Iridescent priced slightly higher ** Crystal – $150.00

MANHATTAN, "HORIZONTAL RIBBED" ANCHOR HOCKING GLASS COMPANY, 1938–1943

Colors: Crystal, pink; some green, ruby, and iridized.

If you find a piece of Manhattan that does not fit the measurements in the list below, then you may have a piece of Anchor Hocking's newer line, Park Avenue. You can see this recent pattern in my book *Anchor Hocking's Fire-King & More.*

Park Avenue was introduced by Anchor Hocking in 1987 to "re-create the Glamour Era of 1938 when Anchor Hocking first introduced a classic" according to the Inspiration '87 catalog issued by the company. Anchor Hocking went to the trouble to preserve the integrity of their older glassware, however! None of the pieces in this line are exactly like the old Manhattan! They are only similar and Manhattan was never made in blue as this line has been. Some collectors of Manhattan have bought this new pattern to augment Manhattan or for use. Thus, everyone remains happy, company and collector alike. Manhattan's collectibility has not been affected by the making of Park Avenue; however, it has caused some chaos with Manhattan cereal bowls. The older **5¼"** cereals are rarely seen, particularly in **mint** condition; Park Avenue line lists a small bowl at 6". All the **original** Manhattan bowls measure **1¹⁵⁄₁₆" high.** If the bowl you have measures more than **two inches,** then you have a piece of Park Avenue! Be especially careful if the bowl is mint! I hope this clears up the measuring problems that people ordering through the mail have had in buying the cereal bowls. You can see an original cereal in the right foreground (bottom photograph). You can also see one pictured beside the Park Avenue bowl in the Fire-King book mentioned previously.

Manhattan cereals do not have handles. The handled berry measures 5⅜". I allude to the measurements because there is an immense price difference. In fact, the reason the 5⅜" handled berry has increased in price so much has come from dealers selling these as cereals! Every Manhattan collector wants the precious cereals!

Manhattan comport price hikes can be directly attributed to margarita or martini drinkers! These were designed for candy or mints at the outset, but you cannot persuade a drinker that these were not designed for mixed drinks!

Metal accessories were made by producers outside the factory. Anchor Hocking sold their wares to other companies who made these accoutrements with tongs or spoons hanging or otherwise attached to them. There is a distant possibility that metal pieces were sold to Hocking; but years ago employees told me that they never fabricated anything but glass at the factory.

Pink Manhattan cups, saucers, and dinner plates do exist, but are rarely seen. A cup is shown in the top photograph. I would like to find a saucer to go with it. The saucer/sherbet plates of Manhattan are like many of Hocking's saucers; they have no cup ring. I have only seen one pink dinner plate. Both sizes of Manhattan Royal Ruby pitchers turn up occasionally. The real mind blower was the Jade-ite large Manhattan pitcher that was bought in Michigan. It is now photographed and will appear in my next book on Fire-King.

Manhattan sherbets have a beaded bottom like the tumblers, but the center insert to the relish tray does not have these beads. These are often confused. Relish tray inserts can be found in crystal, pink, and Royal Ruby. The center insert is always crystal on these relish trays although a pink sherbet was placed in the center of the pink relish at the photo session!

Manhattan is one pattern that is aided by the many look-alike pieces that can be added to it! Some collectors buy Hazel Atlas shakers to use with Manhattan since they are round rather than the original squared ones (pictured) that Hocking made. However, I have deliberately left out all the look-alike Manhattan in these photographs! New collectors were being confused by showing pieces that are not Manhattan. People have a tendency to go by what is pictured — rather than reading what it takes me months to write!

	Item	Crystal	Pink
*	Ashtray, 4" round	12.00	
	Ashtray, 4½" square	18.00	
	Bowl, 4½" sauce, handles	9.00	
	Bowl, 5⅜" berry w/handles	18.00	20.00
	Bowl, 5¼" cereal, no handles	65.00	125.00
	Bowl, 7½" large berry	20.00	
	Bowl, 8", closed handles	25.00	28.00
	Bowl, 9" salad	28.00	
	Bowl, 9½" fruit, open handle	35.00	40.00
	Candlesticks, 4½", square pr.	22.00	
	Candy dish, 3 legs		15.00
**	Candy dish and cover	37.50	
	Coaster, 3½"	16.00	
	Comport, 5¾"	33.00	38.00
	Creamer, oval	12.00	15.00
	Cup	18.00	250.00
	Relish tray, 14", 4-part	30.00	
	Relish tray, 14" with inserts	85.00	85.00
***	Relish tray insert	5.50	8.00
****	Pitcher, 24 oz.	35.00	
	Pitcher, 80 oz., tilted	50.00	70.00
	Plate, 6" sherbet or saucer	8.00	75.00
	Plate, 8½" salad	20.00	
	Plate, 10¼" dinner	25.00	195.00
	Plate, 14" sandwich	25.00	
	Salt & pepper, 2", square, pr.	30.00	50.00
	Saucer/sherbet plate	7.00	75.00
	Sherbet	12.00	18.00
	Sugar, oval	12.00	15.00
*****	Tumbler, 10 oz., ftd.	20.00	22.00
	Vase, 8"	25.00	
**	Wine, 3½"	5.50	

*Ad for Hocking $15.00; ad for others $12.50 **Look-Alike ***Ruby – $4.00 ****Ruby $400.00 ***** Green or iridized – $15.00

MAYFAIR FEDERAL GLASS COMPANY, 1934

Colors: Crystal, amber, and green.

Federal redesigned their Mayfair glass moulds into what finally became known as the Rosemary pattern because Hocking had copyrighted the name **Mayfair** first. I have shown only the old Federal Mayfair pattern before it was altered.

You will have to refer to a previous book to see the transitional period glassware made between the old Federal Mayfair pattern and what was to become known as the Rosemary pattern. These transitional pieces have arching in the bottom of each piece rather than the waffle design, and there is no waffling between the top arches. If you turn to the Rosemary (page 187) for reference, you will see that the design under the arches is entirely plain. Collectors regard these transitional pieces a part of Federal Mayfair rather than Rosemary and that is why they are priced here. As of now, these sell for the price of Mayfair even though they are much more scarce. There does not seem to be enough available to make a set of this transitional ware, but it blends with Mayfair better than Rosemary because of the waffling in the design.

Federal's Mayfair was a very limited production (before limited productions were the mode of selling merchandise). Maybe that's a hint that you ought to start looking at it as another possible set to collect. Amber and crystal are the colors that can be collected (in the true pattern form). Amber cream soups have been found in small numbers and platters in even fewer numbers. Crystal Mayfair can be collected as a set. I had a letter about transitional crystal cream soups but no confirming picture. Green can only be bought in transitional form! Any of those comments can be rebutted should you have anything different than that in your collection.

I, personally, prefer the scalloped lines of Mayfair to those of the plainer Rosemary, but I also prefer the crystal color. Note the red decorated flowers in the second row. I couldn't pass them by, but I have not seen other pieces with that decoration. There may be sets like this or it could be some artist's addition. Mayfair is a challenging set to collect. Once you gather it, you will not be sorry. Mix the transitional with the regular pattern in amber. They go well together and only an experienced collector will recognize the difference.

The Mayfair sugar, like Rosemary, looks like a large sherbet since it does not have handles. There are no sherbets in this pattern. I once bought six sugar bowls from a flea market dealer who sold them as sherbets. I have also seen them labeled "spooners."

Generally, you will find several pieces of Mayfair together, rather than a piece here and there. You can get a brisk beginning to a collection that way.

	Amber	Crystal	Green
Bowl, 5" sauce	9.00	6.50	12.00
Bowl, 5" cream soup	20.00	15.00	22.00
Bowl, 6" cereal	18.00	9.50	20.00
Bowl, 10" oval vegetable	30.00	18.00	35.00
Creamer, ftd.	13.00	10.50	16.00
Cup	9.00	5.00	10.00
Plate, 6¾" salad	7.00	4.50	9.00

	Amber	Crystal	Green
Plate, 9½" dinner	14.00	10.00	14.00
Plate, 9½" grill	14.00	8.50	14.00
Platter, 12" oval	30.00	20.00	35.00
Saucer	4.00	2.50	4.00
Sugar, ftd.	13.00	11.00	16.00
Tumbler, 4½", 9 oz.	30.00	15.00	35.00

MAYFAIR, "OPEN ROSE" HOCKING GLASS COMPANY, 1931–1937

Colors: Ice blue, pink; some green, yellow, and crystal. (See Reproduction Section.)

Mayfair may possibly be the most popular Depression glass pattern in the country, due in part, to Hocking's prolific distribution of it throughout the states. Since it was so widespread, many families still have a piece or two left in their possession. That recognition of something you already have, or that grandma had, may be a determining factor in wanting to buy more. I spend hours answering questions and calls about rare and reproduction pieces in Mayfair. I received an inquiry on the Internet about reproduction shot glasses. It's uncomplicated. The originals have a split stem on the flower design while the reproductions have a single stem. That has never changed since they were first made at Mosser! I have updated the Reproduction Section in the back to take care of the odd colors of cookie jars and shakers now being found. Please read that section if you are having problems!

Some rarely found pieces are pictured on page 124. Be sure to note the blue cup with a pink trim. I studied that piece for a long time to see if I could figure out how or why it was made. It was probably an error, but I suspect it was a worker playing around. In any case, these are the first bi-colored pieces of Mayfair known. There were seven or eight of these found; so, this one is not a fluke! All of those rare items pictured (page 124) have been bought in the last few years. Rare pieces are still being found!

I am repeatedly asked the value of frosted pieces in Mayfair and other Hocking patterns such as Princess. Originally, glass companies dipped glass items in camphoric acid to satinize them. Often, these frosted pieces were hand painted and sold by special order only. As you can see on page 123, there was an extensive line of satin-finished Mayfair. These satinized items are rarer than the regular pieces, but, traditionally there were only a few collectors searching for them; so the prices were frequently lower than the normal Mayfair pieces. However, a mini rush to find satinized pieces has now started! They are presently selling about the same as regular pieces or more with original mint decorations! I suppose that picture of satinized wares in the last book aroused some attention!

Pink Mayfair has a large selection of pieces, including stems and tumblers which enable you to approach collecting from many perspectives. A setting for four with all the pieces in easily found colors is expensive! However, if you try not to buy everything made, you can put a small set together for about the same money as most other patterns. Trying to buy everything available or just buying enough for a small set is a decision that could be determined by the size of your pocketbook. Who knows, you might stumble upon a bargain and enhance your collection all at once.

Yellow and green Mayfair sets can be collected, but it takes considerable time, money, and patience to do so! Of course, that even holds true for pink or blue now.

The 10" celery measures 11½" handle to handle and the 9" one measures 10½" handle to handle. The measurements in this book normally do not include handles unless so noted.

The crystal creamer and butter bottom are rarely seen, but I have only met two collectors of crystal Mayfair. There is a rare covered sugar to match the creamer. A rare piece in an uncollected color does not excite as many collectors as it does the owner. The juice pitcher, shakers, and the divided platter are the commonly seen pieces in crystal. A reader wrote that the divided platter was given as a premium with the purchase of coffee or spices in late 1930s. This platter is often found in a metal holder.

There are a few meaningful details about Mayfair that need to be pointed out. Some stems have a plain foot while others are rayed. Footed iced teas vary in height. Some teas have a short stem above the foot and others have almost none. This stem causes the heights to vary to some extent. It is just a mould variation, which may account for capacity differences, too. Note under measurements on page 5 the listings of tumblers that I have taken from old Hocking catalogs. In two catalogs from 1935, these were listed as 13 ounce; but in 1936, both catalogs listed the tumbler as 15 ounces. I have never found a 13 ounce tumbler.

You may see a price advertised or displayed at shows for more (and sometimes less) than my listed price. You must ultimately decide the worth of an item to you! Being able to see the item before you spend your money is an advantage; you need to consider that, too. A piece might be worth a bit more money actually seeing it in front of you rather than arriving in the mail in who knows what condition. Yes, I've had to go to the bother of returning mailed items, too! Attend a glass show; you'll be glad you did.

	*Pink	Blue	Green	Yellow
Bowl, 5" cream soup	55.00			
Bowl, 5½" cereal	30.00	55.00	85.00	85.00
Bowl, 7" vegetable	30.00	60.00	150.00	150.00
Bowl, 9", 3⅛ high, 3-leg console	5,500.00		5,500.00	
Bowl, 9½" oval vegetable	33.00	80.00	125.00	135.00
Bowl, 10" vegetable	35.00	80.00		135.00
Bowl, 10" same covered	135.00	150.00		995.00
Bowl, 11¾", low flat	60.00	72.50	45.00	195.00
Bowl, 12" deep scalloped fruit	62.50	97.50	45.00	235.00
Butter dish and cover or 7" covered vegetable	75.00	325.00	1,300.00	1,300.00

*Frosted or satin finish items slightly lower if paint is worn or missing

MAYFAIR (Cont.)

	*Pink	Blue	Green	Yellow
Butter bottom with indent				300.00
Butter dish top	45.00	265.00	1,150.00	1,150.00
Cake plate, 10", ftd.	35.00	75.00	150.00	
Candy dish and cover	55.00	315.00	595.00	495.00
Celery dish, 9", divided			195.00	195.00
Celery dish, 10"	50.00	75.00	125.00	125.00
Celery dish, 10", divided	265.00	75.00		
Cookie jar and lid	55.00	295.00	595.00	895.00
Creamer, ftd.	35.00	85.00	225.00	225.00
Cup	20.00	55.00	155.00	155.00
Cup, round	350.00			
Decanter and stopper, 32 oz.	215.00			
Goblet, 3¾", 1 oz. cordial	1,200.00		995.00	
Goblet, 4⅛", 2½ oz.	995.00		950.00	
Goblet, 4", 3 oz. cocktail	100.00		395.00	
Goblet, 4½", 3 oz. wine	110.00		450.00	
Goblet, 5¼", 4½ oz. claret	1,000.00		950.00	
Goblet, 5¾", 9 oz. water	75.00		495.00	
Goblet, 7¼", 9 oz., thin	250.00	225.00		
** Pitcher, 6", 37 oz.	65.00	165.00	550.00	550.00
Pitcher, 8", 60 oz.	75.00	195.00	525.00	525.00
Pitcher, 8½", 80 oz.	125.00	225.00	750.00	750.00
Plate, 5¾" (often substituted as saucer)	15.00	25.00	90.00	90.00
Plate, 6½" round sherbet	15.00			
Plate, 6½" round, off-center indent	25.00	27.50	135.00	135.00
Plate, 8½" luncheon	33.00	55.00	85.00	85.00
Plate, 9½" dinner	60.00	80.00	150.00	150.00
Plate, 9½" grill	50.00	60.00	85.00	85.00
Plate, 11½" handled grill				105.00
Plate, 12" cake w/handles	50.00	75.00	40.00	
*** Platter, 12", oval, open handles	33.00	75.00	165.00	165.00
Platter, 12½", oval, 8" wide, closed handles			235.00	235.00
Relish, 8⅜", 4-part	35.00	75.00	165.00	165.00
Relish, 8⅜" non-partitioned	225.00		295.00	295.00
**** Salt and pepper, flat pr.	65.00	325.00	1,100.00	875.00
Salt and pepper, ftd.	8,500.00			
Sandwich server, center handle	50.00	82.50	40.00	135.00
Saucer (cup ring)	35.00			150.00
Saucer (see 5¾"plate)				
Sherbet, 2¼", flat	195.00	145.00		
Sherbet, 3", ftd.	17.50			
Sherbet, 4¾", ftd.	90.00	80.00	165.00	165.00
Sugar, ftd.	35.00	85.00	210.00	210.00
Sugar lid	1,500.00		1,100.00	1,100.00
Tumbler, 3½", 5 oz. juice	45.00	125.00		
Tumbler, 4¼", 9 oz. water	33.00	110.00		
Tumbler, 4¾", 11 oz. water	225.00	150.00	200.00	200.00
Tumbler, 5¼", 13½ oz. iced tea	65.00	275.00		
Tumbler, 3¼", 3 oz. ftd. juice	85.00			
Tumbler, 5¼", 10 oz., ftd.	45.00	150.00		180.00
Tumbler, 6½", 15 oz. ftd. iced tea	47.50	295.00	275.00	
Vase (sweet pea)	145.00	125.00	295.00	
Whiskey, 2¼", 1½ oz.	67.50			

* Frosted or satin finish items slightly lower if paint is worn or missing
** Crystal – $15.00
*** Divided Crystal – $12.50
**** Crystal – $17.50 pr. – Beware reproductions.

MISS AMERICA (DIAMOND PATTERN) HOCKING GLASS COMPANY, 1935–1938

Colors: Crystal, pink; some green, ice blue, Jade-ite, and Royal Ruby. (See Reproduction Section.)

I wrote about the Miss America pink, five-part relish in the last book and you can see it pictured on a Lazy Susan tray in the bottom row of page 126. Last June, I received a picture of another one from an enterprising auctioneer. He wondered if I would confirm what it was. I did and drove to West Virginia and bought it. It now has very proud new owners in Tennessee. I rarely attend auctions because if I bid, everybody else does, too! However, I made an exception for this rare piece! That relish had been bought in 1967 for $7.00. I didn't even know about Depression glass in 1967.

The Royal Ruby Miss America set (pictured on page 127) is one Royal Ruby pattern where many collectors would love to own just one piece. This red set was bought from the grandson of a former employee who retired in 1962. The 50 pieces contained some surprises! I discovered that there were two styles of water goblets, footed juices, and sherbets! Notice how one of the water goblets and one of the footed juices flare at the top. The sherbets do the same; but, only one style was photographed. This set contained the first Miss America cups, sherbets, and footed and flat juices I had seen in Royal Ruby. It was originally a basic set for eight with cups, saucers, and luncheon plates. A few other pieces turn up occasionally in the market. Butter dishes were reproduced in red in the late 1970s; but they were an amberina red. No original red butter has been seen! Enjoy this one last time, as it is doubtful this much will ever be shown in a book again!

Some pieces of Miss America are found with metal lids. The relish (four-part dish) and cereal bowl are often found that way. Earlier reports said the cereal with a metal lid was a candy instead of a butter, but I have never found documentation to that effect. These pieces were sold to some company who made lids to fit. They are not original factory lids.

Any time a glass pattern was made for several years, it will be possible to find pieces that deviate in design or size. Each item can vary as often as any mould was changed, reworked, or became worn. In talking to the former mould makers for Hocking, I learned that moulds were "cut down" when they wore. When this happened with patterns made for several years, some pieces were made a little smaller each time the moulds were reworked.

Reproductions have been a small problem for the Miss America pattern since the early 1970s. Please refer to page 236 for a complete listing of Miss America reproductions and how to distinguish new from old.

Reproduction shakers have been disconcerting! There are few green shakers available that are old. In fact, I haven't seen an older pair since the early 1970s before reproductions. There are at least four or five generations of reproduction Miss America shakers; it depends upon which one you find as to what to look for on them. There originally were two different moulds used for old shakers. The shakers that are fatter toward the foot are the best ones to buy, since that style has not been reproduced. The shakers that get thin (as shown in the photograph) are the style that has been reproduced. Buy shakers from a **reputable dealer** who will guarantee his merchandise.

There are a few odd-colored or flashed pieces of Miss America that surface occasionally. I have shown some of these in previous editions. Flashed-on red, green, or amethyst make interesting conversation pieces, but are not plentiful enough to collect a set. However, there may be more interest in odd colors in patterns now that rainbow collections are in vogue.

	Crystal	Pink	Green	Royal Ruby
Bowl, 4½" berry			15.00	
Bowl, 6¼" cereal	11.00	28.00	20.00	
Bowl, 8" curved in at top	40.00	90.00		500.00
Bowl, 8¾" straight deep fruit	35.00	80.00		
Bowl, 10" oval vegetable	15.00	40.00		
Bowl, 11", shallow				900.00
*Butter dish and cover	210.00	625.00		
Butter dish bottom	10.00	25.00		
Butter dish top	200.00	600.00		
Cake plate, 12" ftd.	26.00	60.00		
Candy jar and cover, 11½"	65.00	165.00		
***Celery dish, 10½" oblong	16.00	40.00		
Coaster, 5¾"	16.00	35.00		
Comport, 5"	16.00	30.00		
Creamer, ftd.	11.00	22.00		200.00
Cup	11.00	27.00	14.00	250.00
Goblet, 3¾", 3 oz. wine	24.00	110.00		295.00

	Crystal	Pink	Green	Royal Ruby
Goblet, 4¾", 5 oz. juice	27.00	100.00		295.00
Goblet, 5½", 10 oz. water	22.00	52.00		255.00
Pitcher, 8", 65 oz.	50.00	135.00		
Pitcher, 8½", 65 oz., w/ice lip	70.00	210.00		
**Plate, 5¾" sherbet	7.00	12.00	8.00	50.00
Plate, 6¾"			9.00	
Plate, 8½" salad	7.50	27.00	12.00	150.00
***Plate, 10¼" dinner	16.00	36.00		
Plate, 10¼" grill	11.00	27.00		
Platter, 12¼" oval	15.00	40.00		
Relish, 8¾", 4-part	11.00	27.00		
Relish, 11¾" round divided	25.00	5,500.00		
Salt and pepper, pr.	33.00	65.00		
Saucer	4.00	7.00		65.00
**Sherbet	9.00	16.00		135.00
Sugar	9.00	22.00		200.00
***Tumbler, 4", 5 oz. juice	17.00	55.00		225.00
Tumbler, 4½",10 oz. water	16.00	36.00	20.00	
Tumbler, 5¾", 14 oz. iced tea	30.00	95.00		

*Absolute mint price **Also in Ice Blue $50.00 ***Also in Ice Blue $150.00

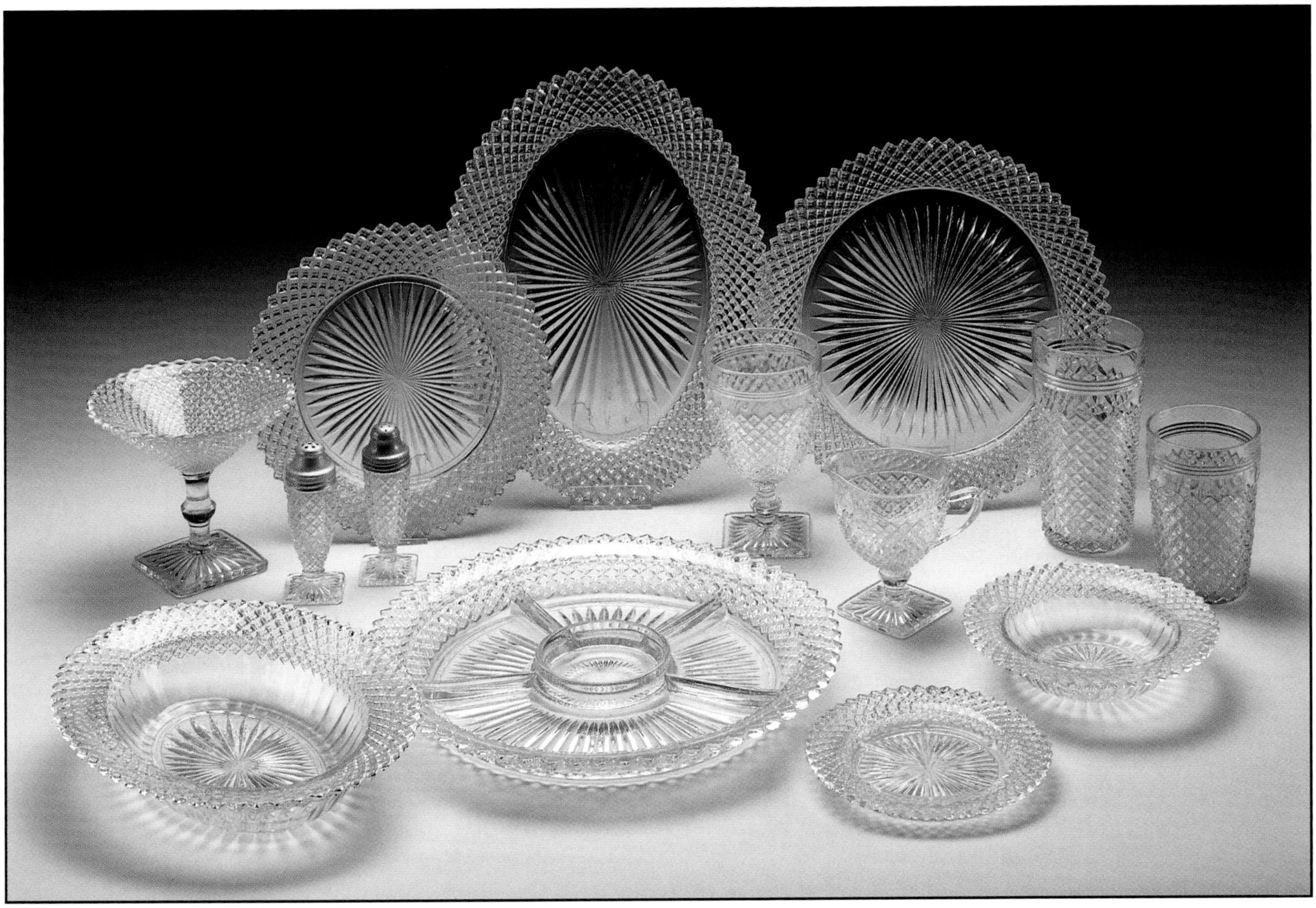

MODERNTONE HAZEL ATLAS GLASS COMPANY, 1934–1942; LATE 1940s–EARLY 1950s

Colors: Amethyst, cobalt blue; some crystal, pink, and Platonite fired-on colors.

Moderntone is greatly admired not only for its color, but for its simplistic pattern. Cobalt and amethyst colored glassware are often displayed in windows for the glass and light to refract the fantastic color. Moderntone is readily found and more economically priced than many of it counterpart patterns.

The certificate below shows a 36 piece set of cobalt blue Moderntone that could be obtained for $1.69 plus freight costs for 24 pounds. Of course, you had to send two or four coupons from flour, also. Note the money back guarantee if the set of dishes did not please you. Of course, $1.69 was more than a day's wages for common laborers of the time.

There is **no true** Moderntone tumbler. Tumblers sold today as Moderntone were once advertised alongside this pattern, but they were never sold as a part of the set. There are even two different style tumblers that have been "adopted" for this set. The water tumbler and the juice to the left of the whiskey on page 129 are paneled and have a rayed bottom. The juice to the right of the whiskey is not paneled and has a plain bottom that is marked **H** over top **A** which is the Hazel Atlas trademark. Either tumbler is acceptable, but the circular paneled one is chosen by most collectors. All sizes of these tumblers are hard to find except for the water. Green, pink, or crystal tumblers are also found, but there is little market for these except the shot or whiskey glass that is sought by those collectors.

I am often asked which lid is the **real lid** for the Moderntone butter or sugar. There is no **true** sugar or butter lid. Evidently, the butter bottom and sugar were sold to some company who made the tops. No one knows whether the lids are supposed to have black, red, or blue knobs, but I have seen all those colors on Moderntone! Red seems to be the dominate color. By adding a lid, mustards were made from the handle-less custard.

There is a punch set being sold as Moderntone which uses a Hazel Atlas mixing bowl and the plain, cobalt, roly-poly cups found with the Royal Lace toddy set. This was not Hazel Atlas factory assembled; but some collectors embrace it to go with Moderntone. My opinion is that it is merely a blue punch set without a piece of Moderntone in it; but if you want one for your Moderntone set, then by all means buy it! People should buy what they like! A similar punch set uses a Hazel Atlas cobalt blue mixing bowl in a metal holder with Moderntone custard cups sitting around the metal rim. That is being accepted as a Moderntone punch set by many collectors; it, at least, uses some Moderntone pieces to make up the set!

In the past, I have shown a boxed set with crystal Moderntone shot glasses in a metal holder that came with a Colonial Block creamer. The box was marked "Little Deb" Lemonade Server Set. That crystal pitcher has turned up in cobalt and several have been found with Shirley Temple's picture! These boxed, crystal children's sets sell in the $75.00 range. Crystal shots go for $15.00 each! Other pieces of crystal Moderntone are found occasionally; and there are a few collectors for it. It brings about one-third the price of amethyst. Flat soups are rare in any color except crystal. Now that collectors are combining colors, perhaps crystal soups will be more desirable to blend in the mixture!

Ruffled cream soups have outdistanced the sandwich plates in price. Sandwich plates can be located, but nearly all are heavily scuffed and worn causing collectors to shun them. When you pick up a blue plate that looks white in the center from years of use, that is not a good sign! A collector gleefully related that she bought nearly a dozen of these sandwich trays on a table in a used furniture store for $18 not too long ago! The cheese dish remains the highest priced piece of Moderntone. There have been some tremendous prices paid for these recently. This cheese dish is essentially a salad plate with a metal cover and wooden cutting board. That cutting board and cover are high priced items!

Green, crystal, and pink ash trays are found occasionally, but there is limited demand for them now. Blue ash trays still command a hefty price for an ash tray. Finding any Moderntone bowls without inner rim roughness (irr) is a difficult task. Prices below are for mint condition pieces. That is why bowls are so highly priced. Used, nicked, and bruised bowls are the norm and should be priced accordingly. Bowls are not rare, but mint condition bowls are!

Platonite Moderntone has been moved into the *Collectible Glassware from the 40s, 50s, 60s...* since it better fits the era covered by that book.

SAVE THIS MONEY VALUE CERTIFICATE

Use Blair's Best or White Fox Flour

This Beautiful 36 PIECE BLUE GLASS DISH SET will be mailed to You for $1.69 FOB Atchison, shipping weight 24 pounds with 2 Yellow Coupons or 4 Blue Coupons. *A Wonderful Gift-- Extraordinary Value.*

Save these Coupons and be sure to mail them in quickly, while the supply lasts.

★

This Beautiful 36-Piece Dinner Set—Consisting of 6-Dinner Plates 6-Cups 6-Sherbets 6-Lunch Salad Plates 6-Saucers 1-Platter 1-Vegetable Dish 1-Salt 1-Pepper 1-Sugar Bowl 1-Creamer

★

Learn the economy of this high grade flour sold under an absolute Money Back Guarantee by the Blair Milling Co., Atchison, Kansas.

If this Dish Set does not more than please you, return it Postpaid and your money gladly refunded—No Obligation

	Cobalt	Amethyst
* Ash tray, 7¾", match holder in center	165.00	
Bowl, 4¾" cream soup	25.00	22.00
Bowl, 5" berry	28.00	25.00
Bowl, 5" cream soup, ruffled	65.00	33.00
Bowl, 6½" cereal	75.00	75.00
Bowl, 7½" soup	150.00	100.00
Bowl, 8¾" large berry	50.00	40.00
Butter dish with metal cover	100.00	
Cheese dish, 7", with metal lid	495.00	
Creamer	12.00	11.00
Cup	12.00	12.00
Cup (handle-less) or custard	22.00	15.00
Plate, 5⅞" sherbet	6.50	5.00
Plate, 6¾" salad	12.50	10.00
Plate, 7¾" luncheon	12.50	9.00
Plate, 8⅞" dinner	21.00	13.00
Plate, 10½" sandwich	60.00	40.00
Platter, 11", oval	50.00	37.50
Platter, 12", oval	80.00	50.00
Salt and pepper, pr.	42.50	35.00
Saucer	5.00	4.00
Sherbet	14.00	12.00
Sugar	12.00	11.00
Sugar lid in metal	37.50	
Tumbler, 5 oz.	65.00	35.00
Tumbler, 9 oz.	38.00	30.00
Tumbler, 12 oz.	125.00	90.00
** Whiskey, 1½ oz.	45.00	

* Pink $75.00; green $95.00

** Pink or green $17.50

MOONDROPS NEW MARTINSVILLE GLASS COMPANY, 1932–1940

Colors: Amber, pink, green, cobalt, ice blue, red, amethyst, crystal, dark green, light green, Jadite, smoke, and black.

Red and cobalt blue are the colors most Moondrops collectors find irresistible. Few search for other colors. Every antique dealer knows that red and cobalt blue glass are expensive colors; therefore, prices are generally high even if they do not recognize Moondrops. Conversely, other colors escape unacknowledged; you might find a bargain if you know what to look for. Amber was the least preferred color for a while, but that is slowly changing, not only in this, but in other patterns as well. Perfume bottles, powder jars, mugs, gravy boats, and triple candlesticks are symbols of more elegant glassware than most of its contemporaries. Bud vases (dark green, page 132), decanters, and "rocket style" stems add a range of unusual pieces from which to choose. Several different colors of "rocket style" decanters are pictured in the *Very Rare* series of glassware books.

Evidently New Martinsville or one of their glass distributors mismatched some of their Moondrops colors. I have found two powder jars with crystal bottoms and cobalt blue tops in antique malls in Ohio and Florida. I recently had a report of another one in Kansas; this may indicate how some of them were sold. I have seen a complete cobalt one. They can be found that way, too!

The butter has to have a matching **glass** top (pictured in amber and dark green on page 132) to obtain the prices listed below. The metal top with a bird finial found on some butter bottoms sells for about $35.00. However, a metal top **with the fan finial** sells for approximately $65.00. Those fan finials are not easily found. Collectors tend to want glass tops on their butter dishes!

	Blue, Red	Other Colors
Ash tray	32.00	17.00
Bowl, 4¼", cream soup	95.00	35.00
Bowl, 5¼" berry	25.00	12.00
Bowl, 5⅜", 3-ftd. tab hndl.	75.00	40.00
Bowl, 6¾" soup	90.00	
Bowl, 7½" pickle	35.00	20.00
Bowl, 8⅜", ftd., concave top	45.00	25.00
Bowl, 8½" 3-ftd. divided relish	40.00	20.00
Bowl, 9½" 3-legged ruffled	70.00	
Bowl, 9¾" oval vegetable	75.00	45.00
Bowl, 9¾" covered casserole	195.00	100.00
Bowl, 9¾" handled oval	52.50	36.00
Bowl, 11" boat-shaped celery	32.00	23.00
Bowl, 12" round 3-ftd. console	85.00	32.00
Bowl, 13" console with "wings"	120.00	42.00
Butter dish and cover	450.00	275.00
Butter dish bottom	75.00	50.00
Butter dish top (glass)	375.00	225.00
Candles, 2", ruffled, pr.	45.00	25.00
Candles, 4½", sherbet style, pr.	30.00	20.00
Candlesticks, 5", ruffled, pr.	40.00	25.00
Candlesticks, 5", "wings," pr.	110.00	60.00
Candlesticks, 5¼", triple light, pr.	150.00	95.00
Candlesticks, 8½", metal stem, pr.	45.00	33.00
Candy dish, 8", ruffled	40.00	20.00
Cocktail shaker with or without hndl., metal top	60.00	35.00
Comport, 4"	27.50	18.00
Comport, 11½"	95.00	55.00
Creamer, 2¾", miniature	18.00	11.00
Creamer, 3¾", regular	16.00	10.00
Cup	18.00	10.00
Decanter, 7¾", small	67.50	38.00
Decanter, 8½", medium	70.00	42.00
Decanter, 11¼", large	100.00	50.00
Decanter, 10¼", "rocket"	450.00	395.00
Goblet, 2⅞, ¾ oz. cordial	40.00	27.50
Goblet, 4", 4 oz. wine	22.00	13.00
Goblet, 4¾" "rocket" wine	60.00	30.00
Goblet, 4¾", 5 oz.	24.00	15.00

	Blue, Red	Other Colors
Goblet, 5¾" 8 oz.	40.00	20.00
Goblet, 5⅛", 3 oz. metal stem wine	16.00	11.00
Goblet, 5½", 4 oz. metal stem wine	20.00	11.00
Goblet, 6¼", 9 oz. metal stem water	23.00	16.00
Gravy boat	195.00	100.00
Mayonnaise, 5¼"	65.00	40.00
Mug, 5⅛", 12 oz.	40.00	23.00
Perfume bottle, "rocket"	250.00	195.00
Pitcher, 6⅞", 22 oz., small	165.00	90.00
Pitcher, 8⅛", 32 oz., medium	185.00	115.00
Pitcher, 8", 50 oz., large, with lip	195.00	115.00
Pitcher, 8⅛", 53 oz., large, no lip	185.00	125.00
Plate, 5⅞"	11.00	8.00
Plate, 6⅛" sherbet	8.00	5.00
Plate, 6" round, off-center sherbet indent	12.00	9.00
Plate, 7⅛" salad	14.00	10.00
Plate, 8½" luncheon	15.00	12.00
Plate, 9½" dinner	30.00	20.00
Plate, 14" round sandwich	45.00	20.00
Plate, 14" 2-handled sandwich	60.00	25.00
Platter, 12", oval	45.00	25.00
Powder jar, 3-ftd.	295.00	160.00
Saucer	6.00	5.00
Sherbet, 2⅝"	16.00	11.00
Sherbet, 4½"	30.00	16.00
Sugar, 2¾"	15.00	10.00
Sugar, 3½"	16.00	11.00
Tumbler, 2¾", 2 oz. shot	20.00	10.00
Tumbler, 2¾", 2 oz. handled shot	16.00	11.00
Tumbler, 3¼", 3 oz. ftd. juice	16.00	11.00
Tumbler, 3⅝", 5 oz.	15.00	10.00
Tumbler, 4⅜", 7 oz.	16.00	10.00
Tumbler, 4⅜", 8 oz.	20.00	11.00
Tumbler, 4⅞", 9 oz., handled	30.00	16.00
Tumbler, 4⅞", 9 oz.	19.00	15.00
Tumbler, 5⅛", 12 oz.	30.00	14.00
Tray, 7½", for mini sugar/creamer	37.50	19.00
Vase, 7¾" flat, ruffled top	60.00	57.00
Vase, 8½", "rocket" bud	275.00	185.00
Vase, 9¼", "rocket" style	250.00	150.00

MT. PLEASANT, "DOUBLE SHIELD" L. E. SMITH GLASS COMPANY, 1920s–1934

Colors: Black amethyst, amethyst, cobalt blue, crystal, pink, green, and white.

Mt. Pleasant is often bought for its cobalt blue and black glass colors rather than for the fact that it is a Depression glass pattern. There are many people who buy some colored glassware for the color alone. At identification tables at shows I see many pieces of Mt. Pleasant brought in to be identified. Usually, the collector is excited to know that this pattern is even in a book! I sell many books to amateur glass buyers who know little about what they already own! You'd be surprised how many people walk into a glass show for the first time not even knowing there are books on the subject. It's gratifying to know there are still so many newcomers discovering our glassware.

Those cobalt blue, leaf-shaped dishes attract non-collectors, also. I received a letter from a lady telling me she had found her cobalt leaf in a friend's book; she had unwrapped a set of one large and six smaller plates as a wedding gift in 1931. The larger leaf measures 11½" and is not easily found.

The picture below illustrates some of the many decorated pieces of Mt. Pleasant that can be found. All these are factory decorations except for the decaled flowers and chickens. Those chicken decals certainly liven up the plain black centers we are used to seeing. A few undecorated white pieces of Mt. Pleasant have been observed, but the black stripes and handles dress up the what is shown. Few pieces of color striped crystal are being seen; but I bought a few for you to enjoy. I have had only occasional reports of pink and green items. Usually these reports are of sugars and creamers. A few pink plates pop up once in a while.

Most cobalt blue Mt. Pleasant is found in the Midwest and in northern New York. Mt. Pleasant was prominently displayed and used for premiums at hardware stores in those areas; black dominates in other areas of the country. Many pieces are found with a platinum (silver) band around them. This decorated band faded with use. Price is generally less for decorated pieces which are worn.

	Pink, Green	Amethyst, Black, Cobalt
Bonbon, 7", rolled-up, hndl.	16.00	23.00
Bowl, 4" opening, rose	18.00	26.00
Bowl, 4⅞", square ftd. fruit	13.00	20.00
Bowl, 6", 2-hndl., square	13.00	18.00
Bowl, 7", 3-ftd., rolled out edge	16.00	25.00
Bowl, 8", scalloped, 2-hndl.	19.00	35.00
Bowl, 8", square, 2-hndl.	19.00	35.00
Bowl, 9", scalloped, 1¾" deep, ftd.		30.00
Bowl, 9¼", square ftd. fruit	19.00	32.00
Bowl, 10", scalloped fruit		42.00
Bowl, 10", 2-hndl. turned-up edge		32.00
Cake plate, 10½", ftd., 1¼" high		37.50
Candlestick, single, pr.	20.00	30.00
Candlestick, double, pr.	26.00	45.00
Creamer	18.00	20.00
Cup (waffle-like crystal)	4.50	
Cup	9.50	14.00
Leaf, 8"		17.50
Leaf, 11¼"		30.00
Mayonnaise, 5½", 3-ftd.	18.00	30.00
Mint, 6", center hndl.	16.00	25.00
Plate, 7", 2-hndl., scalloped	9.00	15.00
Plate, 8", scalloped or square	10.00	15.00
Plate, 8", 2-hndl.	11.00	18.00
Plate 8¼", square w/indent for cup		16.00
Plate, 9" grill		20.00
Plate, 10½" cake, 2-hndl.	16.00	37.00
Plate, 10½", 1¼" high, cake		40.00
Plate, 12", 2-hndl.	20.00	33.00
Salt and pepper, 2 styles	24.00	45.00
Sandwich server, center-hndl.		40.00
Saucer	2.50	5.00
Sherbet, 2 styles	10.00	17.50
Sugar	18.00	20.00
Tumbler, ftd.		25.00
Vase, 7¼"		32.00

MT. VERNON IMPERIAL GLASS COMPANY, LATE 1920s–EARLY 1930s

Colors: Crystal; a few later issued colors.

Cathy and I went out shopping for Mt. Vernon and in about six weeks bought enough for two photographs (without repeating four tumblers to fill the shot). It was all photographed and two pages were set up to place here. Remember that old poem about best laid plans of mice and men "gang aft astray"? One of those photos has never been seen.

The tall celery becomes a pickle by adding a lid; the butter tub becomes a 5" butter dish with lid; both sugar bowls, the 5¾" two-handled bowl and the 69 ounce pitcher were sold with or without lids. Tiffin made a similar looking pattern called Williamsburg in the late 20s in crystal and in the 50s in colors. However, Williamsburg has a rayed "star" bottom design whereas the Mt. Vernon pattern shows a waffled looking design in the bottom of the pieces.

	Crystal
Bon bon, 5¾", one-hndl.	10.00
Bowl, 5", finger	12.00
Bowl, 5¾", two-hndl.	10.00
Bowl, 5¾", two-hndl., w/cover	20.00
Bowl, 6", lily	15.00
Bowl, 7", lily	18.00
Bowl, 8", lily	20.00
Bowl, 10" console	25.00
Bowl, 10", 3-ftd.	25.00
Bowl, punch	30.00
Butter dish, 5"	30.00
Butter dish, dome top	35.00
Butter tub, 5"	15.00
Candlestick, 9"	30.00
Celery, 10½"	22.00
Creamer, individual	8.00
Creamer, large	12.00
Cup, coffee	8.00
Cup, custard or punch	8.00
Decanter	35.00
Oil bottle, 6 oz.	30.00
Pickle jar, w/cover	35.00
Pickle, tall, two-hndl.	20.00
Pickle, 6", two-hndl.	12.00
Pitcher top, for 69 oz.	35.00
Pitcher, 54 oz.	35.00
Pitcher, 69 oz., straight edge	40.00
Plate, 6", bread and butter	5.00
Plate, 8", round	10.00
Plate, 8", square	10.00
Plate, 11" cake	20.00
Plate, 12½" sandwich	25.00
Plate, 13¼" torte	25.00
Plate, 18", liner for punch	20.00
Saucer	2.00
Shaker, pr.	20.00
Spooner	22.00
Stem, 2 oz. wine	12.00
Stem, 3 oz. cocktail	8.00
Stem, 5 oz. sherbet	6.00
Stem, 9 oz. water goblet	10.00
Sugar lid, for individual	8.00
Sugar lid, for large	12.00
Sugar, individual	8.00
Sugar, large	12.00
Syrup, 8½ oz., w/cover	45.00
Tidbit, two tier	30.00
Tumbler, 7 oz. old fashioned	10.00
Tumbler, 9 oz. water	8.00
Tumbler, 12 oz. iced tea	12.00
Vase, 10" orange bowl	50.00

NEW CENTURY, and incorrectly "LYDIA RAY" HAZEL ATLAS GLASS COMPANY, 1930–1935

Colors: Green; some crystal, pink, amethyst, and cobalt.

New Century is the **official** name for this pattern made by Hazel Atlas. "Lydia Ray" was an older name used by collectors and another author.

Green New Century is the chosen color since sets can only be put together in that color. A few pieces are found in crystal, but not enough to assemble a set according to some who tried to do so. Crystal prices are on par with green even with little demand! Years ago, I ran into several crystal powder jars. They were made with a sugar lid on the top of a sherbet. The knob of the sherbet had glass marbles or beads attached by a wire. One of these is pictured on the next page. I have not seen these for a while. You could make a footed powder jar in many patterns (not all) by putting a sugar lid on a sherbet! Cherry Blossom is one pattern where this idea works very well; unfortunately, a lady sent me a picture of one she paid $250.00 for because it was unlisted. A $20.00 investment in a good book is my recommendation!

Only a few collectors are searching for New Century at present; but this pattern is so rarely seen today, that even those few are driving up prices on many hard-to-find items. Bowls are nearly impossible to find. I haven't had a berry bowl to sell for years. Cream soups, casseroles, whiskies, wines, and cocktails are rarely seen. As with Adam, the casserole bottom is harder to find than the top. I saw a chipped lid this morning at a flea market for $10.00. It was only a Depression lid to the dealer; it would have been priced like that no matter what the pattern. When I set it down, he told me any lid was worth that even if it had a few missing pieces. I have never understood what some dealers are thinking when they price damaged merchandise! That casserole lid is a prime example. I bought some Mayfair tumblers for $25.00 each, but left the badly chipped and cracked ones priced for $22.00. Had they been "thrown in" on the deal, I would still have left them since they were beyond repair! Nobody is going to pay $22.00 for damaged $25.00 pieces!

Pink, cobalt blue, and amethyst New Century have only been found in water sets and an occasional cup or saucer. Only **flat** tumblers have been encountered in these colors.

	Green, Crystal	Pink, Cobalt, Amethyst
Ash tray/coaster, 5⅜"	28.00	
Bowl, 4½" berry	20.00	
Bowl, 4¾" cream soup	20.00	
Bowl, 8" large berry	22.00	
Bowl, 9" covered casserole	75.00	
Butter dish and cover	60.00	
Cup	6.50	20.00
Creamer	12.00	
Decanter and stopper	65.00	

	Green, Crystal	Pink, Cobalt, Amethyst
Goblet, 2½ oz. wine	30.00	
Goblet, 3¼ oz. cocktail	30.00	
Pitcher, 7¾", 60 oz., with or without ice lip	35.00	35.00
Pitcher, 8", 80 oz., with or without ice lip	40.00	42.00
Plate, 6" sherbet	5.00	
Plate, 7⅛" breakfast	10.00	
Plate, 8½" salad	13.00	
Plate, 10" dinner	18.00	
Plate, 10" grill	12.00	
Platter, 11", oval	22.00	
Salt and pepper, pr.	35.00	
Saucer	3.00	7.50
Sherbet, 3"	9.00	
Sugar	10.00	
Sugar cover	18.00	
Tumbler, 3½", 5 oz.	15.00	15.00
Tumbler, 3½", 8 oz.	25.00	
Tumbler, 4¼", 9 oz.	20.00	20.00
Tumbler, 5", 10 oz.	20.00	20.00
Tumbler, 5¼", 12 oz.	30.00	33.00
Tumbler, 4", 5 oz., ftd.	20.00	
Tumbler, 4⅞", 9 oz., ftd.	22.00	
Whiskey, 2½", 1½ oz.	20.00	

NEWPORT, "HAIRPIN" HAZEL ATLAS GLASS COMPANY, 1936–1940

Colors: Cobalt blue, amethyst; some pink, Platonite white, and fired-on colors.

In the last book I reported that some Newport collectors were slightly irritated with me for exposing the 5⁄16" difference between a dinner and a luncheon plate! This time I had a dealer tell me that since I pointed out that 5⁄16" difference, his customers were buying luncheon plates and not paying for the higher priced dinners. As an author, I only report what is going on and decisions as to what to buy are entirely up to you.

Originally, most were upset because they now had another piece to find! Others had been trying to buy the dinners for luncheon plate prices. Actually, many collectors found they had a mixture of the two sizes without realizing it. The dinner plate measures 8 13⁄16" while the luncheon plate measures 8½". I only brought the matter up because of problems that dealers who mail order were having! The only official listing I have states plates of 6", 8½", and 11½". However, after obtaining these plates, I found actual measurements quite different as you can see by the size listings in the price guide below. One of the problems with catalog measurements is that they are **not always accurate** and **sometimes not even very close!**

Cereal bowls, sandwich plates, large berry bowls, and tumblers have virtually vanished into collections in all colors. I finally bought a large amethyst berry bowl; but I am having trouble replacing the large cobalt berry bowl that was "annihilated" **before** our photography session. I have run across a few cobalt ones, but not at a reasonable enough price to suit me. Cathy did locate a damaged cobalt blue bowl at an antique show for $25.00. I thought that would fill the hole in the picture until I saw it was missing an entire scallop! There was a 10 percent discount. After all, that **two inch missing piece** didn't matter, because it **was** old. It mattered to me!

More collectors favor cobalt blue than any other color! Of course, cobalt blue seems to be singled out in any pattern that comes in that color. Sets of pink Newport were given away as premiums for buying seeds from a catalog in the 1930s. (See ad below.) Very few of these pink sets are coming into the market; but they are not presently selling very well when they do. That's interesting because pink seems to be the rarest color in Newport. Newport and Moderntone are the only sets you can assemble in amethyst from the Depression glassware. Moroccan Amethyst came much later! Price pink one third of amethyst. I find the shapes of Newport more appealing than those of Moderntone, but that is my preference.

Platonite Newport from the 1950s can be found in my book *Collectible Glassware from the 40s, 50s, 60s....*

	Cobalt	Amethyst
Bowl, 4¾" berry	22.00	17.00
Bowl, 4¾" cream soup	22.00	20.00
Bowl, 5¼" cereal	40.00	35.00
Bowl, 8¼" large berry	42.50	40.00
Cup	14.00	10.00
Creamer	16.00	14.00
Plate, 5⅞" sherbet	9.00	6.00
Plate, 8½" luncheon	16.00	12.00
Plate, 8 13⁄16" dinner	30.00	30.00
Plate, 11¾" sandwich	42.00	38.00
Platter, 11¾" oval	48.00	43.00
Salt and pepper	47.50	40.00
Saucer	5.00	5.00
Sherbet	15.00	13.00
Sugar	16.00	14.00
Tumbler, 4½", 9 oz.	42.00	38.00

32-Piece Rose Crystal Dinner Set
No. 200. LADIES! Here's a gorgeous Dinner Set in that new shade Rose Crystal. It consists of 6 large plates, 6 small plates, 6 cups, 6 saucers, 6 cereal dishes, vegetable dish and large meat platter. This sparkling set, more beautiful than you can imagine, is given for one $4.00 order of Seeds Weight 22 lbs. Sent Express collect.

NORMANDIE, "BOUQUET AND LATTICE" FEDERAL GLASS COMPANY 1933–1940

Colors: Iridescent, amber, pink, and crystal.

Normandie was most often collected in pink; but if you are one of those who like amber colored glassware, you might consider this pattern. Most fundamental pieces can be found economically enough that you will not have to take out an equity loan to compile a setting for six, eight, or even twelve. Buy any hard-to-find items first or whenever you find them! That is exemplary guidance for collecting any pattern. Rarer, harder-to-find items have always increased in price much faster than frequently found ones.

Some iridescent Normandie is being displayed at Depression glass shows. There are people now asking for it, and dealers are heeding those requests. For years, iridescent Normandie sat on shelves unwanted at **any** price. Recently, however, rumors got around that it was getting hard to find and collectors started buying this iridescent color again. There were enough buyers to raise the prices a little. Iridescent is still reasonably priced in comparison to the pink and amber.

Pink Normandie has been very elusive for years for those collectors hunting it. Amber is obtainable in most items; however, tumblers, sugar lids, and dinner-sized plates have become scarce even in this color. All those foregoing items were never copious in pink, even in the good old days! You will notice some lofty prices on pink Normandie. Tumblers are limited enough to approach prices of American Sweetheart; and Normandie collectors are vastly outnumbered by those buying American Sweetheart. Pink pitchers can be bought reasonably when compared to those in American Sweetheart; collectors of pink Normandie come out way ahead on that point!

There have been some fashion color shifts recently. Colors from the 1970s, including gold and greens, are once again showing up. Dealers are becoming aware of a growing interest in the glowing amber and jade wares. Witness the recent rush for Jade-ite due to its continual exposure on a home and garden TV show! We are in for some changes in glass collecting. Are you ready?

That console bowl and candlesticks (occasionally found with sets of iridized Normandie) are Madrid pattern! These were sold about the same time as Normandie. That does not make it Normandie; it is still Madrid! The design on the glass determines pattern, not the color. See Madrid for pricing of these console sets.

	Amber	Pink	Iridescent
Bowl, 5" berry	9.00	10.00	5.00
* Bowl, 6½" cereal	28.00	35.00	8.50
Bowl, 8½" large berry	22.00	30.00	15.00
Bowl, 10" oval veg.	20.00	45.00	18.00
Creamer, ftd.	9.00	14.00	8.00
Cup	7.50	10.00	6.00
Pitcher, 8", 80 oz.	85.00	175.00	
Plate, 6" sherbet	4.50	6.00	3.00
Plate, 7¾" salad	8.50	14.00	
Plate, 9¼" luncheon	8.50	17.00	15.00
Plate, 11" dinner	33.00	115.00	11.50
Plate, 11" grill	15.00	25.00	9.00
Platter, 11¾"	22.00	35.00	12.00
Salt and pepper, pr.	50.00	90.00	
Saucer	2.00	3.00	2.00
Sherbet	6.50	9.00	7.00
Sugar	9.00	12.00	6.00
Sugar lid	95.00	195.00	
Tumbler, 4", 5 oz. juice	35.00	90.00	
Tumbler, 4¼", 9 oz. water	22.00	55.00	
Tumbler, 5", 12 oz. iced tea	40.00	110.00	

* Mistaken by many as butter bottom.

No. 610, "PYRAMID" INDIANA GLASS COMPANY, 1926–1932

Colors: Green, pink, yellow, white, crystal, blue, or black in 1974–1975 by Tiara.

"Pyramid" is the collectors' name for Indiana's pattern No. 610. Indiana gave nearly all their patterns a number rather than a name. Collectors have seldom indulged in calling patterns by numbers; so, most of Indiana's patterns have been given an unofficial designation. "Pyramid" has received acclaim outside Depression glass realms due to its Art Deco styling and prices have advanced with increased demand from that sector. Little is being found, and mint condition "Pyramid" is bringing premium prices.

Crystal pitchers and tumblers in "Pyramid" are more difficult to find than any colored ones! Crystal pitchers are priced higher than all but yellow, even though yellow ones are encountered more often. There are so many collectors of yellow No. 610 that prices continue to increase! Ice buckets turn up often, even in yellow. However, the yellow **lid** to the ice bucket is nearly impossible to find! No other lids have yet been found for the other colors! I had a call recently from someone who found a yellow ice bucket lid with a chip on it. She couldn't comprehend why I would not buy it for book price! I hope she found a buyer at her price, but it wasn't going to be me. The prices below are for **mint** condition glasswares; any with a "ding" or two **should** market for less.

Optimistically, **I hope you read this paragraph about the crystal shaker shown on the next page** and not just look at the picture and say, "I knew that shaker was 'Pyramid'!" This shaker was made by Indiana, and is often misrepresented as "Pyramid," but it is not. If you see one, look at it closely. The design is upside down from that of all No. 610 pieces and slightly different in make-up. It would serve as a great companion item since there are no shakers per se in this older Indiana pattern. I have only seen these shakers in crystal, but they could be found in other colors.

I need to point out that the yellow stand in the top photo is not No. 610. The bona fide stand has **squared** indentations on each side to fit the bottoms of the sugar and creamer. Thanks to a reader for pointing out that mistake!

Oval bowls and pickle dishes are occasionally mixed up inasmuch as both measure 9½". The oval bowl has pointed edges as is shown by bowls in white, green, and yellow. The pickle dish is shown only in pink. The edges of that pickle dish are rounded instead of pointed and it is handled.

Eight ounce tumblers are found with two different sized bases. One has a 2¼" square foot while the other has a 2½" square foot. That inconsistency would never be noticed unless two tumblers with different bases were placed side by side.

No. 610 was, and still is, easily damaged. Be sure to examine all the ridged panels and all the corners on each piece. You will be amazed how often a chipped or cracked piece of "Pyramid" is offered as mint!

Blue and black pieces of "Pyramid" were made by Indiana for Tiara during the 1970s. You will see two sizes of black tumblers, blue berry bowls, and the four-part center-handled relish in either color. If you like these colors, it is fine to buy them! Just realize that they are **not Depression era.** Do not pay antique glass prices for them! That handled, four-part relish is sometimes mistaken for Tea Room, but it is not.

	Crystal	Pink	Green	Yellow
Bowl, 4¾" berry	11.00	20.00	24.00	40.00
Bowl, 8½" master berry	20.00	30.00	45.00	60.00
Bowl, 9½" oval	30.00	40.00	45.00	65.00
Bowl, 9½" pickle, 5¾" wide, hndl.	20.00	35.00	35.00	55.00
Creamer	17.50	35.00	30.00	40.00
Ice tub	85.00	115.00	115.00	225.00
Ice tub lid				650.00
Pitcher	395.00	350.00	225.00	495.00
Relish tray, 4-part, hndl.	23.00	45.00	60.00	65.00
Sugar	17.50	35.00	30.00	40.00
Tray for creamer and sugar	25.00	30.00	30.00	55.00
Tumbler, 8 oz., ftd., 2 styles	55.00	45.00	45.00	75.00
Tumbler, 11 oz., ftd.	75.00	55.00	75.00	95.00

No. 612, "HORSESHOE" INDIANA GLASS COMPANY, 1930–1933

Colors: Green, yellow, pink, and crystal.

The official name for this Indiana pattern is No. 612, but collectors have nicknamed it "Horseshoe." In reality, that design does not fit any form of horseshoe ever made, but I guess that would be considered nit-picking. It's a whimsical horseshoe!

A green "Horseshoe" butter dish is the piece most often lacking from collections, although the footed iced tea tumblers, both flat tumblers, grill plates, and pitchers are becoming scarce! Grill plates are probably harder to find than any of those last pieces, but not all collectors wish to include grill plates in their set. The only "Horseshoe" butter I have seen at a show in the last year was priced about $500.00 above the price where they have been selling. That same butter has made the show tour for five years now without anyone buying it! At least everyone gets to see one that way which is a service to the show-going public. The "Horseshoe" butter dish has always been highly priced. If you can find a first edition of my book, the butter dish was $90.00 back in 1972! That was big bucks for a butter back then.

Yellow pitchers, grill plates, and the footed iced teas also create problems for collectors of that color! I have never pictured a yellow grill plate, but I have finally found one to show later. Amazingly, this yellow grill and a crystal one I found do not have the inner rim roughness (irr) that has been on the six green grill plates I previously owned.

New collectors have avoided "Horseshoe" for years because it was so expensive. However, prices for other patterns have now caught up! Prices are rising on "Horseshoe" for the first time in several years because some newer collectors have stimulated them exploring for hard-to-find pieces. Any pattern you like can give you pleasure in the learning, searching, owning, displaying, or using!

There are two types of plates and platters. Some are plain in the center, while others have a pattern.

Candy dishes only have the pattern on the top. The bottom is plain. A few **pink** candy dishes have been found, but that candy is the only piece to ever surface in pink as far as we know.

	Green	Yellow
Bowl, 4½" berry	28.00	23.00
Bowl, 6½" cereal	30.00	35.00
Bowl, 7½" salad	25.00	25.00
Bowl, 8½" vegetable	40.00	35.00
Bowl, 9½" large berry	45.00	50.00
Bowl, 10½" oval vegetable	30.00	33.00
Butter dish and cover	800.00	
Butter dish bottom	200.00	
Butter dish top	600.00	
Candy in metal holder motif on lid	185.00	
also, pink	160.00	
Creamer, ftd.	18.00	18.00
Cup	12.00	13.00
Pitcher, 8½", 64 oz.	275.00	325.00

	Green	Yellow
Plate, 6" sherbet	8.00	9.00
Plate, 8⅜" salad	12.00	12.00
Plate, 9⅜" luncheon	14.00	16.00
Plate, 10⅜" grill	110.00	135.00
Plate, 11½" sandwich	25.00	25.00
Platter, 10¾", oval	32.00	32.00
Relish, 3-part, ftd.	25.00	40.00
Saucer	5.00	5.00
Sherbet	16.00	18.00
Sugar, open	18.00	17.00
Tumbler, 4¼", 9 oz.	170.00	
Tumbler, 4¾", 12 oz.	170.00	
Tumbler, 9 oz., ftd.	30.00	30.00
Tumbler, 12 oz., ftd.	160.00	175.00

No. 616, "VERNON" INDIANA GLASS COMPANY, 1930–1932

Colors: Green, crystal, yellow.

No. 616 attracts a few collectors. It is another numbered Indiana pattern that was christened "Vernon" in honor of another glass author's spouse. Little is being discovered today; and what is found is quickly bought by collectors looking for it. We once used crystal No. 616 as "every day" dishes. I warn you from experience that there are rough mould lines protruding on the mould seam of the tumblers. After a cut lip or two from using the tumblers, this set was retired to the sale box.

What "Vernon" is turning up today is usually crystal. Some pieces are found trimmed in platinum (silver). Few of these decorated pieces have worn platinum. Evidently, Indiana's process for applying this trim was far better than that of many other glass companies! Crystal is attractive in No. 616. You would be pleased displaying a set of it.

The 11½" sandwich plate is great for dinner or barbecue plates when grilling out. They are certainly lighter than the Fiesta chop plates that are used for grilled steaks and pizza. If you do use this reasonably priced pattern, it is either sandwich plates or the little 8" luncheon. For healthy appetites, that is what is called a "no brainer."

Photographing this pattern is a major obstacle. No. 616 is very delicate and light passes through without picking up the design well. I think we have succeeded this time! My black and white copy looks great!

Yellow and green sets are difficult to complete, but there is even less green than yellow available. I continue to have difficulty locating a green tumbler and creamer.

	Green	Crystal	Yellow
Creamer, ftd.	27.50	12.00	27.50
Cup	17.50	10.00	17.50
Plate, 8" luncheon	9.50	6.00	9.50
Plate, 11½" sandwich	25.00	12.00	25.00
Saucer	4.00	3.00	4.00
Sugar, ftd.	27.50	11.00	27.50
Tumbler, 5" ftd.	40.00	15.00	40.00

No. 618, "PINEAPPLE & FLORAL" INDIANA GLASS COMPANY, 1932–1937

Colors: Crystal, amber; some fired-on red, green, milk white; late 1960s, avocado; 1980s pink, cobalt blue, etc.

Indiana has reissued diamond-shaped comports and 7" salad bowls in "Pineapple and Floral" in a multitude of colors including the original crystal. Most are sprayed-on colors, although the light pink is an excellent transparent color. ("Pineapple and Floral" was never made in pink originally.) Unfortunately, prices on these two older crystal pieces have toppled because of these remakes. Amber and fired-on red are safe colors to collect to avoid reproductions. In crystal, you just have to be careful of those two items.

A crystal "Pineapple and Floral" set is not easily put together; but, it is not impossible. Tumblers, cream soups, and sherbets are the most bothersome pieces to find. As with most of Indiana's patterns, there is some mould roughness on the seams, an impediment for some collectors. This is distinctively true on both sizes of tumblers! Most times this roughness comes from extra glass and not missing glass. Search for the harder-to-find pieces as soon as you can! The set is extraordinarily attractive as a whole due to the design which reflects light vividly.

There are two different plates that have an indented center ring. One is pictured in the foreground of the bottom picture. No one has encountered a top or anything to fit the ring as yet. A cheese dish is the idea most often proposed for this; but no top has turned up. The usual one seen is 11½" in diameter. You may see these advertised as a servitor — which my dictionary says was a human servant! Call it what you wish.

Amber No. 618 is not collected as often as the crystal because there is so little of it available. I have been unable to unearth an amber tumbler. Got one to spare? It is one of the more attractive amber sets if you can find enough to display! Only plates have been found in light green. These are old and will glow under ultraviolet light.

The two-tier tidbit with a metal handle is not priced in my listings although one is pictured. These sell in the $25.00 to $30.00 range. Tidbits were seldom made by the glass companies. They can easily be made today if you can find the metal hardware. Many tidbits are a product of the early 1970s when a dealer in St. Louis would make up any pattern for $10.00 if you furnished the plates. He did a great job!

The fired-on red pitcher that has been found with fired red sets of "Pineapple and Floral" has also been found with sets of fired red Daisy. The color is dull and has no sheen, as is most of this fired-on red. There is a crosshatching design on the base of the pitcher similar to that of No. 618, but that is where the similarity to "Pineapple and Floral" ends. There is no resemblance to Daisy.

There are a few items to be found in milk glass which should please the burgeoning group of collectors for that.

	Crystal	Amber, Red
Ash tray, 4½"	17.50	20.00
Bowl, 4¾" berry	25.00	20.00
Bowl, 6" cereal	30.00	25.00
* Bowl, 7" salad	2.00	10.00
Bowl, 10" oval vegetable	25.00	20.00
* Comport, diamond-shaped	1.00	8.00
Creamer, diamond-shaped	7.50	10.00
Cream soup	22.00	22.00
Cup	11.00	10.00
Plate, 6" sherbet	4.00	5.00
Plate, 8⅜" salad	8.50	8.50
** Plate, 9⅜" dinner	17.50	14.00
Plate, 11½", w/indentation	25.00	
Plate, 11½" sandwich	17.50	16.00
Platter, 11", closed hndl.	17.50	18.00
Platter, relish, 11½", divided	20.00	
Saucer	4.00	4.00
Sherbet, ftd.	22.00	18.00
Sugar, diamond-shaped	7.50	10.00
Tumbler, 4¼", 8 oz.	40.00	25.00
Tumbler, 5", 12 oz.	50.00	
Vase, cone-shaped	55.00	
Vase holder, metal (35.00)		

* Reproduced in several colors **Green $35.00

OLD CAFE HOCKING GLASS COMPANY, 1936–1940

Colors: Pink, crystal, and Royal Ruby.

Old Cafe lamps, pitchers, and dinner plates are the elusive pieces. They are expensive compared to the rest of the pattern! Pitchers were pictured in earlier editions. These pitchers have alternating large panels with two small panels that constitute the make-up of all Old Cafe pieces. The pitcher that is often mislabeled Old Cafe can be seen on pages 171–172 under Hocking's Pillar Optic. Some collectors are mistakenly buying Pillar Optic (evenly spaced panels) for Old Cafe. Many dealers label Pillar Optic pitchers as Old Cafe and price them under market in hopes someone will not know the difference. A dealer's price label is a means to sell glass, and not always correct! The juice pitcher is shaped like the Mayfair juice pitcher.

Lamps are found in Royal Ruby and pink. Lamps were sometimes made by drilling through a vase, but the pink one shown here and the Royal Ruby lamp pictured on page 194 have ball feet to raise them enough to allow the cord to pass under the edge. Bowls have been confusing. The 5" bowl has an open handle while the 4½" bowl has tab handles, as does the 3¾" berry. The **footed** sherbet (pictured in front) also measures 3¾".

Royal Ruby Old Cafe cups are found on crystal saucers. No Old Cafe Royal Ruby saucers have ever surfaced. A 5½" crystal candy with a Royal Ruby lid is also pictured. No Royal Ruby bottom has been spotted.

The low candy is 8⅜", including handles and 6½" without. You can see a pink one on the left and a crystal one standing behind the covered candy in the photograph.

Hocking made a cookie jar (a numbered line) which is an excellent "go-with" piece. It is ribbed up the sides **similar** to Old Cafe but has a crosshatched lid that does not conform to Old Cafe.

	Crystal, Pink	Royal Ruby
Bowl, 3¾" berry	9.00	7.00
Bowl, 4½", tab handles	10.00	
Bowl, 5½" cereal	20.00	13.00
Bowl, 6½", tab handles	25.00	
Bowl, 9", closed handles	12.00	16.00
Candy dish, 8", low, tab handles	12.00	16.00
Candy jar, 5½", crystal with ruby cover		18.00
Cup	10.00	9.00
Lamp	75.00	95.00
Olive dish, 6", oblong	9.00	

	Crystal, Pink	Royal Ruby
Pitcher, 6", 36 oz.	90.00	
Pitcher, 80 oz.	125.00	
Plate, 6" sherbet	2.50	
Plate, 10" dinner	60.00	
Saucer	3.00	
Sherbet, 3¾" low ftd.	14.00	12.00
Tumbler, 3" juice	16.00	16.00
Tumbler, 4" water	20.00	32.00
Vase, 7¼"	40.00	45.00

F.W.WOOLWO
OLD COLONY
The Glass Beautiful
FOR YOUR TABLE
DISPLAYED ON
COUNTER 14
Schreick's Studio
Columbus, Ohio

OLD COLONY "LACE EDGE," "OPEN LACE" HOCKING GLASS COMPANY, 1935–1938

Colors: Pink and some crystal and green.

For those new readers who wonder why "Lace Edge" is listed as **Old Colony** I should explain. I get static from "old time" dealers who hate name changes; but when the real name is discovered, I tend to ignore static. In December 1990, I spent a day at Anchor Hocking going through old files and catalogs. I encountered some old store display photographs (page 149 and 151) promoting the name of this glass as Old Colony. I was thrilled to find the **authentic** name of the pattern! Primarily, this trip was for my new book *Collectible Glassware from the 40s, 50s, 60s…*; but that trip benefited this book also! This corrected pattern name for "Lace Edge" is being accepted by most collectors; but I still get an occasional letter asking why I removed the "Lace Edge" pattern from my book. I merely moved Old Colony to its appropriate alphabetical arrangement! Don't you wish that our ancestors had stocked up on those dime sherbets and underliners? Those underliners look like salad plates! No Old Colony sherbet plate has been seen. Regardless, one engineer wrote that he had tried to gauge the size of those plates by measuring instruments and his supposition was they **were** saucer size. Somebody find one so we will know for sure.

The paramount problem with collecting Old Colony (besides finding it) is the cracked or broken "lace" around the edge. It chipped and fractured, **and still does!** Plates and bowls should be stored carefully. Paper plates between each piece is a must when stacking or packing this pattern. Candlesticks, console bowls, and vases are hard to find in mint condition. It's not that these pieces are unavailable; they are, but with chips and nicks. You will discover extensive price increases on **mint condition** items of Old Colony.

Ribs on the footed tumbler extend approximately half way up the side as they do on the cup. This tumbler on the right side of bottom photo is often confused with the Coronation tumbler that has a similar shape and design. See the Coronation photograph and read there, also. Notice the fine ribbed effect from the middle up on the Coronation tumbler. This upper ribbing is omitted on Old Colony tumblers.

Satinized or frosted pieces presently sell for a fraction of the cost of their unfrosted counterparts in Old Colony. Lack of demand is one reason; but in some pieces, they are more plentiful than non-frosted pieces. Possibly vases and candlesticks are rare because so many of them were satinized. I have shown those two items frosted this time. If satinized pieces still have the original floral decorations, they will fetch up to 25 percent more than the prices listed for them. So far, only a few collectors think frosted Old Colony is beautiful; but I have noticed lately that more are considering it because of price — or perhaps because "blending" has become more legitimate!

Notice the green bowl in the bottom photo. It was found in the basement of a former Anchor Hocking employee. He thought that they made other pieces, but was not sure. It is the only green piece I have ever verified as Hocking. As I write this I cannot recall, but I think it had a ground bottom.

The flower bowl with crystal frog becomes a candy jar with a cover added in place of the frog. It was marketed both ways. That cover is the same as fits the butter dish or bon bon as Hocking actually listed it. The 7" comport becomes a footed candy with a lid added, the cookie lid. This piece was listed as a covered comport; but today, many dealers call it a footed candy jar. Since both these lids fit two items, it doesn't take a genius to figure why there is a lid shortage today. There are two styles of 7¾" and 9½" bowls. Some are ribbed up the side and some are not. The smaller, non-ribbed salad bowl is also the butter bottom. Both sizes of ribbed bowls are harder to find than their non-ribbed counterparts.

The true 9" comport in Old Colony has a **rayed** base. There is a comparable comport that also measures 9". This "pretender" has a plain foot and was probably made by Standard or Lancaster Glass. It has been shown in earlier editions. Both Lancaster and Standard had very similar designs, but their glass generally was better quality and rings when **gently** flipped on the edge with your finger. Hocking's Old Colony makes a thud sound. If the piece is not shown in my listing, or is in any color other than pink or crystal, the likelihood of your having an Old Colony piece is meager at best.

	Pink
* Bowl, 6⅜" cereal	27.00
Bowl, 7¾" ribbed salad	60.00
Bowl, 8¼", crystal	12.00
Bowl, 9½", plain	28.00
Bowl, 9½", ribbed	32.00
** Bowl, 10½", 3 legs (frosted, $65.00)	250.00
Butter dish or bon bon with cover	67.50
Butter dish bottom, 7¾"	27.50
Butter dish top	40.00
** Candlesticks, pr. (frosted $95.00)	325.00
Candy jar and cover, ribbed	50.00
Comport, 7"	30.00
Comport, 7", and cover, ftd.	65.00
Comport, 9"	895.00
Cookie jar and cover (frosted $50.00)	70.00
Creamer	25.00
Cup	28.00
Fish bowl, 1 gal., 8 oz. (crystal only)	30.00

* Officially listed as cereal or cream soup, green – $75.00

	Pink
Flower bowl, crystal frog	30.00
Plate, 7¼" salad	28.00
Plate, 8¼" luncheon	25.00
Plate, 10½" dinner	36.00
Plate, 10½" grill	25.00
Plate, 10½" 3-part relish	26.00
Plate, 13", solid lace	65.00
Plate, 13", 4-part solid lace	65.00
Platter, 12¾"	42.00
Platter, 12¾", 5-part	42.00
Relish dish, 7½", 3-part deep	65.00
Saucer	12.00
** Sherbet, ftd.	115.00
Sugar	25.00
Tumbler, 3½", 5 oz., flat	125.00
Tumbler, 4½", 9 oz., flat	22.00
Tumbler, 5", 10½ oz., ftd.	90.00
Vase, 7" (frosted $90.00)	595.00

** Price is for absolute mint condition

Old Colony
SHERBET and PLATE
Complete 10¢

OLD ENGLISH, "THREADING" INDIANA GLASS COMPANY, Late 1920s

Colors: Green, amber, pink, crystal, crystal with flashed colors, and forest green.

Old English can only be collected in sets of green or amber. All pieces are available in green, though a complete set of amber may not be totally realistic since some pieces have never been seen. That does not suggest that they were never made! Amber Old English is a deep color more indicative of Cambridge or New Martinsville products which collectors find so enticing.

Pink Old English is rarely seen with only the center handled server, cheese and cracker, and sherbets being found periodically. Additional pieces in pink exist, but seldom surface! I did find a pink pitcher and tumbler (page 153) in the St. Louis area last year, but it was only the second pitcher I had seen. Speaking of pitchers, did you see the pitcher and tumblers below with flashed-on black and red decorations? You might also find a vase and candy dish with similar adornments. Crystal Old English must have been admired as decorative ware since several different embellishments are found on pieces today.

Old English footed pieces are more readily available than flat items. I haven't seen a green center-handled server in almost 20 years. There are two styles of sherbets. One is more rounded than the green one pictured. Both large and small berry bowls and the flat candy dish are in meager supply. Sugar and candy jar lids have the same cloverleaf-type knob as the pitcher. The flat candy lid is comparable in size to the pitcher lid that is notched in the bottom rim to allow for pouring. You cannot intermix the two lids since the candy lid is not notched. That flat candy is often found in a metal holder.

Only crystal egg cups have been found. A fan vase is the only piece I have ever seen in dark green! A flashed lavender footed candy bottom has been spotted. Anyone have a lid?

	Pink, Green, Amber
Bowl, 4", flat	20.00
Bowl, 9" ftd. fruit	30.00
Bowl, 9½", flat	35.00
Candlesticks, 4", pr.	38.00
Candy dish & cover, flat	50.00
Candy jar with lid	50.00
Compote, 3½" tall, 6⅜" across, 2-hndl.	22.50
Compote, 3½" tall, 7" across	22.00
Compote, 3½", cheese for plate	16.00
Creamer	17.50
Egg cup (crystal only)	10.00
Fruit stand, 11", ftd.	40.00
Goblet, 5¾", 8 oz.	35.00

	Pink, Green, Amber
Pitcher	65.00
Pitcher and cover	125.00
Plate, indent for compote	20.00
Sandwich server, center hndl.	55.00
Sherbet, 2 styles	20.00
Sugar	17.50
Sugar cover	35.00
Tumbler, 4½", ftd.	25.00
Tumbler, 5½", ftd.	35.00
Vase, 5⅜", fan type, 7" wide	50.00
Vase, 8" ftd., 4½" wide	45.00
Vase, 8¼" ftd., 4¼" wide	45.00
Vase, 12" ftd.	60.00

"ORCHID" PADEN CITY GLASS COMPANY, EARLY 1930s

Colors: Yellow, cobalt blue, crystal, green, amber, pink, red, and black.

Paden City "Orchid" pieces, as other patterns from this company, are making tremendous price jumps! All Paden City patterns were more limited in production runs than those of some of the larger glass companies. Orchid growers and collectors may have sparked the interest for this one pattern. Many of them have completed or nearly completed their sets of Heisey "Orchid" and now are focusing on other Orchid patterns. This "Orchid" pattern was not produced in hundreds of thousands of pieces as was Heisey "Orchid." So far, every piece of "Orchid" we have exhibited at shows has sold not long after the show opened — if not before to a dealer!

It was believed that "Orchid" etched pieces turned up only on #412 Line, the square, Crow's Foot blank made by Paden City. See the yellow sandwich server pictured below. The rounded style, #890 Line (comport in center, bottom of page 155) has now been found with "Orchid"; so, "Orchid" may well turn up on any Paden City line. A few pieces of "Orchid" are being found on black, but only a few. Actually, red and cobalt blue pieces seem to be favored and appear in comparable numbers.

In all likelihood there are three distinct "Orchid" arrangements found on Paden City blanks. Collectors do not mind blending these different "Orchid" varieties because so little of any one is found.

"Orchid" prices have not yet attained the range of those in "Cupid." However, at the rate they are going, it may not be long before they do!

	All Other Colors	Red Black Cobalt Blue
Bowl, 4⅞", square	25.00	50.00
Bowl, 8½", 2-hndl.	75.00	135.00
Bowl, 8¾", square	75.00	125.00
Bowl, 10", ftd., square	95.00	195.00
Bowl, 11", square	85.00	185.00
Cake stand, square, 2" high	75.00	150.00
Candlesticks, 5¾" pr.	110.00	195.00
Candy with lid, 6½", square, 3-part	95.00	195.00
Candy with lid, cloverleaf, 3-part	95.00	195.00
Comport, 3¼" tall, 6¼" wide	25.00	50.00
Comport, 6⅝" tall, 7" wide	65.00	135.00
Creamer	50.00	95.00
Ice bucket, 6"	95.00	195.00
Mayonnaise, 3-piece	85.00	165.00
Plate, 8½", square		100.00
Sandwich server, center hndl.	75.00	125.00
Sugar	50.00	95.00
Vase, 8"	95.00	275.00
Vase, 10"	125.00	295.00

OVIDE, incorrectly dubbed "NEW CENTURY" HAZEL ATLAS GLASS COMPANY, 1930–1935

Colors: Green, black, white Platonite trimmed with fired-on colors in 1950s.

Several varieties of Ovide decorated sets are found. Separating these decorations into time periods for my books has been a gargantuan task. I have selected black and red decorations for this book. Call one "Windmills" and the other "Black, Red, and Gold Trim" for identification purposes due to our lack of actual names. These are listed under the decorated white pattern below.

Hazel Atlas used a gaggle of different patterns on this popular Platonite, including one of flying geese. One of the more popular is the black floral design with red and yellow edge trim. That set covered kitchenware items (stacking sets and mixing bowls) as well as a dinnerware line. Evidently, many people found these patterns pleasing judging from the abundance of pieces now being found. You can see later patterns in *Collectible Glassware from the 40s, 50s, 60s....* For most of those patterns I have found documentation and they are correctly named!

The "Flying Ducks" (geese) set is priced under "Decorated White" and not as "Art Deco." Only the "Art Deco" pieces are priced under that column. The "Art Deco" line is shown in earlier editions and I have been unable to find a single piece of it in the last ten years. You will never be able to sell **any other** decorated Ovide for prices of "Art Deco." The egg cup in the "Flying Ducks" pattern is selling in the $12.00 to $15.00 range. It is peculiar that no other patterns have had egg cups reported. I would not bet against there being some!

Very little black, transparent green, or yellow Ovide are being found, but there are few collectors asking for it. A luncheon set in black or yellow can be assembled; but it would be simpler to put together the same set in black or yellow Cloverleaf. However, Cloverleaf would cost three or four times as much — but it would be more easily found. Depression glass dealers are prone to bring the Cloverleaf pattern to shows, but few exhibit undecorated Ovide. If you want this, you'll have to start requesting it at shows!

	Black	Green	Decorated White	Art Deco
Bowl, 4¾" berry			7.00	
Bowl, 5½" cereal			13.00	
Bowl, 8" large berry			22.50	
Candy dish and cover	45.00	22.00	35.00	
Cocktail, ftd. fruit	5.00	4.00		
Creamer	6.50	4.50	17.50	95.00
Cup	6.50	3.50	12.50	75.00
Plate, 6" sherbet		2.50	6.00	
Plate, 8" luncheon		3.00	14.00	50.00
Plate, 9" dinner			20.00	
Platter, 11"			22.50	
Salt and pepper, pr.	27.50	27.50	24.00	
Saucer	3.50	2.50	6.00	18.00
Sherbet	6.50	3.00	14.00	60.00
Sugar, open	6.50	4.00	17.50	95.00
Tumbler			16.50	95.00

OYSTER AND PEARL ANCHOR HOCKING GLASS CORPORATION, 1938–1940

Colors: Pink, crystal, Royal Ruby, Vitrock, and Vitrock with fired-on pink, blue, and green.

Royal Ruby Oyster and Pearl can be seen under the Royal Ruby pattern shown on page 194, but prices are, also, recorded here. Pink Oyster and Pearl is often used as accessory pieces for other patterns. The pink relish dish and candlesticks sell well since they are fairly priced in comparison to other patterns. These pieces make wonderful gifts because they have an attractive design. We sell almost every Oyster and Pearl relish we get to noncollectors who find it wonderful and inexpensively priced. We regularly try to start newlyweds off with a gift of Depression glass. Cathy encloses a note explaining the derivation of the piece. We have found this custom to be well received!

That Oyster and Pearl relish dish measures 11½" including the handles. I mention that because of letters I receive wondering what piece is 11½" when I list a 10½" relish. All measurements in this book are taken without handles unless otherwise mentioned. Glass companies rarely measured the handles. I have made a point to talk about measurements with handles in my commentary since I have been getting so many letters about measurements on pieces that I have already listed. There is no divided bowl in Oyster and Pearl; it was (and is) listed as a relish!

I had a report of a lamp made from candleholders; but I never saw it nor received any photograph. Many patterns had lamps made out of candle holders or vases. Sometimes these were factory made; more often, these were fabricated by some other company who bought the parts from the factory. Lamps do add appeal to your collection; if you want one, then go for it!

I have seen a few decorated crystal pieces and most of them were trimmed in red. They sell faster than undecorated crystal. The 10½" fruit bowl is a great salad bowl and the 13½" plate makes a wonderful server; several collectors have used these for a small punch bowl and liner! You will have to decide what punch cups to use!

Pink fired-on over Vitrock was called Dusty Rose; the fired-on green was called Springtime Green by Hocking. Most collectors love these shades; but I've met a few who hate them. The undecorated Vitrock is infrequently seen, and not as fascinating. A collector claimed to have found this pattern with fired-on blue; a confirming picture was never received. Have you seen it in blue?

The pink, 6½", deep bowl is often found with metal attached to the handles for holding a spoon. This was another of the marketing gimmicks of that time. With tongs it could serve as a small ice bowl or serving dish. It was another way to retail this bowl!

The spouted, 5½" bowl is often referred to as heart shaped. It might serve as a gravy or sauce boat although most people use them for candy dishes. The same bowl is found without the spout in Royal Ruby. Although pictured in Dusty Rose and Springtime Green, this bowl always has a spout in those particular colors.

	Crystal, Pink	Royal Ruby	White and Fired-On Green Or Pink
Bowl, 5¼" heart-shaped, 1-handled	14.00		10.00
Bowl, 5½", 1-handled		15.00	
Bowl, 6½", deep-handled	18.00	25.00	
Bowl, 10½" deep fruit	25.00	55.00	14.00
Candle holder, 3½" pr.	35.00	60.00	15.00
Plate, 13½" sandwich	20.00	50.00	
Relish dish, 10½" oblong, divided	17.50		

OYSTER AND PEARL

"PARROT," SYLVAN FEDERAL GLASS COMPANY, 1931–1932

Colors: Green, amber; some crystal and blue.

"Parrot" is one of the Depression glass patterns that cycles. Prices reach a plateau and no one wants to buy a piece for a year or so. Then, all of a sudden, everyone seems to want to own "Parrot" and prices rise quickly for months or even a year. Then, just as suddenly, there seem to be no collectors again. The only other pattern that has followed similar paths is cobalt blue Royal Lace. I've watched these patterns for nearly thirty years and it's happened over and over again. Parrot pitcher prices have steadied after more than doubling in price in the last few years. When prices reach the ball park of $3.000.00, there is a limited market! Everyone who was willing to pay that price did; and, right now, other collectors are balking at the current price. After years of pitchers selling in the same price range, suddenly several collectors wanted one and there were few to be found! Now, those that wanted them have them; so, the price has momentarily leveled! Originally, there were 37 pitchers found in the basement of an old hardware store in central Ohio. Today, there are over 30 still in existence. Doubling in price in so short a time is the extraordinary part since the price was already "out of sight" for a majority of collectors. However, I believe we could see much more of that happening in future Depression glass markets because collectors searching for rare items greatly outnumber their supply! Today, there is a large amount of disposable income being wielded about the world.

A few months ago I received a letter from Hawaii from a lady who had 10 or 12 of the high sherbets. Several were damaged, and she told me what she had been offered for them. She wanted to know if I thought the offer was fair, and I told her I thought it was considering the chipped ones. A few weeks later, I received an e-mail message from a dealer who had a bunch of "Parrot" high sherbets. To her surprise, I asked about a Hawaiian connection and found out they had been flown from the Islands. It's a small world, but that was more than anyone had heard of at once since 1973. There were six at the first Depression glass show in Indianapolis. All this proves is that rarely seen glassware is still out there waiting to be found by some lucky collector!

There are two types of "Parrot" hot plates. One is shaped like the Madrid hot plate with the pointed edges. The other is round, and more like the one in Georgian pattern. A collector in Tennessee has found an amber hot plate with pointed edges. That is the only one of those known! I have seen it, and hope to get it photographed one day.

That is still the cracked shaker on the bottom row. It's one way to preserve otherwise useless old glass by giving it a function. Actually, many dealers now offer me damaged, but hard to find pieces, at reasonable prices so I can photograph them for my books. Some items are even gifted. One told me I'd made him enough money over the years that he could afford to give something toward photography! It seems better than having them thrown away or having desirable glass stored in boxes for years with no one able to enjoy it!

The amber butter dish, creamer, and sugar lid are all harder to find than green. There has been only one mint condition butter dish top found in amber. The commonly found butter bottom has an indented ledge for the top. The jam dish is the same as the butter bottom, but without the ledge. The jam dish has never been seen in green. Furthermore, very few mint amber sugar lids have been uncovered. Considering there are fewer collectors of amber "Parrot," prices are not as influenced by demand as are those for green.

Most collectors identify "Parrot" shapes as those found on Madrid. Notice that "Parrot" tumblers are found on Madrid-like moulds except for the heavy footed tumbler. Apparently, the thin, moulded, footed tumbler did not accept the "Parrot" design favorably and the heavier, tumbler was made. The thin, 10 ounce footed tumbler has only been found in amber. Should you see one of these, you will understand when I say it did not accept the design well! The supply of heavy, footed tumblers (in both colors), green water tumblers, and thin, flat iced teas in amber have more than met the demand of collectors. Prices for those last two tumblers have remained steadfast during other "Parrot" price increases. Heavy tumblers are often damaged on the points.

There are quantities of sugar and butter lids found. The dilemma is finding mint condition lids. The pointed edges and ridges chipped! Carefully check these when buying "Parrot." Damaged or repaired glassware should not bring mint prices. Reworked glass should be sold as repaired and priced somewhat less than mint!

	Green	Amber
Bowl, 5" berry	28.00	22.00
Bowl, 7" soup	50.00	35.00
Bowl, 8" large berry	95.00	75.00
Bowl, 10" oval vegetable	65.00	70.00
Butter dish and cover	395.00	1,300.00
Butter dish bottom	65.00	200.00
Butter dish top	330.00	1,100.00
Creamer, ftd.	55.00	75.00
Cup	42.00	42.00
Hot plate, 5", pointed	895.00	950.00
Hot plate, 5", round	995.00	
Jam dish, 7"		35.00
Pitcher, 8½", 80 oz.	2,850.00	
Plate, 5¾" sherbet	35.00	23.00
Plate, 7½" salad	38.00	

	Green	Amber
Plate, 9" dinner	55.00	45.00
Plate, 10½" round grill	32.00	
Plate, 10½" square grill		30.00
Plate, 10¼", square (crystal only)	26.00	
Platter, 11¼", oblong	60.00	75.00
Salt and pepper, pr.	275.00	
Saucer	15.00	15.00
* Sherbet, ftd. cone	25.00	25.00
Sherbet, 4¼" high	1,250.00	
Sugar	40.00	50.00
Sugar cover	160.00	500.00
Tumbler, 4¼", 10 oz.	175.00	125.00
Tumbler, 5½", 12 oz.	195.00	150.00
Tumbler, 5¾", ftd., heavy	165.00	125.00
Tumbler, 5½", 10 oz., ftd. (Madrid mould)		160.00

*Blue – $225.00

"PARROT," SYLVAN

PATRICIAN, "SPOKE" FEDERAL GLASS COMPANY, 1933–1937

Colors: Pink, green, crystal, and amber ("Golden Glo").

Amber Patrician was distributed more than any other Federal pattern save Madrid. This Depression pattern is available to anyone wishing to start a set. Unlike Madrid, this has never been reproduced. Amber is the most collected color, but sets of green or pink Patrician can be assembled with perseverance, and at greater cost. The plentiful 10½" dinner plates were given away with 20 pound sacks of flour as cake plates! Displays of these plates sat on the counter and when you paid for your flour, you were handed one of these as a bonus. That plate has always been specified as a dinner plate since I started buying Depression glass 30 years ago. As I was learning about Depression glass, I discovered my mom had stacks of these and had been giving them away with meals sent home with her day care help. In her collection of 2000 plus pairs of salt and pepper shakers, only amber Patrician represented Depression glass.

The jam dish is a butter bottom without the indented ledge for the top and measures 6¾" wide and stands 1¼" deep. This is the same measurement as the butter bottom, but the cereal bowls are still confused with jam dishes. Cereals are 6" in diameter and 1¾" deep. Prices differ; be aware of which is which!

There is more green Patrician available than pink or crystal. Nevertheless, green dinner plates are infrequently found! Completing a set of pink is difficult, but not yet unfeasible. It might be in crystal. Not all pieces have turned up in crystal.

Amber pitchers were supposedly made in two styles. The one pictured has a moulded handle. If anyone owns an applied handle amber pitcher, let me know as I am beginning to doubt it exists. In crystal and green, the applied handled pitcher is easier to find!

In amber Patrician, mint condition sugar lids, jam dishes, footed tumblers, cookie or butter bottoms, and footed tumblers are harder to find than other pieces. Check sugar lids for signs of repair. Many a glass grinder has cut his teeth on those. That cookie bottom is rare in green. There are several lids found for each bottom. If you have a lid, I know where to find a bottom. This is another pattern where saucers are also harder to find than cups.

	Amber, Crystal	Pink	Green
Bowl, 4¾" cream soup	18.00	22.00	22.00
Bowl, 5" berry	12.50	12.00	12.00
Bowl, 6" cereal	27.00	25.00	30.00
Bowl, 8½" large berry	45.00	30.00	40.00
Bowl, 10" oval vegetable	33.00	30.00	35.00
Butter dish and cover	90.00	225.00	120.00
Butter dish bottom	60.00	175.00	70.00
Butter dish top	30.00	50.00	50.00
Cookie jar and cover	90.00		595.00
Creamer, footed	11.00	12.00	12.00
Cup	9.00	11.00	13.00
Jam dish	30.00	30.00	40.00
Pitcher, 8", 75 oz., moulded handle	125.00	125.00	145.00
Pitcher, 8¼", 75 oz., applied handle	*100.00	150.00	175.00

	Amber, Crystal	Pink	Green
Plate, 6" sherbet	10.00	8.00	8.00
Plate, 7½" salad	15.00	15.00	14.00
Plate, 9" luncheon	12.00	10.00	14.00
Plate, 10½" dinner	7.50	40.00	45.00
Plate, 10½" grill	15.00	15.00	15.00
Platter, 11½", oval	30.00	25.00	32.00
Salt and pepper, pr.	57.50	90.00	65.00
Saucer	9.50	9.50	9.50
Sherbet	13.00	15.00	15.00
Sugar	9.00	9.00	10.00
Sugar cover	60.00	65.00	75.00
Tumbler, 4", 5 oz.	33.00	33.00	33.00
Tumbler, 4¼", 9 oz.	30.00	26.00	25.00
Tumbler, 5½", 14 oz.	47.00	40.00	45.00
Tumbler, 5¼", 8 oz., ftd.	55.00		65.00

*Crystal only

“PATRICK” LANCASTER GLASS COMPANY, EARLY 1930s

Colors: Yellow and pink.

Yellow “Patrick” luncheon sets are being found, but other pieces are difficult. I had reports of some crystal turning up, but was unable to confirm this sighting by a photo. Look for a piece for me. Some pink “Patrick” luncheon sets have turned up, but the cost has scared away all but fervent collectors. Prices have eased a bit for pink; but I have seen little available recently which could account for that. This is a very limited pattern; production was small before anyone ever came up with the idea of limited productions in order to sell you something. Jubilee was distributed heavily in the Northwest and Florida, but “Patrick” seems scarcely found anywhere.

Pink “Patrick” sugar or creamers were selling for $75.00 each, but that has been wavering some as new collectors seem to get “sticker shock” when asked that price. I only record market prices, not make them. The “Patrick” three-footed candy is shaped just like the Jubilee one shown in the twelfth edition of this book.

“Patrick” serving dishes are rare! The pattern is bold and large on the 11" console bowl. I bought one not long ago from a dealer who “knows everything” about Depression glass (except what “Patrick” looks like). I've learned never to skip a booth just because there will probably not be any bargains to be had. There are similar serving pieces to be had from other patterns cut on the same blanks used for “Patrick” and Jubilee. However, these similar pieces should sell at more reasonable prices than the very collectible ones with true “Patrick” and Jubilee etches.

	Pink	Yellow
Bowl, 9" handled fruit	175.00	135.00
Bowl, 11" console	140.00	135.00
Candlesticks, pr.	195.00	150.00
Candy dish, 3-ftd	175.00	175.00
Cheese & cracker set	150.00	125.00
Creamer	75.00	37.50
Cup	65.00	35.00
Goblet, 4" cocktail	80.00	80.00
Goblet, 4¾", 6 oz. juice	80.00	75.00
Goblet, 6", 10 oz. water	80.00	70.00

	Pink	Yellow
Mayonnaise, 3-piece	195.00	135.00
Plate, 7" sherbet	20.00	12.00
Plate, 7½" salad	25.00	20.00
Plate, 8" luncheon	45.00	27.50
Saucer	20.00	12.00
Sherbet, 4¾"	75.00	60.00
Sugar	75.00	37.50
Tray, 11", 2-handled	75.00	60.00
Tray, 11", center-handled	155.00	110.00

"PEACOCK REVERSE" PADEN CITY GLASS COMPANY, LINE #411, #412 & #991, 1930s

Colors: Cobalt blue, red, amber, yellow, green, pink, black, and crystal.

Paden City's Line #412 ("Crow's Foot"), Line #991 ("Penny Line"), and Line #411 (square shapes with the corners cut off) compose the blanks on which "Peacock Reverse" has been found. Paden City lines have various etched patterns; it is not unknown to recognize a blank only to notice that it does not have the etched design you want! (Those designs which show white in the photograph have been highlighted with chalk so you can see them better!)

That pink, eight-sided plate is the only pink piece I have seen, and it is the only plate I have seen in this pattern. There are bound to be others! Red seems to be the most available and most desired color. That blue sugar is the only blue piece I have found with "Peacock Reverse" etch except for vases. We have found two colored sugars, but have yet to spot a creamer in 12 years of searching. A newly discovered, lipped, footed comport measures 4¼" tall and 7⅜" wide. It is pictured in the back on the right.

There are two styles of candy dishes. Notice that both have patterns only on the lids. The plain bottoms can be discovered with lids wearing other etches or even without an etch. That should make bottoms easier to find; but that hasn't been the case, so far.

Prices for "Peacock Reverse" are not established by color as much as other patterns. Collectors welcome any piece in any color revealed!

"Peacock Reverse" could conceivably be etched on almost any piece listed under "Crow's Foot" (squared) or "Orchid." Let me know what unlisted pieces or colors you encounter!

	All Colors
Bowl, 4⅞", square	42.00
Bowl, 8¾", square	115.00
Bowl, 8¾", square with handles	110.00
Bowl, 11¾" console	125.00
Candlesticks, 5¾", square base, pr.	150.00
Candy dish, 6½", square	175.00
Comport, 3¼" high, 6¼" wide	75.00
Comport, 4¼" high, 7⅜" wide	85.00
Creamer, 2¾", flat	95.00
Cup	90.00

	All Colors
Plate, 5¾" sherbet	22.50
Plate, 8½" luncheon	60.00
Plate 10⅜", 2-handled	95.00
Saucer	25.00
Sherbet, 4⅝" tall, 3⅜" diameter	65.00
Sherbet, 4⅞" tall, 3⅝" diameter	65.00
Server, center-handled	75.00
Sugar, 2¾", flat	95.00
Tumbler, 4", 10 oz., flat	85.00
Vase, 10"	225.00

"PEACOCK & WILD ROSE," "NORA BIRD" PADEN CITY GLASS COMPANY, LINE #300, 1929–1930s

Colors: Pink, green, amber, cobalt blue, black, light blue, crystal, and red.

An interesting observation about Paden City's "Peacock and Wild Rose" and "Nora Bird" is that they are virtually the same pattern with "Nora Bird" being a condensed (or sectioned off) version of the "Peacock and Wild Rose" design. If you have a chance to examine a tall vase, you will see the small bird at the bottom of the design that appears on the pieces formerly known as "Nora Bird." The bird on each piece can be found in flight or getting ready to take flight. Obviously, the whole pattern would not fit on the smaller pieces; so, a condensed version was designed! That is why creamers, sugars, and luncheon pieces have never been discovered in "Peacock and Wild Rose." These pieces have formerly been attributed to another pattern, "Nora Bird." Both are etched on Line #300 which is the same line on which most "Cupid" pieces appear. Thus, I have assimilated both patterns into only "Peacock and Wild Rose."

The abundant auxiliary pieces of "Peacock and Wild Rose" can now combine with the cups, saucers, creamers, sugars, and luncheon plates of "Nora Bird" to give a fairly comprehensive pattern! I had suggested a mixture of these two Paden City peacock patterns previously, but not for this reason! I was just positive that they looked fine together!

It has been insinuated that this bird is, in fact, a pheasant. That may be true since several pheasant patterns were made by other glass companies during this era. Pheasants supposedly represented health and happiness; and since America was captivated with influences from the Orient, this Oriental bird lore may have been adopted for glass. I'm told by a reader that the old time plant workers referred to any of the bird etches as "pheasant line."

Note the pink, **octagonal** flat candy dish on the bottom of page 165! This is not a part of the #300 line as is the footed, 5¼" candy dish. The flat, three-part candy dish is not pictured this time, but the lids to those two candy dishes are interchangeable. Finding a candy in "Peacock and Wild Rose" **should** be easier now with three from which to choose! Alas, finding only one is not an easy achievement. A few pieces of light blue have been found.

There are two styles of creamers and sugars in pink. These two types are also found with "Cupid" etch. So far, we have only discovered the round handled set in green "Peacock and Wild Rose." Recently, I ran across an individual (smaller) sugar and creamer in green. I had not seen these in any Paden City pattern before. They have the round style handles. Additionally, a collector in Texas has found two green tumblers that are different from those listed. They are 2¼", 3 ounces; and 5¼", 10 ounces.

Be sure to check out the 8½", 64 ounce pitcher in *Very Rare Glassware of the Depression Years, Sixth Series.* There are possibly more pieces in this pattern than I have listed; please let me know if you find something else.

	All Colors
Bowl, 8½", flat	125.00
Bowl, 8½", fruit, oval, ftd.	195.00
Bowl, 8¾", ftd.	175.00
Bowl, 9½", center-handled	165.00
Bowl, 9½", ftd.	185.00
Bowl, 10½", center-handled	125.00
Bowl, 10½", ftd.	195.00
Bowl, 10½", fruit	185.00
Bowl, 11", console	175.00
Bowl, 14", console	195.00
Candlestick, 5" wide, pr.	165.00
Candlesticks, octagonal tops, pr.	195.00
Candy dish w/cover, 6½", 3-part	195.00
Candy dish w/cover, 7"	250.00
Candy with lid, ftd., 5¼" high	195.00
Cheese and cracker set	185.00
Comport, 3¼" tall, 6¼" wide	125.00
Creamer, 4½", round handle	55.00
Creamer, 5", pointed handle	55.00
Cup	70.00
Ice bucket, 6"	210.00

	All Colors
Ice tub, 4¾"	195.00
Ice tub, 6"	195.00
Mayonnaise and liner	110.00
Pitcher, 5" high	265.00
Pitcher, 8½", 64 oz.	350.00
Plate, 8"	25.00
Plate, cake, low foot	145.00
Relish, 3-part	110.00
Saucer	15.00
Sugar, 4½", round handle	55.00
Sugar, 5", pointed handle	55.00
Tray, rectangular, handled	195.00
Tumbler, 2¼", 3 oz.	50.00
Tumbler, 3"	55.00
Tumbler, 4"	65.00
Tumbler, 4¾", ftd.	75.00
Tumbler, 5¼", 10 oz.	75.00
Vase, 8¼", elliptical	395.00
Vase, 10", two styles	250.00
Vase, 12"	295.00

"PEBBLED RIM" Line #707 L. E. SMITH GLASS COMPANY, 1930s

Colors: Amber, green, pink

"Pebbled Rim" is a small L. E. Smith pattern that collectors are beginning to notice because, generally speaking, it is graceful and still economically priced. However, I do know of one dust catching set being offered in an antique mall I visit once or twice a year at a ridiculous price. I trust the owner believes since its pink Depression glass, it must be worth a mint! Right now, there are only a few collectors searching for it; thus, "mint" status is hardly its realm.

The large ruffled edge bowl and the platter seem to be the hardest pieces to find, although any green seems to be harder to come by than the pink. This is another pattern that can be mixed with other patterns or blended with patterns for accessory pieces. In fact, I'm fairly certain that accounts for the dearth of the above two pieces. People are using them with other sets.

	All colors
Bowl, 9½", oval	25.00
Bowl, berry	8.00
Bowl, ruffled edge vegetable, deep	30.00
Bowl, ruffled edge vegetable, shallow	28.00
Candleholder	20.00
Cream	12.50
Cup	7.50

	All colors
Plate, 6" bread/butter	5.00
Plate, 7" salad	6.00
Plate, 9" dinner	10.00
Plate, 9", two-hndl.	20.00
Platter, oval	25.00
Saucer	2.00
Sugar	12.50

PETALWARE MacBETH-EVANS GLASS COMPANY, 1930–1950

Colors: Monax, Cremax, pink, crystal, cobalt and fired-on red, blue, green, and yellow.

The red-trimmed Petalware, Mountain Flowers, continues to be the preferred decoration of all the different Petalware designs. Original boxed sets of sherbets revealed the design name, "Mountain Flowers"; that's how I will refer to it from now on. Since it has been pictured here for years and on the cover of both this book and the *Pocket Guide,* I am letting it rest so you can see some other decorations on Petalware. Mountain Flowers Petalware has three sizes of decorated tumblers, a pitcher, and sherbets to match it. These are possibly Libbey decorated since many of these tumblers are found in northern Ohio. I have listed the two sizes of tumblers I own. You can find these tumblers in both frosted or unfrosted versions. I saw a Mountain Flowers decorated pitcher, however, which was a frosted Federal Star juice pitcher.

Collectors are also smitten with other decorated Petalware patterns. That was abundantly evident in Michigan last November. We had just photographed for the book and decided to sell most all the pieces we had accumulated and buy different ones for future books. We sold over 60 different pieces since I only buy one of anything to photograph. Many collectors and dealers left our booth with smiling faces.

Florette is the second most collected design. It is the pointed petal, red flower decoration without the red edge trim. It is pictured on the second and third shelves on page 169. Notice the flat soup on the third row. Soups are rarely seen in Petalware, let alone decorated as Florette! One batch of these were found in Pennsylvania about 10 years ago. This is one of that group; few others have ever been seen. Since I have now found a 1949 company magazine showing a lady painting this design on stacks of plates, this Florette pattern will probably move to the 50s book hereafter.

Monax and Ivrene are names given the Petalware colors by MacBeth-Evans. Ivrene refers to the opaque beige colored Petalware shown on page 168 and Monax is the whiter color shown in all the other pictures. Pastel decorated Ivrene shown in the middle row on page 168 is the pattern being currently pursued. I have been continually asked for it at shows. Considering little of it is found, prices are rising! Notice the crystal tumblers with matching pastel bands in that photo. These are found in three sizes, all presently selling in the $7.00 to $10.00 range. No pitchers were originally made, but banded, decorated tumblers to match were advertised with the set in 1939. However, those 1939 tumblers were all straight sided and probably nearly impossible to locate now.

I have tried to show as wide a variety of decorated Petalware focusing in on fruits and some florals this time. We had additional pictures, but I had to limit my choice to three in order to add other new patterns to the book. Look back over the last few editions for additional designs. There are different series of fruits, birds, and flowers. Fruit-decorated Petalware (with printed names of fruits) is found in sets of eight. One such set consists of plates showing cherry, apple, orange, plum, strawberry, blueberry, pear, and grape. You may find other sets with different fruits. Some plates have labels which read "Rainbow Hand Painted." Others have colored bands or 22K gold trim. All series of fruit- and bird-decorated Petalware sell well!

Pink Petalware (top 169) has captivated some collectors. I previously suggested that pink Petalware was inexpensive and an excellent pattern for beginning collectors. This pink is still less costly than most other pink patterns in Depression glass.

The 9" berry bowl varies from 8¾" at times. You will find other quarter inch variances on many larger pieces in this pattern. It was made for a long time and replacing worn moulds caused some size discrepancies. Very few 4" Monax sherbets have been seen in recent years. The last one I owned (in 1976) was a casualty of my concrete basement floor!

	Crystal	Pink	Cremax Monax Plain	Cremax, Monax Florette, Fired-On Decorations	Red Trim Floral
Bowl, 4½" cream soup	4.50	17.50	12.00	15.00	
Bowl, 5¾" cereal	4.00	14.00	8.00	14.00	40.00
Bowl, 7" soup			60.00	75.00	
*Bowl, 9" large berry	8.50	25.00	18.00	35.00	135.00
Cup	3.00	9.00	5.00	10.00	27.50
**Creamer, ftd.	3.00	8.00	6.00	12.50	35.00
Lamp shade (many sizes) $8.00 to $15.00					
Mustard with metal cover in cobalt blue only, $10.00					
Pitcher, 80 oz. (crystal decorated bands)	25.00				
Plate, 6" sherbet	2.00	2.50	2.50	6.00	22.00
Plate, 8" salad	2.00	6.00	4.00	10.00	25.00
Plate, 9" dinner	4.00	14.00	13.00	16.00	37.50
Plate, 11" salver	4.50	15.00	10.00	25.00	
Plate, 12" salver		11.00	18.00		40.00
Platter, 13", oval	8.50	25.00	15.00	25.00	
Saucer	1.50	2.00	2.00	3.50	10.00
Saucer, cream soup liner			18.00		
Sherbet, 4", low ftd.			30.00		
**Sherbet, 4½", low ftd.	3.50	10.00	8.00	12.00	38.00
**Sugar, ftd.	3.00	9.00	6.00	10.00	35.00
Tidbit servers or Lazy Susans, several styles 12.00 to 17.50					
Tumbler, 3⅝", 6 oz.					35.00
Tumbler, 4⅝", 12 oz.					37.50
***Tumblers (crystal decorated pastel bands) 7.50 to 10.00					

*Also in cobalt at $65.00 **Also in cobalt at $35.00 ***Several sizes

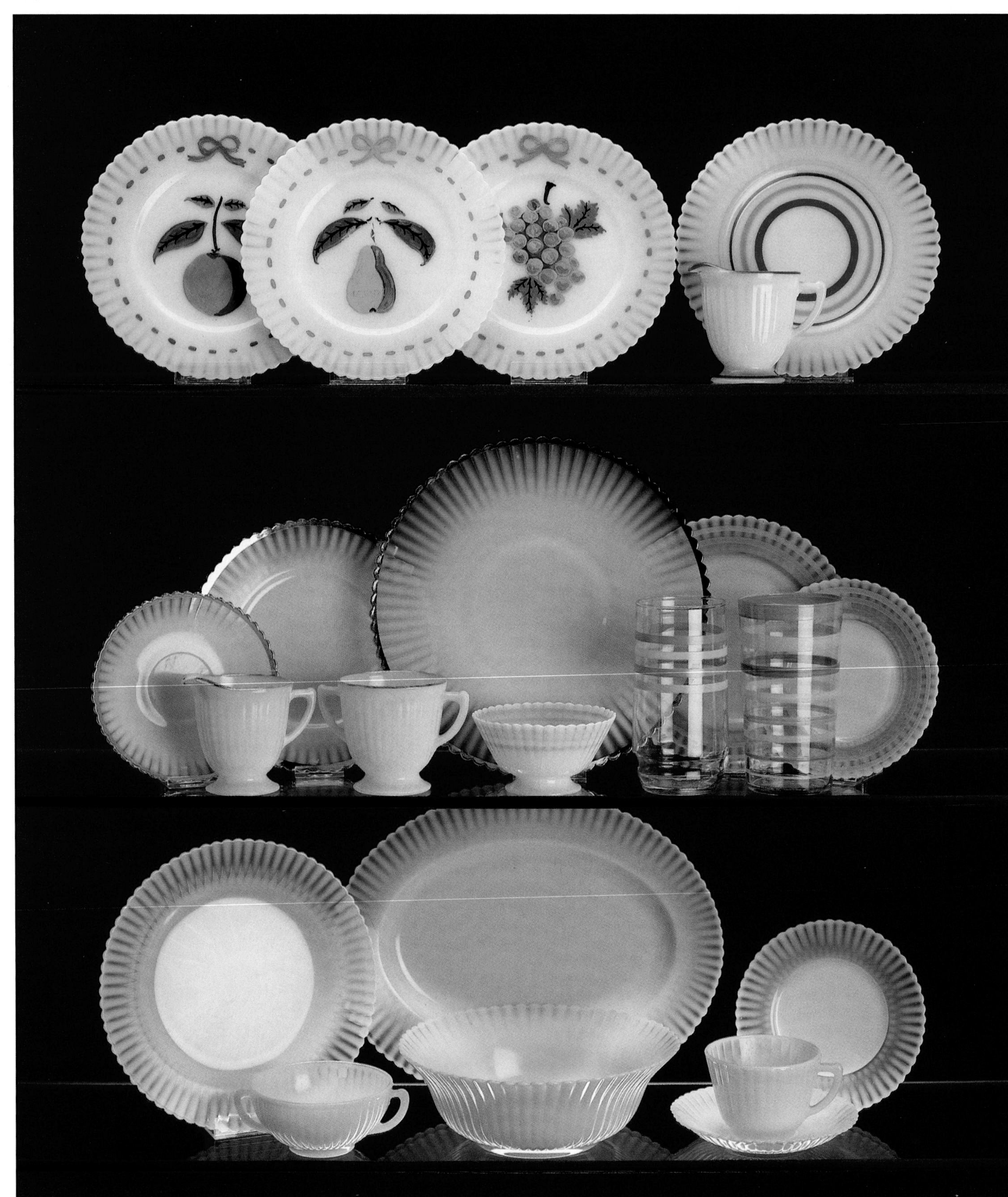

PETALWARE

PILLAR OPTIC, "LOGS," "LOG CABIN" ANCHOR HOCKING GLASS COMPANY, 1937–1942

Colors: Crystal, green, pink, Royal Ruby; amber and iridescent, possible Federal Glass Co.

I found the name for this Hocking pattern while researching old catalog files for the Fire-King book. Up until this point, I'd heard it mostly referred to as "Log Cabin" glass. I have shown the 60 ounce pitcher in three colors, and two 80 ounce ones are shown below. The panels of the Pillar Optic are evenly spaced (note pretzel jars) and not like Old Cafe's alternating large panel with two small ones. Hopefully, everyone will pay attention to this new pattern and not buy Pillar Optic as Old Cafe. Fourteen of the last fourteen pitchers I have seen labeled as Old Cafe have not been. Notice in the photo below that there were two styles of Pillar Optic pitchers manufactured.

Most of you who have been collecting for sometime will recognize this Pillar Optic pattern from my Kitchenware book. Hocking promoted a beer and pretzel set with mugs and the pretzel jar. Most collectors call the 130 ounce jar a cookie, but it was not offered as such. The top is hard to find mint and, as you can see, it is totally missing in pink in my picture.

Amber, Royal Ruby, and iridescent items are hard to find. I have only observed flat tumblers in amber and the iridescent water shown here. However, Federal Glass Company is known to have manufactured like patterned tumblers and it's possible amber and iridescent wares came from them rather than Anchor Hocking. I have seen Royal Ruby Pillar Optic in four items, the three footed tumblers like those found in Colonial and the 9" two-handled bowl. Let me hear from you if you know of others.

There are two styles of cups, the rounded cup pictured in green and the flatter pink one is more reminiscent of Colonial styled cups. I finally found a green saucer, but no pink one as yet. I have not seen flat green cups or rounded pink ones. The pink sugar and creamer came out of the attic of a former Hocking employee. It is the only creamer and sugar that I have found.

Tumblers in crystal in this line have been a stable in Hocking's production for years. In fact, in one or their later catalogs, it's shown under the heading "Old Reliable." Many restaurants still use them today.

	Crystal	Amber Green Pink	Royal Ruby
Bowl, 9", two-hndl.		65.00	95.00
Creamer, ftd.		45.00	
Cup	10.00	15.00	
Mug, 12 oz.	10.00	30.00	
Pitcher, w/o lip, 60 oz.	25.00	45.00	
Pitcher, w/lip, 80 oz.	30.00	55.00	
Pitcher, 80 oz., tilt	35.00	65.00	
Plate, 8" luncheon	8.00	12.00	
Pretzel Jar, 130 oz.	60.00	125.00	
Saucer	2.00	4.00	
Sugar, ftd.		45.00	
Tumbler, 1½ oz. whiskey	10.00	15.00	
Tumbler, 7 oz. old fashioned	10.00	15.00	
Tumbler, 9 oz. water	2.50	20.00	
Tumbler, 11 oz., ftd., cone	12.00	20.00	
Tumbler, 13 oz. tea	4.00	25.00	
Tumbler, 3¼", 3 oz., ftd.	8.00	12.50	25.00
Tumbler, 4", 5 oz. juice, ftd.	10.00	15.00	30.00
Tumbler, 5¼", 10 oz., ftd.	12.00	25.00	35.00

PILLAR OPTIC

PRIMO, "PANELED ASTER" U.S. GLASS COMPANY, EARLY 1930s

Colors: Green and yellow.

Primo was sold in 1932 as a 14-piece bridge set (with plates, cups, saucers, and sugar and creamer), a 16-piece luncheonette (with grill plates, tumblers, cups, and saucers), an 18-piece occasional set (with plates, tumblers, sugar, creamer, cup, and saucer), a 19-piece hostess set (add a tray), and a 7-piece berry set. A new find has been reported, the two-handled tray. The recently listed (last edition) 11" three-footed console bowl (large berry in old ads) has created a stir among collectors of this smaller pattern. No one seemed too excited about the 6¼" sherbet plate which had not been previously listed. Oh, I got excited enough for everybody when I first spied them in that antique mall. I bought the sherbet plates, but had to take the sherbets to get them. The large berry (console) bowl is beat up, but I had to pay the $20.00 asked because "it had to be rare since it wasn't in Gene Florence's book," according to the proprietor. A friend who decided to collect yellow Primo asked me to watch for this pattern and for over five years, I have looked for it. Any bowls, dinner, grill, or cake plates will take some searching. Though I did discover two new pieces, I have not yet found a green berry bowl to photograph!

An aggravation to buying Primo comes from mould roughness and inner rim damage on pieces that have rims. There seems to be more Primo along the Gulf Coast than any place I have looked. I have seen several sets in antique malls between Florida and Texas, but a majority of the pieces were very rough or chipped. Prices marked were for mint pieces! I wonder if anyone buys damaged Primo (substitute any pattern) that way? Since the pieces were still on the shelves, I surmise not. My theory is that if you see a piece priced for sale and it is still there a year or more later, then no one has wanted to pay that price!

The tumbler exactly fits the coaster/ash tray! These coasters have been found in boxed sets with Primo tumblers that were advertised as "Bridge Service Sets." The coasters are also found in pink and black, but no Primo design is found on the coasters.

	Yellow, Green
Bowl, 4½"	22.00
Bowl, 7¾"	35.00
Bowl, 11", 3-footed	45.00
Cake plate, 10", 3-footed	35.00
Coaster/ash tray	8.00
Creamer	12.00
Cup	12.00
Plate, 6¼"	10.00

	Yellow, Green
Plate, 7½"	12.00
Plate, 10" dinner	25.00
Plate, 10" grill	16.00
Saucer	3.00
Sherbet	14.00
Sugar	12.00
Tray, 2-hndl. hostess	35.00
Tumbler, 5¾", 9 oz.	30.00

PRINCESS HOCKING GLASS COMPANY, 1931–1935

Colors: Green, Topaz yellow, apricot yellow, pink, and light blue.

I wrote in the last book that I had received a picture of a blue Princess 8¾" square, three-footed bowl which stands only 1½" high. I said it was like the pink one pictured in *Very Rare Glassware of the Depression Years, Fourth Series,* but I was wrong. It is divided into three sections unlike the pink which was undivided. You can see the blue one in *Very Rare Glassware of the Depression Years, Sixth Series.* Newly discovered pieces of Princess continue to surface! Blue Princess pieces are discovered on rare occasions. The cookie jar, cup and saucer, and dinner plate are finding a ready market by collectors of those items. Last April there was an **erroneous report** in some publication that Princess dinner plates had been reproduced in blue. No reproductions of anything in Depression glass have ever come close to that real blue color pictured on page 175. Blue Princess suffers the fate of many seldom-found patterns or colors of Depression glass. It seems too rare to collect a set! Keep looking, though, because you never know these 65 or 70 years later what is still awaiting discovery. Reproduction cobalt blue and amber (candy dishes) have been reported to me however.

Finding mint condition Princess bowls presents a problem due to inner rim roughness. If you see an ad that says "irr" next to the item, it means inner rim roughness. Some new collectors are always writing for these explanations; you do **have to read each pattern** to catch all these little asides. Some of this "irr" damage was caused by stacking the bowls together over the years; but some destruction was created by the very sharply defined inner rim itself. The undivided Princess relish is touted as a soup bowl by some dealers. To me, it does not seem deep enough for a soup bowl.

Footed iced tea tumblers and all bowls are hard to find in all colors of Princess. Besides the previously mentioned items, green Princess collectors have to search long and hard for the undivided relish and the elusive, square foot pitcher with tumblers to match. Collectors of pink Princess have problems finding coasters, ash trays, and the squared foot pitchers with matching tumblers. The hardest to find yellow pieces include the butter dish, juice pitcher, undivided relish, 10½" handled sandwich plate, coasters, and ash trays. I bought two of the yellow handled trays out of an antique mall in Kentucky. This plate is just like the handled grill plate without the dividers. You can see one in the background of the photograph at the bottom of page 175. I had a customer who had been looking for one for eight years.

There is some extreme color variation in yellow Princess. Topaz is the official color listed by Hocking, and it is a bright, attractive shade of yellow. However, some yellow turned out amber and has been dubbed "apricot" by collectors. Most favor the Topaz which makes the darker, amber shade hard to sell. The colors are so mismatched that it is almost as if Hocking meant to have two distinct colors. For some reason (probably distribution) yellow Princess bowls and sherbets prevail in the Detroit area. Almost all yellow Princess juice pitchers have been found in northern and central Kentucky.

The grill plate without handles and dinner plate have been corrected to read 9½" in the listing instead of the 9" listed in Hocking catalogs. Measure perpendicularly and not diagonally!

	Green	Pink	Topaz, Apricot
Ash tray, 4½"	75.00	95.00	110.00
Bowl, 4½" berry	30.00	30.00	55.00
Bowl, 5" cereal or oatmeal	40.00	40.00	35.00
Bowl, 9" octagonal salad	40.00	40.00	140.00
Bowl, 9½", hat-shaped	55.00	50.00	140.00
Bowl, 10" oval vegetable	30.00	28.00	65.00
Butter dish and cover	100.00	115.00	750.00
Butter dish bottom	35.00	40.00	250.00
Butter dish top	65.00	75.00	500.00
Cake stand, 10"	33.00	33.00	
*Candy dish and cover	65.00	70.00	
Coaster	42.00	85.00	115.00
**Cookie jar and cover	60.00	70.00	
Creamer, oval	16.00	15.00	18.00
***Cup	13.00	12.00	8.00
Pitcher 6", 37 oz.	55.00	65.00	695.00
Pitcher, 7⅜", 24 oz., ftd.	525.00	475.00	
Pitcher, 8", 60 oz.	58.00	58.00	100.00
****Plate, 5½" sherbet	10.00	10.00	3.00
Plate, 8" salad	14.00	16.00	15.00
****Plate, 9½" dinner	30.00	25.00	15.00
**Plate, 9½" grill	15.00	15.00	5.50
Plate, 10¼" handled sandwich	16.00	28.00	175.00
Plate, 10½" grill, closed handles	10.00	12.00	5.50
Platter, 12", closed handles	27.00	27.00	65.00
Relish, 7½", divided	26.00	28.00	100.00
Relish, 7½", plain	195.00	195.00	250.00
Salt and pepper, 4½" pr.	60.00	55.00	85.00
Spice shakers, 5½" pr.	40.00		
***Saucer (same as sherbet plate)	10.00	10.00	3.00
Sherbet, ftd.	25.00	25.00	35.00
Sugar	10.00	12.00	8.50
Sugar cover	25.00	22.00	17.50
Tumbler, 3", 5 oz. juice	33.00	33.00	33.00
Tumbler, 4", 9 oz. water	28.00	28.00	25.00
Tumbler, 5¼", 13 oz. iced tea	50.00	32.00	33.00
Tumbler, 4¾", 9 oz., sq. ftd	65.00	60.00	
Tumbler, 5¼", 10 oz., ftd.	30.00	30.00	21.00
Tumbler, 6½", 12½ oz., ftd.	110.00	95.00	165.00
Vase, 8"	40.00	45.00	

*Beware reproductions in cobalt blue and amber
**Blue $895.00
***Blue $125.00
****Blue $60.00
**** Blue $200.00

QUEEN MARY (PRISMATIC LINE), "VERTICAL RIBBED"

ANCHOR HOCKING GLASS COMPANY, 1936–1949

Colors: Pink, crystal, and some Royal Ruby.

Crystal Queen Mary is attracting as many new collectors as pink. Price is the principal reason, but availability and its somewhat Deco look are others. Nothing is as irksome to ferret out as pink Queen Mary dinner plates and footed tumblers; and prices for those same items in crystal are increasing, but will have a way to go to catch the pink! A crystal set can still be accomplished at reasonable prices!

As far as I can determine, the pink **footed** creamer and sugar pictured here is Anchor Hocking, but there is no listing for them in any catalog I have. They have all the characteristics of Queen Mary! A set was found in crystal and is pictured in *Very Rare Glassware of the Depression Years, Fifth Series.* A crosshatched vase (shaped like Old Cafe with a 400 line number) is pictured with Queen Mary items in Hocking catalogs.

The 6" cereal bowl has the same shape as the butter bottom. Butter dishes were called preserve dishes in Hocking catalogs. There are two sizes of cups. The smaller sits on the saucer with cup ring. The larger cup rests on the combination saucer/sherbet plate. Lately, the pink smaller cup and saucer have outdistanced the larger in price. The 5½" tab-handled bowl is being called a cream soup by some dealers. Calling it that doesn't make it so, but the price on that bowl has gone up rather dramatically.

The frosted crystal butter dish with metal band looks somewhat like a crown. I was informed that these were made about the time of the English Coronation in the mid-1930s. I have seen these priced as high as $150.00 in an Art Deco shop, but I had to think before paying $25.00 for the one pictured in the last book! A pair of lamp shades were found made from frosted candy lids (with metal decorations similar to the butter). Someone had fun designing these items. I wish we could find out who.

In the 1950s, the 3½" ash tray in the Queen Mary pattern was made in forest green and Royal Ruby. The 2" x 3¾" ash tray and oval cigarette jar have been found together labeled "Ace Hi Bridge Smoking Set" and may be Hazel Atlas manufactured. I am now sure the little colored shakers pictured were Hazel Atlas; keep that in mind if they are offered to you as Queen Mary. They, alas, are not!

	Pink	Crystal
Ash tray, 2" x 3¾", oval	5.00	3.00
*Ash tray, 3¼", round		3.00
Ash tray, 4¼", square (#422)		4.00
Bowl, 4", one-hndl. or none	5.00	3.50
Bowl, 4½" berry	6.00	4.00
Bowl, 5" berry, flared	12.00	6.00
Bowl, 5½", two hndl.	20.00	6.50
Bowl, 6", cereal	25.00	6.00
Bowl, deep, 7½" (#477)	12.00	7.00
Bowl, 8¾" large berry (#478)	20.00	15.00
Butter dish or preserve and cover (#498)	150.00	25.00
Butter dish bottom (#498)	40.00	6.50
Butter dish top (#498)	110.00	18.50
Candy dish and cover, 7¼" (#490)	40.00	22.00
**Candlesticks, 4½" double branch, pr.		20.00
Celery or pickle dish, 5" x 10" (#467)	25.00	11.00
Cigarette jar, 2" x 3", oval	7.50	5.50
Coaster, 3½"	5.00	3.00
Coaster/ash tray, 3¼", round (#419)	6.00	5.00
Comport, 5¾"	25.00	15.00

*Royal Ruby $5.00; Forest Green $3.00 ** Royal Ruby $75.00

	Pink	Crystal
Creamer, ftd.	50.00	25.00
Creamer, 5½", oval (#471)	12.00	5.50
Cup, large	7.00	5.50
Cup, small	10.00	8.00
Mayonnaise, 5" x 2¾" h, 6" plate	30.00	15.00
Plate, 6⅝"	6.00	4.00
Plate, 8¾" salad (#438)		5.50
Plate, 9¾" dinner (#426)	60.00	18.00
Plate, 12" sandwich (#450)	22.00	12.00
Plate, 14" serving tray	22.00	12.00
Relish tray, 12", 3-part	18.00	9.00
Relish tray, 14", 4-part	20.00	12.00
Salt and pepper, 2½", pr. (#486)		19.00
Saucer/cup ring	5.00	2.50
Sherbet, ftd.	9.00	5.00
Sugar, ftd.	50.00	25.00
Sugar, 6", oval (#470)	12.00	4.50
Tumbler, 3½", 5 oz. juice	12.00	4.00
Tumbler, 4", 9 oz. water	17.00	6.00
Tumbler, 5", 10 oz., ftd.	70.00	33.00
Vase, 6½" (#441)		10.00

RADIANCE NEW MARTINSVILLE GLASS COMPANY, 1936–1939

Colors: Red, cobalt and ice blue, amber, crystal, pink, and emerald green.

Radiance punch, cordial, and condiment sets continue to be evasive. Some new items have been found. A Texas reader reported a crystal cake stand, 11½" x 4" tall. If you are collector of Radiance and do not have my *Very Rare Glassware of the Depression Years, Sixth Series,* you ought to get a copy. There is an 8" red candlestick with matching boboches, a 5" red ball candle, and several odd colored vases.

The punch set is hard to find, but the punch ladle is the Achilles' heel of this set. The ladle was made by adding a long handle to a punch cup. If not broken years ago, collectors and dealers have added to their demise by traveling with them over recent years. I have been told more than once that the handle comes loose from the cup very easily. The dealer who relayed that information should know; he did it — twice! He must pack even worse than I.

Those crystal punch bowl sets being found on emerald green and black plates were made by Viking after they bought out New Martinsville. One such emerald green set was pictured previously. These are found rather frequently — unlike their older counterparts! I saw a black punch bowl in Seattle. I suspect that too is Viking! If Viking, it probably has a crystal plate and cups; but this is only speculation!

A few collectors have tenaciously implied that Radiance is too elegant a glassware to be included in this book. They believe it was more superior glassware than those mass-produced wares of the Depression era and belongs in my *Elegant Glassware of the Depression Era.* They are probably right. However, Radiance was collected as Depression glass long before the word "Elegant" was ever coined to identify that type of glassware.

Red and ice blue are the most coveted Radiance colors; enjoy what I have pictured this time. The most troublesome pieces to find in red and ice blue include the butter dish, pitcher, handled decanter, and the five-piece condiment set. Vases have been found made into lamps. I question this being a factory project, but it could have been.

A few pieces are being found in pink including creamer, sugar, tray, cup, saucer, vase, and shakers. These are selling in the same range as the red since they are scarce at this time.

Price crystal about 50 percent of amber. Only the crystal pieces that item collectors seek sell very well. These include pitchers, butter dishes, shakers, sugars, creamers, and cordials.

	Ice Blue, Red	Amber
Bowl, 5" nut, 2-hndl.	20.00	10.00
Bowl, 6" bonbon	30.00	15.00
Bowl, 6" bonbon, footed	32.00	17.50
Bowl, 6" bonbon w/cover	95.00	45.00
Bowl, 7" relish, 2-part	30.00	18.00
Bowl, 7" pickle	25.00	15.00
Bowl, 8" relish, 3-part	45.00	30.00
* Bowl, 9" punch	200.00	100.00
Bowl, 10" celery	30.00	18.00
Bowl, 10", crimped	45.00	25.00
Bowl, 10", flared	42.00	22.00
Bowl, 12", crimped	50.00	30.00
Bowl, 12", flared	47.50	27.50
Butter dish	465.00	200.00
Candlestick, 6", ruffled, pr.	175.00	80.00
Candlestick, 8", pr.	125.00	60.00
Candlestick, 2-lite, pr.	150.00	70.00
Cheese/cracker (11" plate) set	110.00	30.00
Comport, 5"	30.00	18.00
Comport, 6"	35.00	22.00
Condiment set, 4-piece w/tray	295.00	160.00
Creamer	25.00	15.00
Cruet, indiv.	75.00	36.00
Cup, ftd.	18.00	12.00
Cup, punch	15.00	7.00
** Decanter w/stopper, hndl.	195.00	100.00
Goblet, 1 oz. cordial	35.00	25.00
Ladle for punch bowl	135.00	95.00
Lamp, 12"	110.00	56.00
Mayonnaise, 3-piece, set	95.00	40.00
*** Pitcher, 64 oz.	295.00	150.00
Plate, 8" luncheon	16.00	10.00
**** Plate, 14" punch bowl liner	85.00	45.00
Salt & pepper, pr.	95.00	50.00
Saucer	8.50	5.50
Sugar	25.00	15.00
Tray, oval	40.00	24.00
***** Tumbler, 9 oz.	30.00	20.00
****** Vase, 10", flared or crimped	100.00	55.00
Vase, 12", flared or crimped	150.00	

* Emerald green $125.00
** Cobalt blue $185.00
*** Cobalt blue $350.00
**** Emerald green $25.00
***** Cobalt blue $28.00
****** Cobalt blue $75.00

RADIANCE

RAINDROPS, "OPTIC DESIGN" FEDERAL GLASS COMPANY, 1929–1933

Colors: Green and crystal.

As I wrote about raindrops falling outside my office window two years ago, it is hard to remember what it looked like then. We have had less than two inches of rain this entire year and Florida could turn into another fire zone again this year. For elementary collectors please heed that Raindrops has rounded bumps and not elongated ones. Elongated bumps belong to another pattern usually referred to as "Thumbprint." Almost all Raindrops pieces are embossed on the bottom with Federal's trademark of an F inside a shield.

The 7½" berry bowl price continues to climb and is now the second most expensive piece in Raindrops. It has overtaken the price of the sugar bowl lid. However, both of these pieces have to take a back seat to the shakers. In actuality, Raindrops sugar lids have turned out to be common in comparison to shakers! Consequently, the price of shakers has skyrocketed over the last few years. A couple of shaker collectors have told me that these are harder to find than yellow and green Mayfair! Both collectors had at least one of those elusive shakers, but neither one had the Raindrops. One of them told me to name my price for the one shown. If I did, you might never be able to see one pictured again. I have never seen a Raindrops shaker for sale at any show I have attended if that makes any kind of impression on you as to how rare it is. I have owned the one footed Mayfair shaker and have held both genuine pairs of pink Cherry Blossom shakers known. One Raindrops shaker is all I have seen, though I have heard of others!

Raindrops makes a great little luncheon or bridge set. It even has a few accessory pieces that other smaller sets do not. You can find three sizes of bowls in Raindrops. The 7½" bowl will be the one you will probably find last. Raindrops will blend well with many other green sets; so, give that a try if you want additional pieces.

There are two styles of cups. One is flat bottomed and the other has a slight foot. The flat bottomed is 2⁵⁄₁₆" high and the footed is 2¹¹⁄₁₆" (reported by a Raindrops collector). I have not measured them myself. Prices for crystal tumblers run from 50 to 60 percent less than for green.

	Green
Bowl, 4½" fruit	6.00
Bowl, 6" cereal	10.00
Bowl, 7½" berry	50.00
Cup	5.50
Creamer	7.50
Plate, 6" sherbet	2.50
Plate, 8" luncheon	6.00
Salt and pepper, pr.	325.00
Saucer	2.00
Sherbet	7.00

	Green
Sugar	7.50
Sugar cover	40.00
Tumbler, 3", 4 oz.	5.00
Tumbler, 2⅛", 2 oz.	5.00
Tumbler, 3⅞", 5 oz.	6.50
Tumbler, 4⅛", 9½ oz.	9.00
Tumbler, 5", 10 oz.	9.00
Tumbler, 5⅜", 14 oz.	12.00
Whiskey, 1⅞", 1 oz.	7.00

"RIBBON" HAZEL ATLAS GLASS COMPANY, EARLY 1930s

Colors: Green; some black, crystal, and pink.

"Ribbon" bowls are among the most difficult to find in all of Depression glass. They are even more scarce than those of its sister pattern, Cloverleaf. The mould shapes are the same. Were there more collectors for Ribbon, it would be interesting to see where the price of bowls would level off considering the prices brought by Cloverleaf bowls with tons of collectors. Several collectors informed me that they lusted over the display of both the berry and the cereal in my previous book. I had a letter from a long-time collector who had an older book explaining that I was wrong in listing the cereal because it didn't exist. I suggested he order the current book to see one. He did and called to ask how much for that bowl? The cereal and berry are sitting flat in this photo since they looked ovoid when sitting on their sides in the last book. I found four of the berry bowls and kept one for photography. A dealer bought the other three for her sister's collection. Sorry, that's all the berry bowls I have ever owned; and you are looking at the only cereal I have seen!

I rarely see "Ribbon" for sale at shows. "Ribbon" is another of the patterns that is not found in the West according to dealers who travel those areas.

Tumblers, sugars, and creamers are not yet as hard to find as bowls, but even they are beginning to be in lesser supply. The candy dish prevails as the repeatedly seen piece of "Ribbon." Freely found and inexpensively priced, it makes an excellent, functional gift!

Two bowl designs were made for the 8" berry. The normally found smaller bowls have evenly spaced small panels on them while the panels on some larger bowls expand in size as it approaches the top of the bowl. This makes the larger bowl flare at the top while the smaller bowls are more straight sided. You can see this flare on the large bowl below. It is also prominent on the tumbler, creamer, and sugar which are all larger at the top than the bottom! There is an 8" bowl with sides straight up like the berry and cereal. This bowl is analogous to a Cloverleaf bowl.

I have never been convinced that the shakers exist in green. All those represented as "Ribbon" have always made me wonder if they are. Notice I do not have one pictured!

	Green	Black
Bowl, 4" berry	30.00	
Bowl, 5" cereal	40.00	
Bowl, 8" large berry, 2 styles	35.00	35.00
Candy dish and cover	40.00	
Creamer, ftd.	15.00	
Cup	5.00	
Plate, 6¼" sherbet	3.00	
Plate, 8" luncheon	5.00	14.00
*Salt and pepper, pr.	30.00	45.00
Saucer	2.50	
Sherbet, ftd.	5.50	
Sugar, ftd.	14.00	
Tumbler, 6", 10 oz.	33.00	

*Pink — $35.00

RING, "BANDED RINGS" HOCKING GLASS COMPANY, 1927–1933

Colors: Crystal, crystal w/pink, red, blue, orange, yellow, black, silver, etc. bands; green, pink, "Mayfair" blue, and Royal Ruby.

Crystal Ring with colored bands fascinates more collectors than the ever abundant, ordinary crystal. Crystal with platinum (silver) bands is the second most collected form of crystal Ring. Worn trims aggravate collectors. Colored rings do not seem to suffer from that problem. It may be because the paint did not decorate the rims as did platinum; but, I surmise that painted trims proved more impervious to wear than metal ones.

Colored Ring enthusiasts usually start by collecting one specific color sequence. There is a predominant arrangement involving black, yellow, red, and orange rings in that order. Those other assortments drive the punctilious crazy!

A reader enlightened me that obtaining a subscription to *Country Gentleman* in the 1930s got you a green Ring berry bowl set consisting of an 8" berry and six 5" berry bowls. That must not have been too enticing since I have seen few green bowls over the years. You could put a set of green together over time. You will notice that my green accumulation is not building up very fast though, thanks to a reader, I now have two berry bowls!

Pink pitcher and tumbler sets are the only pieces I see in that color. A Wisconsin collector reported that the pink pitchers were given away as a dairy premium. The tumblers were packed with cottage cheese and she could not remember what you had to do to receive the pitcher! Pink sets are plentiful only in that part of the country!

A few pieces of Ring are discovered occasionally in Royal Ruby and "Mayfair" blue. The luncheon plate and 10 ounce tumbler are fairly common in Royal Ruby, but flat juice tumblers and cups have turned up in inadequate quantities. I have had no reports of saucers to go with those cups. Let me know if you spot any Royal Ruby or blue Ring saucer/sherbet plates.

You may spot items painted with Ring-like colors, only to find that these pieces have no actual rings moulded into the design. A reader sent me an ad from the mid-30s which described these as Fiesta! Hocking had a number of different striped patterns in ads of this period. I assume the Fiesta was one version of those.

	Crystal	Green/Dec.
Bowl, 5" berry	4.00	7.00
Bowl, 7" soup	10.00	14.00
Bowl, 5¼", divided	12.00	40.00
Bowl, 8" large berry	7.00	12.00
Butter tub or ice tub	22.00	35.00
Cocktail shaker	20.00	27.50
** Cup	5.00	5.00
Creamer, ftd.	4.50	6.00
Decanter and stopper	25.00	40.00
Goblet, 7¼", 9 oz.	10.00	15.00
Goblet, 3¾", 3½ oz. cocktail	11.00	18.00
Goblet, 4½", 3½ oz. wine	13.00	20.00
Ice bucket	20.00	35.00
Pitcher, 8", 60 oz.	17.50	25.00
* Pitcher, 8½", 80 oz.	22.00	33.00
Plate, 6¼" sherbet	2.00	2.50
Plate, 6½", off-center ring	5.00	7.00
***Plate, 8" luncheon	2.50	4.50
Plate, 11¼" sandwich	7.00	14.00
****Salt and pepper, pr., 3"	20.00	45.00
Sandwich server, center handle	16.00	27.50
Saucer	1.50	2.00
Sherbet, low (for 6½" plate)	8.00	18.00
Sherbet, 4¾", ftd.	6.00	9.00
Sugar, ftd.	4.50	5.50
Tumbler, 3", 4 oz.	4.00	9.00
Tumbler, 3½", 5 oz.	5.00	9.00
Tumbler, 4", 8 oz. old fashioned	15.00	17.50
Tumbler, 4¼", 9 oz.	4.50	10.00
Tumbler, 4¾", 10 oz	7.50	
* Tumbler, 5⅛", 12 oz.	8.00	10.00
Tumbler, 3½" ftd. juice	6.00	10.00
Tumbler, 5½" ftd. water	6.00	12.00
Tumbler, 6½" ftd. iced tea	8.00	15.00
Vase, 8"	17.50	35.00
Whiskey, 2", 1½ oz.	7.00	14.00

* Also found in pink. Priced as green. Red $7.50 ** Red $65.00. Blue $45.00 ***$17.50 **** Green $55.00

ROCK CRYSTAL, "EARLY AMERICAN ROCK CRYSTAL" McKEE GLASS COMPANY, 1920s and 1930s in colors

Colors: Four shades of green, aquamarine, Canary yellow, amber, pink and frosted pink, red slag, dark red, red, amberina red, crystal, frosted crystal, crystal with goofus decoration, crystal with gold decoration, amethyst, milk glass, blue frosted or "Jap" blue, and cobalt blue.

Rock Crystal is an attractive pattern as numerous new collectors for it attest. Crystal production started about 1915 and lasted into the 1940s. Unfortunately, catalogs illustrating **all** the pieces do not exist. Colored glassware production years are fairly well authenticated, but new pieces are always showing up. A red syrup pitcher turned up a few years ago, but the time period that red was presumably made and the time period that syrup pitchers were made supposedly did not overlap. Thus, a red syrup pitcher should not have been made; but it was; and that gives hope for red shakers, cruets, and other pieces that have not yet been seen in red. You can see this syrup in *Very Rare Glassware of the Depression Years, Fourth Series*. We bought a large collection of red Rock Crystal from a former McKee employee in the late 1970s. He had eight or nine flat candy bottoms which he explained were soup bowls. I gather that may have been a method to get rid of excess stock.

Red, crystal, and amber sets can be completed with tenacity. There are so many diverse pieces available that you need to determine how much you are willing to spend on a set by selecting what items you want. Instead of buying every tumbler and stem made, you can pick a couple of each (choose which styles you prefer) and buy only them. Even collectors with limited budgets can start a small crystal or amber set. Red will take a deeper pocket! One drawback to some in collecting red is color variances. Red runs from very light to a very deep red that almost looks black. We collected it for about 20 years and tried to match all our glass to a middle range of the color hues. Many times we passed on a piece we needed because it was too dark or too light, a practice I wouldn't follow today. Amazingly, we were able to find red regularly. Now, that is not so easily accomplished.

Rock Crystal pieces are often bought by collectors of other patterns to use as accessory items. Vases, cruets, candlesticks, and an abundance of serving pieces are some of the items obtained. Serving pieces abound; enjoy using them!

Remember, there are two different sizes of punch bowls. The recent purchase of a smaller-based bowl absolutely confirms this. The base for the larger bowl has an opening 5" across, and stands 6 1/16" tall. This base fits a punch bowl that is 4 3/16" across the bottom. The other style base has only a 4 3/16" opening but also stands 6 1/16" tall. The bowl to fit this base is only 3 1/4" across the bottom.

The egg plate is shown standing up in the rear of the photo on page 184. Often these are found with gold trim; so, they may have been a promotional item. The oval piece in front of that is the 13" roll or bread tray. In this part of Florida, I find Lazy Susans quite often. They consist of a revolving metal stand with a Rock Crystal relish for a top. I have only found these here; so, they may have been a give-away or premium.

In the 20s and 30s, Tiffin also made a Rock Crystal similar to McKee's. Their wares had one 8-to-11-petaled daisy flower with ruffled rim lines above it, rounded pedestal feet and ribbed type handles. Too, McKee, itself, made a similar pattern to their Rock Crystal which was called Puritan. It had two 11-petaled daisy flowers, honeycombed effect stems, and ribbed handles, but no long, "S" type scrolls surrounding the (five-petaled) flower that enhances the Rock Crystal design. I'm beginning to get letters about these "almost" Rock Crystal finds. It may interest you to know that the Rock Crystal design itself was reportedly inspired by hand-cut wares made for a king's table centuries ago. **Now** you know why you chose it!

	Crystal	All Other Colors	Red
* Bon bon, 7½", s.e.	22.00	35.00	60.00
Bowl, 4", s.e.	12.00	22.00	32.00
Bowl, 4½", s.e.	14.00	22.00	32.00
Bowl, 5", s.e.	16.00	24.00	42.00
** Bowl, 5" finger bowl with 7" plate, p.e.	30.00	45.00	85.00
Bowl, 7" pickle or spoon tray	25.00	40.00	65.00
Bowl, 7" salad, s.e.	24.00	37.50	65.00
Bowl, 8" salad, s.e.	27.50	37.50	75.00
Bowl, 8½", center hndl.			225.00
Bowl, 9" salad, s.e.	25.00	50.00	110.00
Bowl, 10½" salad, s.e.	25.00	50.00	90.00
Bowl, 11½" 2-part relish	30.00	50.00	75.00
Bowl, 12" oblong celery	27.50	45.00	85.00
*** Bowl, 12½" ftd. center bowl	85.00	125.00	295.00
Bowl, 12½", 5-part relish	45.00		
Bowl, 13" roll tray	35.00	60.00	125.00
Bowl, 14" 6-part relish	37.50	65.00	
Butter dish and cover	335.00		
Butter dish bottom	200.00		
Butter dish top	135.00		
**** Candelabra, 2-lite, pr.	40.00	105.00	275.00
Candelabra, 3-lite, pr.	52.50	125.00	350.00
Candlestick, flat, stemmed, pr.	40.00	65.00	125.00
Candlestick, 5½", low, pr.	40.00	65.00	175.00
Candlestick, 8" tall, pr.	100.00	150.00	425.00
Candy and cover, ftd., 9¼"	70.00	90.00	250.00
Candy and cover, round	65.00	85.00	195.00
Cake stand, 11", 2¾" high, ftd.	35.00	52.50	125.00
Comport, 7"	35.00	52.50	95.00
Creamer, flat, s.e.	37.50		
Creamer, 9 oz., ftd.	20.00	32.00	67.50
Cruet and stopper, 6 oz. oil	100.00		
Cup, 7 oz.	17.50	27.50	70.00
Egg plate	35.00		
Goblet, 7½ oz., 8 oz., low ftd.	18.00	27.50	57.50
Goblet, 11 oz. low ftd. iced tea	20.00	30.00	67.50
Ice dish (3 styles)	40.00		
Jelly, 5", ftd., s.e.	18.00	27.50	52.50
Lamp, electric	250.00	395.00	695.00
Parfait, 3½ oz., low ftd.	25.00	37.50	75.00
Pitcher, qt., s.e.	165.00	225.00	
Pitcher, ½ gal., 7½" high	110.00	195.00	
Pitcher, 9", large covered	175.00	330.00	700.00
Pitcher, fancy tankard	195.00	695.00	995.00
Plate, 6" bread and butter, s.e.	6.00	9.50	20.00
Plate, 7½", p.e. & s.e.	8.00	12.00	21.00
Plate, 8½", p.e. & s.e.	9.00	12.50	30.00
Plate, 9", s.e.	18.00	22.00	55.00
Plate, 10½", s.e.	25.00	30.00	65.00
Plate, 10½" dinner, s.e. (large center design)	47.50	70.00	195.00
Plate, 11½", s.e.	18.00	25.00	57.50
Punch bowl and stand, 14" (2 styles)	650.00		
Punch bowl stand only (2 styles)	225.00		
Salt and pepper (2 styles) pr.	75.00	125.00	
Salt dip	40.00		
Sandwich server, center-hndl.	30.00	45.00	145.00

* s.e. McKee designation for scalloped edge
** p.e. McKee designation for plain edge
*** Red Slag – $350.00 Cobalt – $325.00
**** Cobalt – $325.00

ROCK CRYSTAL (Cont.)

	Crystal	All Other Colors	Red
Saucer	7.50	8.50	22.00
Sherbet or egg, 3½ oz., ftd.	15.00	25.00	60.00
Spooner	45.00		
Stemware, 1 oz. ftd. cordial	22.00	45.00	65.00
Stemware, 2 oz. wine	18.00	28.00	50.00
Stemware, 3 oz. wine	22.00	33.00	60.00
Stemware, 3½ oz. ftd. cocktail	15.00	21.00	43.00
Stemware, 6 oz. ftd. champagne	16.00	23.00	35.00
Stemware, 7 oz.	16.00	25.00	52.50
Stemware, 8 oz. large ftd. goblet	18.00	26.00	57.50
Sundae, 6 oz., low ftd.	12.00	18.00	35.00
Sugar, 10 oz., open	15.00	22.00	40.00
Sugar, lid	35.00	50.00	135.00
Syrup with lid	165.00		750.00
Tray, 5⅜" x 7⅜", ⅞" high	65.00		
Tumbler, 2½ oz. whiskey	22.00	30.00	55.00
Tumbler, 5 oz. juice	16.00	25.00	57.50
Tumbler, 5 oz. old fashioned	18.00	27.50	60.00
Tumbler, 9 oz., concave or straight	18.00	26.00	52.50
Tumbler, 12 oz., concave or straight	25.00	35.00	67.50
Vase, cornucopia	80.00	115.00	200.00
Vase, 11", ftd.	60.00	110.00	195.00

"ROMANESQUE" L. E. SMITH GLASS COMPANY, EARLY 1930s

Colors: Black, amber, crystal, yellow, and green.

"Romanesque" is one of those smaller Depression glass patterns that magnetizes people. Every time my wife ventures near a piece, it draws her like a magnet. You can imagine, then, how this jewel-like pattern came to be written up in this book.

There is a 10½" console bowl that is not footed, but comes in two parts. The bowl rests on a plain, detached base. I imagine this may have been a tad precarious; but, a number of companies made bowls during this era which resided on matched or different colored stands. You may find the bowl separate from the base these days, making it appear something like a turned edge plate.

Green and amber seem to be the prevalent colors; we have, so far, spotted plates, candles, ruffled sherbets, and the bowl part of the console in amber. I see amber more than green in my travels. The yellow is a bright, canary yellow that is often called vaseline by collectors. Those tri-cornered candles stand 2½" high.

As I write this, I am awaiting a faxed copy of a piece being used as a pattern shot which was described as a three-part piece looking like Mickey Mouse ears; I am assuming it's a snack tray which I did not have listed. Glass descriptions are entertaining from non-collectors. Presumably, there should be a cup for the snack tray. Have you seen such?

Black pieces have the design on the bottoms; thus, the cake plate was turned over so you could see the pattern. I had earlier only seen bowls in black before the cake plate appeared at a show. If you have any other information or pieces not listed in this pattern, please let me know!

	* All Colors
Bowl, 10", ftd., 4¼" high	55.00
Bowl, 10½"	40.00
Cake plate, 11½" x 2¾"	35.00
Candlestick, 2½", pr.	25.00
Plate, 5½", octagonal	5.00
Plate, 7", octagonal	7.00
Plate, 8", octagonal	10.00
Plate, 8", round	9.00
Plate, 10", octagonal	22.00
Tray, snack	15.00
Sherbet, plain top	8.00
Sherbet, scalloped top	10.00
Vase, 7½", fan	45.00

*Black — add 30%

ROSE CAMEO BELMONT TUMBLER COMPANY, 1931

Color: Green.

Rose Cameo was patented in 1931 by Belmont Tumbler Company according to records previously verified. I believe that the actual production was done at Hazel Atlas. Glass shards have been found in excavations at a Hazel Atlas factory site in West Virginia. Contrarily, a yellow Cloverleaf shaker was dug up at the site of Akro Agate's factory in Clarksburg, West Virginia; and we believe Akro had nothing to do with making Cloverleaf. (Did you know some glass collectors apparently engage in archaeological pursuits of glass?) Actually, the more we learn about how the companies farmed out their moulds and/or, contract glass runs, anything is possible. It was often easier (and more economical) to come to some arrangement with another company making the buyers requested color run than to change over vats to run it themselves.

All three Rose Cameo bowls are difficult to find, with the smaller berry being the easiest. The straight sided 6" bowl is not being found by most collectors. That is the bowl sitting on its edge on the right making it look like a plate. This little set only has six pieces, but it will probably take at least six months of searching to assemble one of each piece, although with the Internet buying done now, maybe not!

Rose Cameo is not puzzling new collectors as it once did. Cameo, with its dancing girl, and this cameo encircled rose were often confused in bygone days. An informed collecting public rarely makes those mistakes today.

There are two styles of tumblers; one flares and one does not. Some day I'll find the other style and show them together. Got an extra?

Item	Price
Bowl, 4½" berry	12.00
Bowl, 5" cereal	20.00
Bowl, 6", straight sides	25.00
Plate, 7" salad	14.00
Sherbet	14.00
Tumbler, 5", ftd. (2 styles)	25.00

ROSEMARY, "DUTCH ROSE" FEDERAL GLASS COMPANY, 1935–1937

Colors: Amber, green, pink; some iridized.

The story of Rosemary's becoming a separate pattern redesigned from Federal's Mayfair can be read on page 118. Rosemary pattern came about because of Hocking's earlier patent to the Mayfair name.

Collectors who saw gathering pink Rosemary as a challenge tell me they have been stymied; so, I am picturing some for you to see. Pink is being found in minute amounts at shows! I haven't seen a pink tumbler in quite some time. It is joyless to try to collect a pattern that is not being found at any price!

On the other hand, an amber set can be assembled; there are only a few pieces being found irregularly. I cannot remember when I have seen an amber cereal or a green cream soup! The transitional green cream soups could be substituted for Rosemary in a pinch. A set of green Rosemary will probably take quite a bit of time to gather.

Cereal bowls, cream soups, grill plates, and tumblers are few and far between. I noticed a want list for green Rosemary cream soups on the Internet last night! I wish I had one for photography! New collectors should know that grill plates are the divided plates usually associated with diners or grills (restaurants) in that time. Food was kept from flowing together by those raised partitions (normally three). These are especially laborious to find in pink.

The sugar has no handles and is often mislabeled as a sherbet. There is no sherbet known in Rosemary! Those sugars could serve as large sherbets if you could locate enough of them. My father-in-law would approve their size for dessert!

Rosemary is an engaging pattern. I've never heard anybody say they were sorry they chose it to collect — even those still searching for pieces.

	Amber	Green	Pink
Bowl, 5" berry	6.00	9.00	13.00
Bowl, 5" cream soup	18.00	25.00	32.00
Bowl, 6" cereal	30.00	35.00	45.00
Bowl, 10" oval vegetable	17.00	27.50	42.00
Creamer, ftd.	9.00	12.50	20.00
Cup	7.50	9.50	10.00
Plate, 6¾" salad	6.00	8.50	12.00
Plate, dinner	10.00	15.00	23.00
Plate, grill	10.00	15.00	22.00
Platter, 12", oval	17.00	22.00	32.00
Saucer	5.00	5.00	6.00
Sugar, ftd.	9.00	12.50	20.00
Tumbler, 4¼", 9 oz.	32.00	35.00	60.00

ROULETTE, "MANY WINDOWS" HOCKING GLASS COMPANY, 1935–1939

Colors: Green, pink, and crystal.

Roulette is the bona fide name of this pattern which collectors formerly had called "Many Windows." Several collectors have told me they favor that terminology rather than the real name! A gambling reader said the name probably came from the indentations like those on a roulette wheel. Makes sense! Was the original designer a gambler?

Pink pitchers and tumblers are easier to find than green ones, but pink Roulette was only made in those pieces. Both colors are similarly priced. There are five sizes of pink, **flat** tumblers; but I have never found a pink footed tumbler. Have you?

Cups, saucers, sherbets, and luncheon plates can be found in green rather easily. The 12" sandwich plate and fruit bowl are seldom encountered. After finding those, comes the fun of shopping for the various six tumblers! A lady at a show in Tulsa told me she had finally completed her tumblers at that show! Juice tumblers and the old fashioned are the most elusive. I still have not found a green juice tumbler. Thanks to a reader I was able to, finally, buy a green whiskey, although too late for this photograph. Only the juice and the whiskey are missing in that photo of green. The whiskeys sell very well to the shot glass collecting group that is making its increasing presence known in our collecting world.

Crystal tumbler and pitcher sets are very seldom found; however, there is limited demand for the few that have surfaced. Some crystal sets are decorated with colored stripes. In fact, this striped effect gives them an Art Deco look. I am impressed with these decorated crystal pitchers!

	Crystal	Pink, Green
Bowl, 9" fruit	9.50	25.00
Cup	4.00	7.00
Pitcher, 8", 65 oz.	30.00	40.00
Plate, 6" sherbet	3.50	4.50
Plate, 8½" luncheon	5.00	7.00
Plate, 12" sandwich	11.00	16.00
Saucer	1.50	3.50

	Crystal	Pink, Green
Sherbet	3.50	5.50
Tumbler, 3¼", 5 oz. juice	7.00	25.00
Tumbler, 3¼", 7½ oz. old fashioned	23.00	45.00
Tumbler, 4⅛", 9 oz. water	13.00	25.00
Tumbler, 5⅛", 12 oz. iced tea	16.00	33.00
Tumbler, 5½", 10 oz., ftd.	14.00	32.00
Whiskey, 2½", 1½ oz.	14.00	18.00

"ROUND ROBIN" MANUFACTURER UNKNOWN, PROBABLY EARLY 1930s

Colors: Green, iridescent, and crystal.

"Round Robin" is another small mystery pattern whose manufacturer remains undiscovered. Its always looked like Imperial's ware to me. In the 30 plus years that Depression glassware has been collected, it is surprising how little we know about some of the patterns. Someone please find a boxed set, an ad, or a labeled piece.

The Domino tray is the fancier, unanticipated piece in this small pattern. Hocking's Cameo is another pattern in Depression glass which offers a sugar cube tray. This tray has, so far, only been found in green "Round Robin." It is shown standing up behind the creamer and sugar in the picture. For new readers, the Domino tray held the creamer in the center ring with sugar cubes surrounding it. Sugar cubes were made by a famous sugar company, and the tray became synonymous with this name. I have seen few of these over the years. A damaged one sold for $50.00 recently. Grab one if you can!

Sherbets and berry bowls are the most difficult green pieces to come across in "Round Robin" outside the Domino tray. I have not even found a green berry bowl myself. Sherbets and berry bowls are plentiful in iridescent. Saucers seem to be harder to find than the cups. Only a few patterns can claim that. The "Round Robin" cup is one of the few footed ones available in Depression glass. I have not found an iridescent cup and saucer. Do you have one?

Some crystal "Round Robin" is found today. Crystal was sprayed and baked to accomplish the iridized look. Obviously, not all the crystal was sprayed, since we find it occasionally. Too, Cathy just found a "Round Robin" creamer that is top half irridized and bottom half crystal. Their spraying hand, or technique, wasn't too precise, either!

	Green	Iridescent
Bowl, 4" berry	10.00	9.00
Cup, ftd.	7.00	7.00
Creamer, ftd.	10.00	9.00
Domino tray	95.00	
Plate, 6" sherbet	2.50	2.50
Plate, 8" luncheon	4.00	4.00
Plate, 12" sandwich	12.00	10.00
Saucer	2.00	2.00
Sherbet	9.00	10.00
Sugar	10.00	9.00

ROXANA HAZEL ATLAS GLASS COMPANY, 1932

Colors: "Golden Topaz," crystal, and some white.

Roxana always seemed to be more prevalent in Michigan. Thanks to a couple of Michigan collectors, we now know why. They supplied the information exhibited on page 191. If you ate Star Brand Oats, you were able to receive one piece of "Golden Topaz" table glassware in every package. This "Golden Topaz" is what we now call Roxana. This ad may show why the deep 4½" bowl and the 5½" plate are so hard to find. They were not packed as a premium in these oats! I am presuming that the plate shown on the ad is the 6" one for the sherbet.

The "saucer" listed in earlier editions is actually a 5½" plate! I had to buy a set before I realized that mistake. All seven recognized pieces are shown! For those who counted eight, I pictured a plate **with its design highlighted in gold** in hopes the pattern would show better in the photograph. This weak pattern is difficult to captivate on film since the light shade of yellow has a inclination to vanish under bright lights. Notice that the pattern nearly disappeared in the original advertisement! Now you know why even silhouettes are important for identification.

Roxana was only chronicled by Hazel Atlas for one year. It is a truly limited pattern when compared to the thousands of pieces made in other patterns over years. Unfortunately, there are so few pieces available that most collectors ignore it. The plentiful sherbets would be fun to blend with other patterns — or to use as "nut" cups.

Only the 4½" deep bowl has been found in white.

	Yellow	White
Bowl, 4½" x 2⅜"	15.00	15.00
Bowl, 5" berry	15.00	
Bowl, 6" cereal	20.00	
Plate, 5½"	10.00	
Plate, 6" sherbet	10.00	
Sherbet, ftd.	12.00	
Tumbler, 4¼", 9 oz.	22.00	

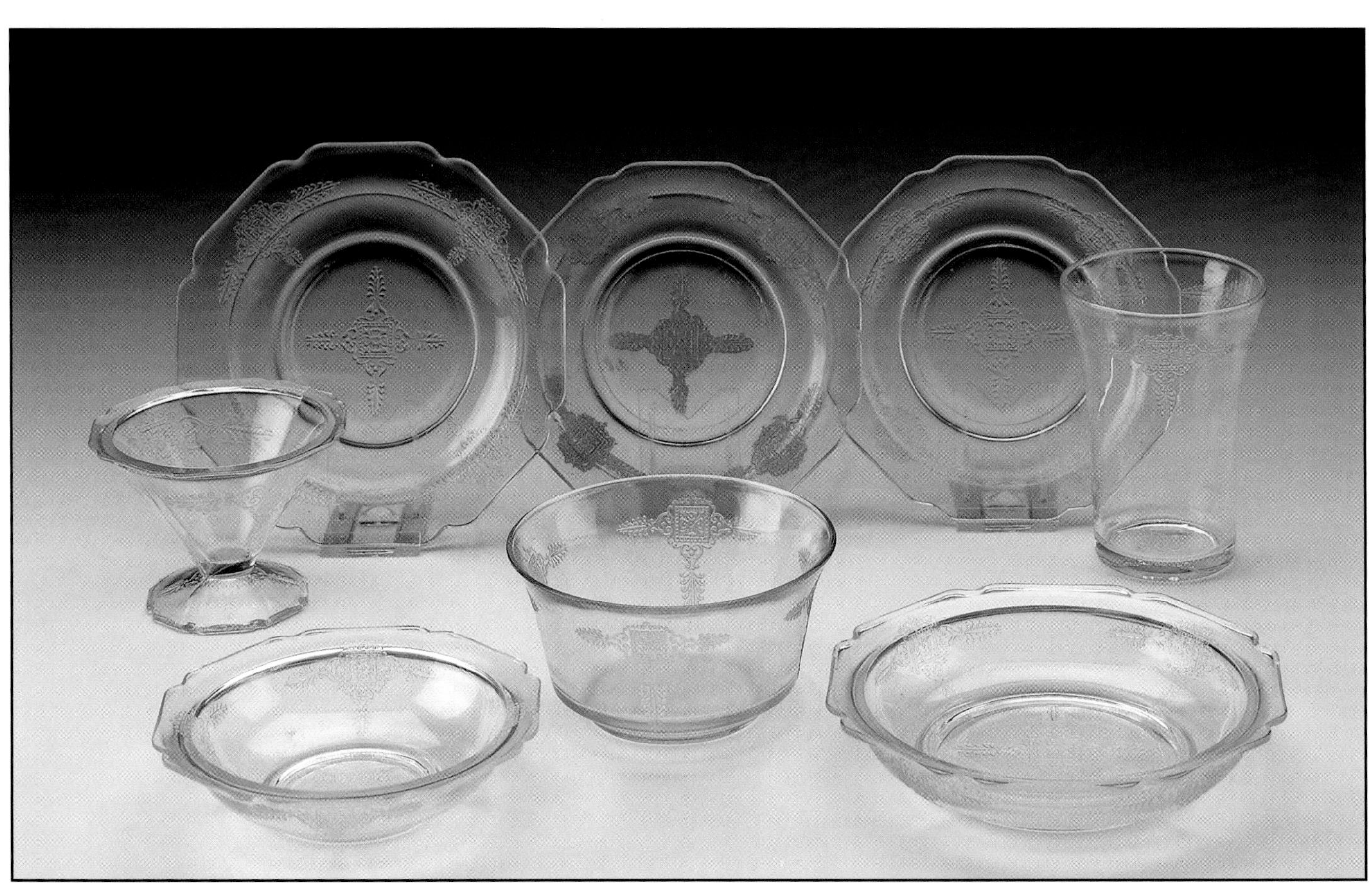

ONE OF THESE PIECES OF
GOLDEN TOPAZ
GLASSWARE
IN EVERY PACKAGE
The cost of the ware is included in the price of the package and we hereby authorize your grocer to show it to you

STAR A STAR

BRAND

NEW PROCESS

OATS

WITH GOLDEN TOPAZ

TABLE GLASSWARE

PACKED FOR

SYMONS BROS. & CO.

SAGINAW, JACKSON, ALMA

ROYAL LACE HAZEL ATLAS GLASS COMPANY, 1934–1941

Colors: Cobalt blue, crystal, green, pink; some amethyst. (See Reproduction section.)

Royal Lace in cobalt blue color **continues** to be one of the most alluring patterns in Depression glass. On my summer lay-off from teaching in 1970, I found out that dealers in the South and Midwest were paying big prices for this cobalt glass; I started buying as much as I could and shipping it as I found it. By 1971, you could sell a straight-sided blue Royal Lace pitcher for $30.00, and the **most** you could expect to pay in my area was $12.00 to $15.00. As a mathematics teacher in Kentucky earning $7200, I found doubling my insubstantial moneys was an acceptable notion! Since teachers only received 10 paychecks, I found summers of buying and selling were necessary if we wanted to eat. I went to Springfield, Missouri, in May 1971 to attend my first Depression glass show. I delivered enough glass to dealers that I made several hundred dollars on that trip after all expenses; and that show was my crash course in glass buying and selling. I sold a Miss America butter dish for $35.00 and an extra top for $12.00 (I did not know the top was the rare part). I parted with several boxes of cobalt Royal Lace! One dealer asked me if I were making it, and I didn't know whether he was joking or not. Depression glass could be found in my area, there was a market for it — and our newest addition was racing through those expensive baby shoes every three or four months.

Since I have pictured cobalt blue in previous books, I am now showing green. There are almost as many collectors for green Royal Lace as for blue. Green is found in quantity in England. A wealth of basic "tea" sets are there, i.e. cups, saucers, creamers, and sugars. I had a source for a couple of years that shipped me American Depression glass from there. I never received a sugar lid, but a lot of topless sugars. Perhaps, the lid got in the way of spooning sugar in that strong tea or maybe the lids were never sent to England! The straight-sided pitcher must be prevalent in England as I bought six or seven of those in a couple of years. I never bought any other style pitcher and only water tumblers. Shakers with original Hazel Atlas labels proclaiming "Made in America" were on several sets of those which I purchased! You have to wonder if Hazel Atlas named this pattern specifically for this "royal" market! It seems likely since this would have been before the coronation or abdication of the throne that so enthralled everybody.

There were five different pitchers made in Royal Lace: a) 48 ounce, straight side; b) 64 ounce, 8", no ice lip; c) 68 ounce, 8", w/ice lip; d) 86 ounce, 8", no ice lip; e) 96 ounce, 8½", w/ice lip. The 10 ounce difference in the last two listed is caused by the spout on the pitcher without lip dipping below the top edge of the pitcher. This causes the liquid to run out before you get to the top. All spouted pitchers will vary in ounce capacity (up to eight ounces) depending upon how the spout tilts or dips. Always measure ounce capacities until no more liquid can be added without running out.

Crystal, pink, and blue pitchers can be found in all five styles. Green can only be found in four styles. There is no 68 ounce with ice lip in green.

The 4⅞", ten ounce tumblers remain almost impossible to find; but the number of iced teas and juice tumblers is waning. Some collectors only purchase water tumblers and the straight-sided pitcher for their collections. This style of pitcher and water tumblers is more prolific and, therefore, more economically priced; but demand continues to drive up the price!

Be aware that **the cookie jar, juice and water tumblers have been reproduced** in a very dark cobalt blue. Know your dealer and if it is priced below market, beware!

Both a rolled-edge console bowl and rolled-edge candlesticks have been found in amethyst! The only other amethyst pieces are the sherbets in metal holders and the cookie jar bottom used for toddy sets. There were **reports** of shakers.

Collectors used to prefer all glass sherbets to the ones found in metal holders; like everything else, this is beginning to change. We've recently sold and had requests for the metal holder type sherbets.

	Crystal	Pink	Green	Blue
Bowl, 4¾" cream soup	15.00	30.00	35.00	47.00
Bowl, 5" berry	15.00	33.00	35.00	52.00
Bowl, 10" round berry	20.00	35.00	30.00	65.00
Bowl, 10", 3-legged straight edge	30.00	55.00	65.00	95.00
* Bowl, 10", 3-legged rolled edge	225.00	95.00	125.00	600.00
Bowl, 10", 3-legged ruffled edge	45.00	95.00	125.00	700.00
Bowl, 11" oval vegetable	28.00	35.00	40.00	65.00
Butter dish and cover	75.00	195.00	275.00	650.00
Butter dish bottom	45.00	140.00	180.00	450.00
Butter dish top	30.00	55.00	95.00	200.00
Candlestick, straight edge, pr.	40.00	65.00	85.00	165.00
** Candlestick, rolled edge, pr.	60.00	135.00	150.00	500.00
Candlestick ruffled edge, pr.	40.00	135.00	150.00	500.00
Cookie jar and cover	35.00	60.00	100.00	375.00
Cream, ftd.	15.00	22.00	28.00	60.00
Cup	9.00	20.00	20.00	40.00
Nut bowl	250.00	400.00	400.00	1,500.00
Pitcher, 48 oz., straight sides	40.00	90.00	120.00	195.00

	Crystal	Pink	Green	Blue
Pitcher, 64 oz., 8", w/o lip	45.00	110.00	120.00	275.00
Pitcher, 8", 68 oz., w/lip	50.00	115.00		295.00
Pitcher, 8", 86 oz., w/o lip	50.00	135.00	175.00	375.00
Pitcher, 8½", 96 oz., w/lip	65.00	150.00	160.00	450.00
Plate, 6", sherbet	7.00	9.00	12.00	15.00
Plate, 8½" luncheon	8.00	15.00	16.00	38.00
Plate, 9⅞" dinner	16.00	30.00	35.00	45.00
Plate, 9⅞" grill	11.00	22.00	28.00	40.00
Platter, 13", oval	20.00	38.00	42.00	60.00
Salt and pepper, pr.	42.00	65.00	130.00	295.00
Saucer	5.00	7.00	9.00	12.50
Sherbet, ftd.	17.00	19.00	25.00	50.00
*** Sherbet in metal holder	3.50			40.00
Sugar	11.00	15.00	22.00	35.00
Sugar lid	20.00	60.00	60.00	195.00
Tumbler, 3½", 5 oz.	20.00	33.00	35.00	60.00
Tumbler, 4⅛", 9 oz.	16.00	28.00	32.00	50.00
Tumbler, 4⅞", 10 oz.	35.00	75.00	75.00	130.00
Tumbler, 5⅜", 12 oz.	35.00	65.00	65.00	120.00
**** Toddy or cider set: includes cookie jar metal lid, metal tray, 8 roly-poly cups, and ladle				250.00

* Amethyst $900.00 ** Amethyst $900.00 *** Amethyst $40.00 **** Amethyst $195.00

ROYAL RUBY ANCHOR HOCKING GLASS COMPANY, 1938–1940

Color: Ruby red.

Anchor Hocking inaugurated the Royal Ruby color in 1938 using their contemporary moulds. I am identifying only pieces of Royal Ruby introduced before 1940 in my listing. Royal Ruby pieces made after 1940 are now in the *Collectible Glassware from the 40s, 50s, 60s....* Remember, only Anchor Hocking's red can rightfully be called Royal Ruby. That name was patented by them and no other company was able to use it for their red.

Oyster and Pearl, Old Cafe, and Coronation were among the patterns used in the original Royal Ruby campaign in 1938. A smattering of pieces in Royal Ruby have been found in other Anchor Hocking lines including Colonial, Ring, Manhattan, Queen Mary, and Miss America. These Royal Ruby pieces are generally considered rare in these major collected patterns and most are of exceptional quality for Anchor Hocking, having ground bottoms which are usually not found on the normal mass-produced glassware. There were other designs produced that were never given pattern names. None of these items are priced in the listing below.

I suspect that the name of the color was inspired by our country's enchantment with the English coronation of Edward VIII in 1936 and his ensuing relinquishing of that royal crown. Witness our fascination, still, with Princess Diana in today's world and you have an inkling of the impact that event had 60 some years ago; and Diana wasn't even an American as was Wallace, who made headlines back then.

Item	Price
Bonbon, 6½"	8.50
Bowl, 3¾" berry (Old Cafe)	7.00
Bowl, 4½", handled (Coronation)	7.00
Bowl, 4⅞", smooth (Sandwich)	12.50
Bowl, 5¼" heart-shaped, 1-handled (Oys & Prl)	20.00
Bowl, 5¼", scalloped (Sandwich)	20.00
Bowl, 5½" cereal (Old Cafe)	13.00
Bowl, 5½", 1-handled (Oys & Prl)	15.00
Bowl, 6½", deep-handled (Oys & Prl)	25.00
Bowl, 6½", handled (Coronation)	18.00
Bowl, 6½", scalloped (Sandwich)	27.50
Bowl, 8", handled (Coronation)	15.00
Bowl, 8", scalloped (Sandwich)	37.50
Bowl, 9", closed handles (Old Cafe)	18.00
Bowl, 10½" deep fruit (Oys & Prl)	55.00
Candle holder, 3½", pr. (Oys & Prl)	60.00
Candle holder, 4½", pr. (Queen Mary)	75.00
Candy dish, 8" mint, low (Old Cafe)	16.00
Candy jar, 5½", crys. w/Ruby cov. (Old Cafe)	18.00
Cigarette box/card holder, 6⅛" x 4" crys. w/Ruby top	65.00
Creamer, ftd.	9.00
Cup (Coronation)	6.50
Cup (Old Cafe)	9.00
Cup, round	6.00
Goblet, ball stem	12.00
Jewel box, 4¼", crys. w/Ruby cov.	12.50
Lamp (Old Cafe)	150.00
Marmalade, 5⅛", crys. w/Ruby cov.	7.50
Plate, 8½" luncheon (Coronation)	10.00
Plate, 9⅛" dinner, round	11.00
Plate, 13½" sandwich (Oys & Prl)	50.00
Puff box, 4⅝", crys. w/Ruby cov.	9.00
Relish tray insert (Manhattan)	4.00
Saucer, round	2.50
Sherbet, low ftd. (Old Cafe)	12.00
Sugar, ftd.	7.50
Sugar, lid	11.00
Tray, 6" x 4½"	12.50
Tumbler, 3" juice (Old Cafe)	16.00
Tumbler, 4" water (Old Cafe)	22.00
Vase, 7¼" (Old Cafe)	45.00
Vase, 9", two styles	17.50

"S" PATTERN, "STIPPLED ROSE BAND" MacBETH-EVANS GLASS COMPANY, 1930–1933

Colors: Crystal; crystal w/trims of silver, blue, green, amber; pink; some amber, green, fired-on red, Monax, and light yellow.

"S" Pattern with platinum or pastel bands commands more respect than does plain crystal. The dilemma in collecting pastel banded "S" Pattern is that there are limited amounts available! Amber, blue, or green banded crystal was made; you might follow an ever-growing trend and collect various colors! You can find crystal; so, mix some color with that. I found a 14-piece luncheon set of amber band last Monday at the flea market (in amongst the Beanie Babies, socks, and imports).

The solid amber "S" Pattern coloration causes many pieces to look more yellow than amber. The discrepancy is almost as distinct as in Hocking's Princess; however, amber "S" Pattern collectors do have a dinner plate to use! Neither crystal nor crystal-trimmed dinner plates have been found. Crystal luncheon plates would be striking against a colored dinner plate of some variety.

A pink or green pitcher and tumbler set still shows up once in a while; but the demand is not what it once was. Years ago, there were a number of pitcher collectors; rare pitchers sold fast in the $200.00–500.00 range. Today, some are commanding prices of two to three times that. That makes for a limited market at best.

If you find a pink tumbler that has a moulded pattern, it will be a "Dogwood" moulded tumbler and not "S" Pattern. The only pink tumblers found in "S" Pattern have an applied, silk screened design onto the glass.

Fired-on red and true red "S" Pattern items both fit the rare classification; however, there are fewer collectors excited by them. The first red "S" Pattern luncheon plates discovered sold for $65.00 each in the early 1970s. Today, those red "S" Pattern plates are a difficult sell at $40.00. That could change, of course!

	Crystal	Yellow, Amber, Crystal W/ Trims
*Bowl, 5½" cereal	5.00	9.00
Bowl, 8½" large berry	13.00	18.00
*Creamer, thick or thin	6.00	7.00
*Cup, thick or thin	3.50	4.50
Pitcher, 80 oz. (like "Dogwood")		
(green or pink 550.00)	55.00	125.00
Pitcher, 80 oz. (like "American		
Sweetheart")	75.00	
Plate, 6" sherbet (Monax 8.00)	2.50	3.00
**Plate, 8¼" luncheon	5.00	6.00
Plate, 9¼" dinner		9.00

	Crystal	Yellow, Amber, Crystal W/Trims
Plate, grill	6.50	8.00
Plate, 11¾" heavy cake	40.00	50.00
***Plate, 13" heavy cake	65.00	75.00
Saucer	2.00	2.50
Sherbet, low ftd.	4.50	7.00
*Sugar, thick and thin	5.50	6.50
Tumbler, 3½", 5 oz.	5.00	8.00
Tumbler, 4", 9 oz. (green or		
pink 50.00)	6.00	8.00
Tumbler, 4¾, 10 oz.	8.00	9.00
Tumbler, 5", 12 oz.	10.00	15.00

* Fired-on red items will run approximately twice price of amber **Red – $40.00; Monax – $10.00 ***Amber – $77.50

SANDWICH INDIANA GLASS COMPANY, 1920s–1980s

Colors: Crystal late 1920s–today; teal blue 1950s–1980s; milk white mid-1950s; amber late 1920s–1980s; red 1933,1969–early 1970s; Smokey Blue 1976–1977; pink, green 1920s–early 1930s.

Since green Indiana Sandwich was chosen for the cover of my latest *Pocket Guide,* I have received numerous calls and letters from people who think they have old Sandwich, but who actually have Tiara's 1980s version called Chantilly. On the bottom of page 197, I have attempted to show an old Sandwich and a new Chantilly decanter with a black light below them. None of the Tiara green will glow under ultraviolet light. Thus, if you have doubts as to age of this particular green Sandwich, give it the "black light" test. I hasten to add that this is *not* a general test for age of glass. There is glass made yesterday which will glow under black light. It is a test for this particular green Sandwich vs. Chantilly pattern.

Amber is priced here with crystal. Realize that most all amber found today is from the Tiara issues and is not Depression era glass. There is no easy way to distinguish old crystal from new.

Any green piece that has no price listed is presumably new! Indiana also made a lighter pink in recent years.

Only six items in red Sandwich date from 1933, i.e., cups, saucers, luncheon plates, water goblets, creamers, and sugars. In 1969, Tiara Home Products marketed red. Today, there is no difference in pricing red unless you have some marked 1933 Chicago World's Fair which will fetch considerably more!

	Amber Crystal	Teal Blue	Red	Pink/ Green
Ash trays(club, spade, heart, diamond shapes, ea.)	3.25			
Basket, 10" high	35.00			
Bowl, 4¼" berry	3.50			
Bowl, 6"	4.00			
Bowl, 6", hexagonal	5.00	14.00		
Bowl, 8½"	11.00			
Bowl, 9" console	16.00			40.00
Bowl, 11½" console	18.50			50.00
Butter dish and cover, domed	22.00	*155.00		
Butter dish bottom	6.00	42.50		
Butter dish top	16.00	112.50		
Candlesticks, 3½", pr.	16.00			45.00
Candlesticks 7", pr.	30.00			
Creamer	9.00		45.00	
Celery, 10½"	16.00			
Creamer and sugar on diamond shaped tray	16.00	32.00		
Cruet, 6½ oz. and stopper	26.00	135.00		175.00
Cup	3.50	8.50	27.50	
Decanter and stopper	22.00		80.00	125.00
Goblet, 9 oz.	13.00		45.00	
Mayonnaise, ftd.	13.00			35.00
Pitcher, 68 oz.	22.00		130.00	
Plate, 6" sherbet	3.00	7.00		
Plate, 7" bread and butter	4.00			
Plate, 8" oval, indent for cup	5.50			15.00
Plate, 8⅜" luncheon	4.75		20.00	
Plate, 10½" dinner	8.00			20.00
Plate, 13" sandwich	12.75	24.00	35.00	25.00
Puff box	16.00			
Salt and pepper pr.	17.50			
Sandwich server, center	18.00		45.00	35.00
Saucer	2.50	4.50	7.50	
Sherbet, 3¼"	5.50	12.00		
Sugar, large	9.00		45.00	
Sugar lid for large size	13.00			
Tumbler, 3 oz. ftd. cocktail	7.50			
Tumbler, 8 oz. ftd. water	9.00			
Tumbler, 12 oz. ftd. iced tea	10.00			
Wine, 3", 4 oz.	6.00		12.50	25.00

*Beware recent vintage sell $22.00

SHARON, "CABBAGE ROSE" FEDERAL GLASS COMPANY, 1935–1939

Colors: Pink, green, amber; some crystal. (See Reproduction Section.)

Sharon prices have remained steady except for rarely found items which are rising, as usual. Prices for the cheese and other elusive pieces ever ascend! Of course, that upward direction is true of **all major patterns** right now. That has not always been the case, but prices on rarely found items in collectible patterns have increased dramatically in the last few years. Amber footed teas are the most scarce of **all** Sharon tumblers; but fewer collectors of amber Sharon have been making this tumbler an option at today's prices. They are truly under priced for their paucity! You will see ten green Sharon tumblers for every one amber footed tea. Amber Sharon pitchers with ice lip are more than twice as difficult to find as pink; but prices are not indicative of that. Calls for pink Sharon by the abundance of those collectors propels pink prices.

Pink Sharon suffered a shortage of collectors for a few years due to reproductions. Pink was the color hit hardest by the spurious tricksters since it was the most desirable. Due to education about the differences between old and new (page 237–238), attraction to Sharon has again been bolstered! It was not that people stopped collecting as much as newer collectors would not hazard starting it. Without fresh collecting blood, basic pieces stopped selling and dealers, in turn, stopped buying them. It beget a cycle with only rarely found and bargain pieces selling. Today, every dealer who bought into this pessimism is lamenting that he cannot find enough pink or green Sharon to meet the demand!

Amber Sharon is again pictured to go with the ad showing a coupon exchange for amber Sharon. We reproduced only parts of this advertisement. The numbers in the right column under Golden Glow tableware represent the number of coupons from large cans needed to order the item. Labels from small cans only were worth one half. The problem being that I have no idea as to cans of what. This ad was given to me and the product was not shown on the part I have. In any case, most of the items shown were for amber Sharon and Patrician or, as listed, Golden Glow dinnerware. This ad also listed pieces from Hocking (Manhattan), Jeannette (Jennyware), and McKee (Glass Bake), although the major portion of the ad was for Federal wares. The refrigerator containers are priced in my *Kitchen Glassware of the Depression Years.* The pitcher, without design, sells in the $35.00 range, but with little demand.

The Sharon cereal was redesigned into a child's feeding dish. One is pictured on the bottom of page 199. I have only seen this bowl in amber and few of those!

The price for a pink Sharon cheese dish has finally crossed into the four figure range. The top for the cheese and butter dish are the **same** piece. The bottoms are different. The butter bottom is a 1½" deep bowl with an indented ledge while the cheese bottom is a salad plate with a raised band of glass on top of it. The lid fits inside this raised band. The bottom is the rare part of this cheese. Amber cheese dishes can be found. There is no cheese dish in the original green.

Infrequently found Sharon pink pieces include flat, thick iced teas and jam dishes. The jam dish is like the butter bottom except it has **no indentation** for the top. It differs from the 1⅞," deep soup bowl by standing only 1½" tall. Once in a while, you can find a jam dish priced as a soup bowl; but that happens rarely now.

Green Sharon pitchers and tumblers in all sizes are difficult to find. Surprisingly, the green pitcher without ice lip is rarer than the one with an ice lip. There are no green soup bowls, only jam dishes.

You will find thick or thin flat iced teas and waters. The thick tumblers are easier to find in green; and the price reflects that. In amber and pink, the heavy iced teas are more rarely seen than the waters. I have seen some large prices on the pink, thick iced teas recently. Although I have not seen anyone paying them. You can see all sorts of prices on items, but what it **actually** sells for is what matters.

	Amber	Pink	Green
Bowl, 5" berry	8.50	15.00	17.00
Bowl, 5" cream soup	28.00	50.00	55.00
Bowl, 6" cereal	22.00	27.50	27.50
Bowl, 7¾" flat soup, 1⅞" deep	52.50	60.00	
Bowl, 8½" large berry	6.00	35.00	35.00
Bowl, 9½" oval vegetable	20.00	35.00	35.00
Bowl, 10½" fruit	21.00	45.00	42.50
Butter dish and cover	47.50	60.00	90.00
Butter dish bottom	24.00	30.00	40.00
Butter dish top	23.50	30.00	50.00
* Cake plate, 11½", ftd.	27.50	45.00	65.00
Candy jar and cover	45.00	50.00	160.00
Cheese dish and cover	195.00	1,200.00	
Creamer, ftd.	14.00	20.00	22.50
Cup	9.00	14.00	20.00
Jam dish, 7½"	40.00	250.00	55.00

	Amber	Pink	Green
Pitcher, 80 oz., with ice lip	145.00	185.00	450.00
Pitcher, 80 oz., without ice lip	140.00	175.00	475.00
Plate, 6" bread and butter	5.00	8.00	9.00
** Plate, 7½" salad	15.00	23.00	22.50
Plate, 9½" dinner	11.00	20.00	22.50
Platter, 12½", oval	18.00	32.00	32.50
Salt and pepper, pr.	40.00	55.00	70.00
Saucer	6.50	12.00	12.00
Sherbet, ftd.	13.00	18.00	37.50
Sugar	9.00	14.00	16.00
Sugar lid	22.00	32.50	40.00
Tumbler, 4⅛", 9 oz., thick	30.00	42.00	75.00
Tumbler, 4⅛", 9 oz., thin	30.00	42.00	80.00
Tumbler, 5¼", 12 oz., thin	55.00	52.00	110.00
Tumbler, 5¼", 12 oz., thick	65.00	85.00	110.00
*** Tumbler, 6½", 15 oz., ftd.	125.00	57.50	

*Crystal $8.00 **Crystal $13.50 ***Crystal $15.00

Golden Glow Tableware

No.	Item	Price
*101	Cup and Saucer	20
*102	Drinking Set, Ice Lip Jug and 6 Tumblers	110
*104	Salt and Pepper Shakers....pair	22
*108	Bowl, 8½ inch	22
*113	Fruit Dish, 5 inch	8
*116	Plate, 6 inch	10
*117	Plate, 9½ inch	20
*118	Sherbet	10
*121	Sugar and Creamer	30
*122	Vegetable Dish, 9½ inch	22
*123	Meat Platter, 12½ inch	28
*124	Cream Soup, Handled	12
*127	Butter Dish	24

*Items not mailable. See page 31.
†Coupons from Small Cans count ½ Coupon.

"SHIPS" or "SAILBOAT" also known as "SPORTSMAN SERIES"
HAZEL ATLAS GLASS COMPANY, LATE 1930s

Colors: Cobalt blue w/white, yellow, and red decoration, crystal w/blue.

Moderntone decorated with "Ships" is, now, seldom found. Sherbet plates are harder to find than dinner plates, but both have disappeared into collections! Prices below are for **mint** pieces (white, not discolored beige). Discolored or worn items **should sell for less.** I have been running into quite a bit of this pattern in Florida. I looked at several pieces yesterday that were priced at "book," but were badly worn. When the "Ships" pattern is partially missing, it would be easier to sell if the whole ship had sunk and you only had a cobalt blue piece to sell. I've had several dealers tell me they can't sell "Ships"; but when I look at their prices and how worn the designs are, I can see why. Worn designs on this pattern are like trying to sell chipped pieces in other patterns. Unless it is cheaply priced, it is not going to sell! There is no ship on the Moderntone cup that fits the saucer with a "Ships" decoration. It is a regular cup; I have not pictured it here.

The confusing "Ships" shot glass is shown on page 201 next to the pitcher in the top row. It is the smallest (2¼", two ounce) tumbler, **not** the heavy bottomed tumbler shown next to it that holds four ounces and is 3¼" tall. I have letters from people who purchased this four ounce tumbler under the impression (or having been told) it was a shot glass! You will notice there is a large price difference between the authentic, two ounce shot and the four ounce tumbler! The price for that four ounce tumbler has increased, but not to the level of the tiny shot glass.

The yellow "Ships" old-fashioned tumbler next to the ice bucket on the bottom row is not a discoloration. It really is "raincoat" yellow! Observe the pieces with red and white "Ships" or crystal tumblers with a blue boat.

Pictured below are other items in the "Sportsman Series." (My computer's grammar editing just told me to change that "man" to "sports lover" or "sport enthusiast" to be politically accurate!) People who collect Dutch-related glassware enjoy the "Windmills." There are nursery rhymes, dogs, fish, horses, hunting, skiing, golfing, or dancing!

I am fond of the decorations that have the red boats with white sails. Only pitchers and tumblers seem to be found with this design. To collect dinnerware in this pattern, you will have to stick to decorated Moderntone.

I might mention that **no red pitcher** has ever been found to go with the **red "Ships" tumblers** ($9.00)! I must get 40 letters a year and a dozen calls regarding those. They seem to be popular with men.

	Blue/White		Blue/White		Blue/White
Cup (Plain) "Moderntone"	11.00	Plate, 8" salad	28.00	Tumbler, 5 oz., 3¾" juice	14.00
Cocktail mixer w/stirrer	30.00	Plate, 9" dinner	35.00	Tumbler, 6 oz. roly poly	11.00
Cocktail shaker	38.00	Saucer	17.00	Tumbler, 8 oz., 3⅜" old fashioned	18.00
Ice bowl	38.00	Tumbler, 2 oz., 2¼" shot glass	195.00	Tumbler, 9 oz., 3¾" straight water	14.00
Pitcher w/o lip, 82 oz.	65.00	Tumbler, 3½" whiskey	27.50	Tumbler, 9 oz., 4⅝" water	11.00
Pitcher w/lip, 86 oz.	75.00	Tumbler, 4 oz., heavy bottom	27.50	Tumbler, 10½ oz., 4⅞" iced tea	16.00
Plate, 5⅞" sherbet	30.00	Tumbler, 4 oz., 3¼", heavy bottom	27.50	Tumbler, 12 oz. iced tea	25.00

SIERRA, "PINWHEEL" JEANNETTE GLASS COMPANY, 1931–1933

Colors: Green, pink, and some Ultra Marine.

Sierra is becoming hard to find in both colors. Prices for rarely found pieces are pursuing that upward trend of all Depression glass. Pink and green pitchers, tumblers, and oval vegetable bowls have disappeared into collections and few are being marketed. You can stumble upon one of these pieces in pink once in a while with persistent shopping, but finding them in green at any price, is a major accomplishment! Impassioned Sierra collectors tell me that being able to purchase the green oval vegetable is dubious; but finding six or eight tumblers takes even more time and a bundle of money! An unparalleled problem is finding **mint** conditioned items. If they were used much, one of those pointed protrusions customarily became chipped, nicked, or chunked! The points have to be carefully inspected! Look underneath as well as on the top.

Sugar bowls are harder to find than lids. It is the pointed extremities on the sugar bowl (which chip) that make this bowl so hard to obtain. Always examine any pink Sierra butter dishes to check for the Adam/Sierra combination. That is the way I found my first one. Be sure to read about this elusive and pricey butter under Adam. You can see one pictured in *Very Rare Glassware of the Depression Years, Fifth Series.*

Wrong cups are often found on Sierra saucers. For some reason pink cups of nondescript origin are usually used atop the saucers. You have to be vigilant when you are out shopping! Saucers are becoming harder to find than cups because of damaged points. The cups, pitchers, and tumblers all have smooth edges instead of the serrated edges of the other pieces. Without smooth edges, these cups and tumblers would be "dribble" glasses.

There have been three Sierra Ultra Marine cups found, but no saucer has been spotted! Why? Were these an experimental run? Perhaps a sample run of Sierra was made at the time Jeannette was producing Doric and Pansy or Swirl in Ultra Marine. You might even find some fired-on colors of Sierra. They have been reported, though I have not seen any yet.

	Pink	Green
Bowl, 5½" cereal	16.00	18.00
Bowl, 8½" large berry	35.00	40.00
Bowl, 9¼" oval vegetable	65.00	135.00
Butter dish and cover	70.00	75.00
Creamer	20.00	22.50
Cup	13.00	16.00
Pitcher, 6½", 32 oz.	115.00	135.00
Plate, 9" dinner	22.00	24.00

	Pink	Green
Platter, 11" oval	50.00	60.00
Salt and pepper, pr.	45.00	45.00
Saucer	8.00	9.00
Serving tray, 10¼", 2 handles	20.00	20.00
Sugar	20.00	26.00
Sugar cover	16.00	16.00
Tumbler, 4½", 9 oz., ftd.	65.00	85.00

SPIRAL HOCKING GLASS COMPANY, 1928–1930

Colors: Green, crystal, and pink.

Hocking's Spiral is one of many serpentine patterns from the Depression era which have their roots in older, pattern glass lines. Availability of Spiral in pink is limited; but green can be collected with some effort. The difficulty lies in recognizing Hocking's Spiral among all the others. Notice several pieces of Spiral are shaped like Cameo including the ice tub, platter, creamer, and sugar. The platter is not often found. It has closed or tab handles as do many platters in patterns made by Hocking.

Again, a luncheon set can, slowly but surely, be acquired rather inexpensively in Spiral. This is not a pattern that most dealers carry to glass shows. You will have to request it.

A few pieces of Spiral can be found in crystal. However, I have never been approached by collectors searching for any color other than green.

The Spiral center-handled server has a solid handle and the Twisted Optic center-handled server has an open handle if you have trouble distinguishing those patterns from each other. Note the two pitchers. One has the "rope" top treatment that is found in Cameo.

I have always included a Twisted Optic piece in my Spiral pictures for comparison to the Spiral. It is the covered candy on the right. Remember that Spiral swirls go to the left or clockwise while Twisted Optic spirals go to the right or counter-clockwise. In the center-handled server, the actual pattern is on the bottom which makes the spiral right. Green Twisted Optic pieces have a yellow tint missing from Spiral.

	Green
Bowl, 4¾" berry	5.00
Bowl, 7" mixing	10.00
Bowl, 8" large berry	12.50
Creamer, flat or ftd.	7.50
Cup	5.00
Ice or butter tub	27.50
Pitcher, 7⅝", 58 oz.	32.00
Plate, 6" sherbet	2.50
Plate, 8" luncheon	3.50
Platter, 12"	30.00

	Green
Preserve and cover	32.00
Salt and pepper, pr.	35.00
Sandwich server, center handle	25.00
Saucer	2.00
Sherbet	5.00
Sugar, flat or ftd.	7.50
Tumbler, 3", 5 oz. juice	4.50
Tumbler, 5", 9 oz. water	7.50
Tumbler, 5⅞", ftd.	18.00
Vase, 5¾", ftd.	50.00

STARLIGHT HAZEL ATLAS GLASS COMPANY, 1938–1940

Colors: Crystal, pink; some white, cobalt.

Prices on crystal Starlight are indicating new collecting attention. This small pattern has never been gathered by large numbers of collectors; but enough are purchasing pieces now to show some deficiencies in inventories. Answers to finding sherbets, cereals, and the large salad bowls are not forthcoming. Few 13" sandwich plates are being seen and those that appear at shows are eagerly bought. That plate, along with the 12" deep bowl, makes a great salad set. You might even be able to use it as a small punch bowl should the occasion arise. This pattern was utilitarian; watch for use marks on those large plates.

I have had several collectors trying to buy my Starlight punch bowl set pictured in an earlier edition. This set was similar in make up to the Royal Lace toddy set. As with other Hazel Atlas sets, this punch bowl was made by putting a bowl in a metal holder and extending the metal to accommodate cups. A metal ladle with a red knob rests in the bowl. I owe that find to an eagle-eyed collector who bought it just for me to use in my book! These gestures are mightily appreciated.

The 5½" cereal is handled and measures 6" including the handles. All measurements in this book do not include handles, unless directly noted.

Starlight can be collected without having to borrow money, but difficulty (nearly 30 years into Depression glass mania) comes in finding it to buy. Pink and blue bowls make nice accessory pieces that can be used alongside the crystal or even with other patterns. Only bowls are available in those colors.

I often pondered why Starlight shakers were found with a one hole shaker top. I now know. It was a specially designed top made to keep the salt "moisture proof." Airko shakers with these tops are often seen in southern areas where the humid air caused shaker holes to clog. One of these moisture-proof shakers is pictured here with an original label.

	Crystal, White	Pink
Bowl, 5½" cereal, closed handles	7.00	12.00
* Bowl, 8½", closed handles	10.00	20.00
Bowl, 11½" salad	28.00	
Bowl, 12", 2¾" deep	35.00	
Creamer, oval	8.00	
Cup	5.00	
Plate, 6" bread and butter	3.00	
Plate, 8½" luncheon	5.00	
Plate, 9" dinner	7.50	
Plate, 13" sandwich	15.00	18.00
Relish dish	15.00	
Salt and pepper, pr.	22.50	
Saucer	2.00	
Sherbet	15.00	
Sugar, oval	8.00	

* Cobalt $32.50

STRAWBERRY U.S. GLASS COMPANY, EARLY 1930s

Colors: Pink, green, crystal; some iridized.

Strawberry and Cherryberry are divided into two individual patterns because today's collectors consider these to be two separate patterns and not one. Strawberry has more supporters than Cherryberry.

There are two very extraordinary pitchers shown in the photograph. Those crystal and iridescent pitchers are in few collections! Iridescent Strawberry pitchers and tumblers are quite rare! Carnival collectors cherish this pitcher more highly than do Depression glass collectors. By cherish, I mean will pay more for it. The paramount carnival glass test is that it has to have full, vivid color and not color fade out toward the bottom, as many do. Iridescent carnival pieces with faded colors or lack of color near the bottom are avoided by them. I'm wondering if this prejudice will hold with Depression glass collectors since the movement for bi-colored wares is beginning to unfold. Time will tell! The **rare** crystal pitcher is not popular with collectors, but should be!

Green Strawberry demands more attention than pink. Matching color tones of green seems to be an insignificant issue. Green or pink Strawberry can be collected in a set; however, as with other U.S. Glass patterns, there are no cups, saucers, or dinner-sized plates; and if mould roughness offends your collecting sensibilities, then this pattern needs to be avoided. Even pieces that are considered mint may have roughness on a seam where it came out of the mould. Often this is extra glass and not chips or missing glass.

Crystal is priced along with iridescent because it is, categorically, rare. There are few crystal Strawberry collectors. Strawberry sugar covers and the 6¼", 2" deep bowl are missing from most collections. I found a second, 2" deep green bowl (reported last fall) to show to you in the future. If you find a copy of my *Collector's Encyclopedia of Depression Glass, Fifth Edition,* you can see the first one found! Some of the uneducated mistakenly label the sugar with missing lid as a spooner. It is a sugar bowl without handles often found in earlier glassware.

Strawberry has a plain butter dish bottom that is adaptable to other U.S. Glass patterns! This is the pattern for which other U.S. Glass butter dish bottoms were borrowed to use with Strawberry tops. That custom left many other butters bottomless! Strawberry butter dishes have always been beloved by collectors.

	Crystal, Iridescent	Pink, Green
Bowl, 4" berry	6.50	12.00
Bowl, 6¼", 2" deep	55.00	125.00
Bowl, 6½" deep salad	15.00	25.00
Bowl, 7½" deep berry	20.00	30.00
Butter dish and cover	135.00	195.00
Butter dish bottom	77.50	100.00
Butter dish top	57.50	75.00
Comport, 5¾"	14.00	25.00
Creamer, small	12.00	22.00
Creamer, 4⅝", large	22.50	40.00
Olive dish, 5", one-hndl.	9.00	20.00
Pickle dish, 8¼", oval	9.00	20.00
Pitcher, 7¾"	175.00	175.00
Plate, 6" sherbet	5.00	12.00
Plate, 7½" salad	12.00	18.00
Sherbet	8.00	10.00
Sugar, small, open	12.00	22.00
Sugar, large	22.00	40.00
Sugar cover	38.00	65.00
Tumbler, 3⅝", 8 oz.	20.00	38.00

"SUNBURST," "HERRINGBONE" JEANNETTE GLASS COMPANY, LATE 1930s

Colors: Crystal.

"Sunburst" is a pattern I pursued for a few years in order to add it to my book. I have ascertained that candlesticks are the most commonly found pieces. This is surprising because there are few patterns where candlesticks are seen more often than other pieces. Imperial's Crocheted Crystal is the only other pattern that comes to mind.

I can tell you that sherbets, dinner plates, and tumblers are the hard to find items. I have not found much "Sunburst" to sell; but the little I have found sold briskly!

This smaller pattern was made from the same shaped moulds as Iris. A divided relish and "Sunburst's" form of berry bowl would have made sensational pieces for Iris! Look this pattern over carefully, since inner rims are easily nicked. Collectors would probably not have noticed "Sunburst" had it not been for the popular Iris.

I have been trying to find a catalog or advertisement to tell the true name of this pattern which I have heard called both "Sunburst" and "Herringbone." I do not know which, if either, is correct; but more people use "Sunburst."

I am listing only pieces I have found or pieces that have been in photographs sent me over the years. I will not be surprised by additional finds! Let me know what you have in your collections! I promise to show a tumbler next time. It is similar in style to the flat Iris.

Item	Price
Bowl, 4¾" berry	8.00
Bowl, 8½" berry	18.00
Bowl, 10¾"	25.00
Candlesticks, double, pr.	30.00
Creamer, footed	10.00
Cup	10.00
Plate, 5½"	7.00
Plate, 9¼" dinner	20.00
Plate, 11¾" sandwich	20.00
Relish, 2-part	12.00
Saucer	4.00
Sherbet	15.00
Sugar	10.00
Tray, small oval	12.00
Tumbler, 4", 9 oz., flat	25.00

SUNFLOWER JEANNETTE GLASS COMPANY, 1930s

Colors: Pink, green, some Delphite; some opaque colors and Ultra Marine.

Sunflower is a well recognized pattern of Depression glass. The ubiquitous cake plate may help explain that since they were packed in 20 pound bags of flour for many years during the 1930s. Everyone bought flour in large quantities because home baking was the norm then — the way bread came to the table. A pink cake plate is shown in the center of the picture. If you look closely you can see a couple of the legs showing through. A quandary occurring with the green cake plate is that many are found in a deep, dark green that does not even approximate the coloration of other pieces of green Sunflower shown here. No other pieces of green are found in this hue, but there were large quantities of cake plates made in that color. The heavy, round piece in the center is a paperweight found in a former Jeannette employee's home.

There is some bafflement over the cake plate and the rarely found Sunflower trivet. The **7" trivet** has an edge that is **slightly upturned** and it is three inches smaller than the omnipresent **10" cake plate.** You would consider three inches is enough difference to keep this mistake from happening, but some folks find it hard to believe that they find common pieces and not just rare ones! The 7" trivet remains the most elusive piece of Sunflower. Collector demand for the trivet keeps prices accelerating. Green Sunflower pieces are found less often than pink as evidenced by my photo; consequently, prices for green are greater than those of pink. Both colors make impressive looking sets.

Sunflower suffers a lack of saucers in both colors. The last few groups of Sunflower I have seen have had more cups than saucers. Two lots of green had no saucers at all. In total, there were 29 cups and only 13 saucers. Maybe the cups were a premium which never offered saucers or the cups were offered longer than the saucers. If you run into a stack of Sunflower saucers, remember that they could be a prudent buy if the price is right.

The Ultra Marine ash tray pictured is the only piece I have found in that color. Opaque colors show up sporadically, usually creamers and sugars. Only a creamer, plate, 6" tab-handled bowl, cup, and saucer have been spotted in Delphite blue. You can see all but the creamer in *Very Rare Glassware of the Depression Years, Fifth Series.*

	Pink	Green
* Ash Tray, 5", center design only	9.00	12.00
Cake Plate, 10", 3 legs	15.00	15.00
** Creamer (opaque $85.00)	22.00	22.00
Cup (opaque $75.00)	16.00	18.00
Plate, 8" luncheon	35.00	
Plate, 9" dinner	22.00	22.00
Saucer	8.00	10.00
Sugar (opaque $85.00)	22.00	22.00
Tumbler, 4¾", 8 oz., ftd.	35.00	35.00
Trivet, 7", 3 legs, turned up edge	325.00	335.00

* Found in Ultra Marine $25.00 **Delphite $85.00

SWANKY SWIGS 1930s–EARLY 1940s

"Why, I remember those! We used them when I was a child!" is a comment I often hear when Swankies are spotted. Larger and smaller sizes are what all collectors are seeking.

See *Collectible Glassware from the 40s, 50s, 60s...* for later made Swankys and a display of their collectible metal tops.

Top Row:

Band No.1	Red & Black	3⅜"	2.00–3.00
	Red & Blue	3⅜"	3.00–4.00
	Blue	3⅜"	3.50–5.00
Band No.2	Red & Black	4¾"	4.00–5.00
	Red & Black	3⅜"	3.00–4.00
Band No.3	Blue & White	3⅜"	3.00–4.00
Circle & Dot:	Blue	4¾"	8.00–10.00
	Blue	3½"	5.00–6.00
	Red, Green	3½"	4.00–5.00
	Black	3½"	5.00–6.00
	Red	4¾"	8.00–10.00
Dot	Black	4¾"	7.00–9.00
	Blue	3½"	5.00–6.00

2nd Row:

Star	Blue	4¾"	6.00–7.00
	Blue, Red, Green, Black	3½"	3.00–4.00
	Cobalt w/White Stars	4¾"	18.00–20.00
Centennials	W.Va. Cobalt	4¾"	22.00–25.00
	Texas Cobalt	4¾"	35.00–38.00
Texas	Blue, Black, Green	3½"	35.00–38.00
Checkerboard	Blue, Red	3½"	27.50–30.00

3rd Row:

Checkerboard	Green	3½"	30.00–32.50
Sailboat	Blue	4½"	12.00–15.00
	Blue	3½"	10.00–12.00
	Red,Green	4½"	12.00–15.00
	Green, Lt. Green	3½"	10.00–15.00
Tulip No.1	Blue, Red	4½"	17.50–20.00
	Blue, Red	3½"	3.00–4.00

4th Row:

Tulip No.1	Green	4½"	17.50–20.00
	Green, Black	3½"	3.00–4.00
	Green w/Label	3½"	10.00–12.00
*Tulip No.2	Red, Green, Black	3½"	30.00–32.50
Carnival	Blue, Red	3½"	5.00–7.00
	Green, Yellow	3½"	5.00–7.00
Tulip No. 3	Dk. Blue, Lt. Blue	3¾"	2.50–3.50

*West Coast lower price

SWIRL, "PETAL SWIRL" JEANNETTE GLASS COMPANY, 1937–1938

Colors: Ultra Marine, pink, Delphite; some amber and "ice" blue.

Ultra Marine Swirl pitchers (pictured in previous editions) are found once in a blue moon. Only three have turned up! So far, none have been discovered in pink. (Today really is the second blue moon of 1999; there will not be another for almost 20 years.) Some collectors of Swirl combine this pattern with Jeannette's "Jennyware" kitchenware line that does have a **flat,** 36 ounce pink pitcher in it! If you find mixing bowls, measuring cups, or reamers, then you have crossed over into the kitchenware line and out of the Swirl dinnerware set. See *Kitchen Glassware of the Depression Years* for complete "Jennyware" listings.

Swirl candy and butter dish bottoms are more plentiful than are tops. They had a habit of getting dropped. Remember that before you buy only the bottom! Having said that, I found an Ultra Marine candy bottom with good color at the flea market, today, priced right and I went ahead and bought it. That dearth of tops holds true for 90 percent of the butter and candy dishes in Depression glass. Unless you are good at remembering color hues, it might be sensible to take your half with you to match this Ultra Marine color.

Swirl has some green-tinged pieces as well as the normally found color. This green tint is hard to match, and some collectors avoid this shade. Because of this, there are many times you can buy this green tint at a bargain price if you are willing to accumulate that shade. This problem occurs with all Jeannette patterns made in Ultra Marine. In the future this color might be what collectors seek. The smaller, flat tumbler and the 9" rimmed salad bowl beside it in the picture below, have this green tint. A boxed console set labeled "One 1500/3 Console Set, Ultra Marine from Jeannette Glass Co., Jeannette, Pa." was bought for my candlestick book. The set was sent to "Jno. Curtis Extract Co., 322 Broadway, Hanover, Pa." It has the footed console and a pair of candles in the green shade of Ultra Marine.

Pink candle holders are not considered rare even though they were omitted from some of my earlier editions. **Omissions on my part do not make a piece rare.** Sorry!

The pink coaster, shown in the left foreground of page 210, is usually found inside a small rubber tire and used for ash trays. These tires were advertisements distributed by tire manufactures and neighborhood garages which have, themselves, become collectible. Those with a tire manufacturer's name on the glass insert are more in demand; but those with a non-advertising glass insert (such as this coaster) are collected if the miniature tire is embossed with the name of a tire company. Many of these tires dried up or decayed over the years leaving only the glass inserts as reminders. I certainly see few in Florida, but they are seen frequently in Ohio and Pennsylvania. Rubber in Florida heat rapidly breaks down.

Swirl was produced in several scarce colors. A smaller set can be assembled in Delphite blue; it would only have basic pieces and a serving dish or two. Vegetable bowls (9") were made in several trial colors. A recent find is a small amethyst berry bowl pictured in *Very Rare Glassware of the Depression Years, Fifth Series.*

Almost all pieces of Swirl can be found with two different borders, ruffled and plain. Pink comes mostly with plain borders while Ultra Marine comes with both. This makes a big difference if you mail order or shop the Internet for your pattern. It is **your** responsibility to specify what style you want. The seller has no idea what you want unless you spell it out. Either style is pleasing to most collectors, but some do not like to mix shapes. If you only want plain edged pieces, please tell the dealer before he ships your order. This is not a problem, of course, when you can see the merchandise displayed at shows.

SWIRL (Cont.)

	Pink	Ultra Marine	Delphite
Bowl, 4⅞" & 5¼" berry	14.00	16.00	14.00
Bowl, 9" salad	26.00	32.00	30.00
Bowl, 9" salad, rimmed	30.00	32.00	
Bowl, 10" ftd., closed handles	35.00	35.00	
Bowl, 10½" ftd. console	20.00	30.00	
Butter dish	210.00	265.00	
Butter dish bottom	35.00	40.00	
Butter dish top	175.00	225.00	
Candle holders, double branch, pr.	70.00	60.00	
Candle holders, single branch, pr.			125.00
Candy dish, open, 3 legs	15.00	20.00	
Candy dish with cover	115.00	170.00	
Coaster, 1" x 3¼"	13.00	16.00	
Creamer, ftd.	10.00	16.00	12.00
Cup	10.00	16.00	10.00
Pitcher, 48 oz., ftd.		1,750.00	

	Pink	Ultra Marine	Delphite
Plate, 6½" sherbet	7.00	8.00	6.00
Plate, 7¼"	10.00	15.00	
Plate, 8" salad	10.00	15.00	9.00
Plate, 9¼" dinner	17.00	22.00	12.00
Plate, 10½"			25.00
Plate, 12½" sandwich	22.00	32.00	
Platter, 12", oval			38.00
Salt and pepper, pr.		45.00	
Saucer	3.00	4.00	5.00
Sherbet, low ftd.	17.00	22.50	
Soup, tab hndl. (lug)	35.00	40.00	
Sugar, ftd.	10.00	16.00	12.00
Tray, 10½", 2-hndl.			27.50
Tumbler, 4", 9 oz.	22.00	35.00	
Tumbler, 4⅝", 9 oz.	20.00		
Tumbler, 5⅛", 13 oz.	55.00	120.00	
Tumbler, 9 oz., ftd.	22.00	45.00	
Vase, 6½" ftd., ruffled	23.00		
Vase, 8½" ftd., two styles		30.00	

TEA ROOM INDIANA GLASS COMPANY, 1926–1931

Colors: Pink, green, amber, and some crystal.

Tea Room prices perpetually increase, but they are not soaring as they once did. Prices do not increase rapidly when fewer sales are being transacted due to a lack of merchandise in the market. This sometimes occurs when newer collectors cannot find enough to start a set. Rarely found pieces are not coming on the market unless a previously collected set is being dispersed. Established collectors, anticipating new finds, are not augmenting their sets very quickly either.

The dilemma in gathering Tea Room is finding **mint condition** pieces to buy. The underneath sides of flat pieces are inclined to chip and flake on all the unprotected points, of which there are many. I had the privilege to witness the opening of an original box of Tea Room that had 32 each cups, saucers, and luncheon plates. There were less than a dozen mint condition (as we define it today) pieces out of the 96 in the box. The $1,000.00 for the box had seemed a good deal, until I saw the pieces. These had never been used; so, there was doubtless a mould problem with Tea Room initially. It's perfectly fine to buy and use the flawed pieces; just don't pay mint prices for them.

Green Tea Room is sought more than pink; and some people are starting to request crystal. Crystal pieces are fetching about 75 to 80 percent of the pink prices listed except for the commonly found 9½" ruffled vase and the rarely found pitcher, priced separately below. That crystal pitcher is even harder to find than the amber one. I have bought and sold four amber pitchers, but only one crystal. I have only seen two! Amber pitchers and tumblers are often found in the Atlanta metro area. I was told they were Coca-Cola premiums. Creamers and sugars emerge occasionally in amber. After that, amber has not been seen in any other item. You can see all four amber pieces on page 212.

A couple of pink parfaits turned up in Houston. I bought one for a future book. These are usually found highly priced and badly damaged. There are two styles of banana splits. Both the footed and flat are very desirable pieces of Tea Room to own in any color! The green, flat one is the hardest to find. Many times you can find banana splits priced reasonably because they are not recognized as Tea Room! A footed green one is pictured on the right side of page 212. That is the celery in front. A flat banana split is pictured in the photo of pink, right of the shaker.

The flat sugar and marmalade bottom are the same. However, the marmalade has a notched lid; the sugar lid is not notched. Finding either is not an easy task! The mustard comes with a plain or notched lid. As the name suggests, Tea Room was intended to be used in the tea rooms and ice cream parlors of the day. That is why you find so many soda fountain items in this pattern. Tea Room was **used** which accounts for some imperfections.

Some interesting lamps are showing up which used frosted Tea Room tumblers in their makeup. We recently photographed a chandelier which employed a ruffled top vase. The regular lamp is not as plentiful as it once was. It has been a while since I have seen one in green.

Prices are for mint items. These prices are high because **mint condition items are difficult to obtain!** I cannot emphasize that too much! Damaged pieces are often bought to supplement sets until mint items can be found. Not everyone can afford to buy only mint items, and they are willing to accept Tea Room pieces with some minor flaws at lesser prices. New collectors may have to accept some damage on items or do without.

TEA ROOM (Cont.)

	Green	Pink
Bowl, finger	60.00	60.00
Bowl, 7½" banana split, flat	120.00	115.00
Bowl, 7½" banana split, ftd.	85.00	75.00
Bowl, 8¼" celery	35.00	27.50
Bowl, 8¾" deep salad	85.00	70.00
Bowl, 9½" oval vegetable	75.00	65.00
Candlestick, low, pr.	70.00	70.00
Creamer, 3¼"	27.50	27.50
Creamer, 4½", ftd. (amber $75.00)	20.00	20.00
Creamer, rectangular	25.00	20.00
Creamer & sugar on tray, 4"	85.00	75.00
* Cup	60.00	60.00
Goblet, 9 oz.	75.00	65.00
Ice bucket	60.00	52.50
Lamp, 9", electric	135.00	110.00
Marmalade, notched lid	195.00	160.00
Mustard, covered	150.00	125.00
Parfait	95.00	95.00
** Pitcher, 64 oz. (amber $500.00)	140.00	125.00
Plate, 6½" sherbet	32.00	30.00
Plate, 8¼" luncheon	35.00	30.00
Plate, 10½", 2-hndl.	48.00	43.00
Relish, divided	25.00	20.00

	Green	Pink
Salt and pepper, pr.	65.00	50.00
* Saucer	30.00	30.00
Sherbet, low, ftd.	25.00	22.00
Sherbet, low flared edge	30.00	26.00
Sherbet, tall ftd.	50.00	50.00
Sugar w/lid, 3"	110.00	100.00
Sugar, 4½", ftd. (amber $75.00)	20.00	20.00
Sugar, rectangular	25.00	20.00
Sugar, flat with cover	195.00	160.00
Sundae, ftd., ruffled top	95.00	75.00
Tray, center-hndl.	210.00	155.00
Tray, rectangular sugar & creamer	50.00	40.00
Tumbler, 8 oz., 4³⁄₁₆", flat	110.00	120.00
Tumbler, 6 oz., ftd.	35.00	35.00
Tumbler, 8 oz., 5¼", high, ftd. (amber $95.00)	33.00	33.00
Tumbler, 11 oz., ftd.	50.00	45.00
Tumbler, 12 oz., ftd.	75.00	70.00
Vase, 6½", ruffled edge	100.00	100.00
*** Vase, 9½", ruffled edge	120.00	120.00
Vase, 9½", straight	95.00	90.00
Vase, 11", ruffled edge	250.00	295.00
Vase, 11", straight	140.00	150.00

* Prices for absolutely mint pieces
** Crystal – $400.00
*** Crystal – $16.00

THISTLE MacBETH-EVANS, 1929–1930

Colors: Pink, green; some yellow and crystal.

Thistle pattern is definitely the nettle that every photographer whom I have worked with since 1972 hates to see placed before them. Originally, we decorated all the faint patterns with Bon Ami® cleanser which took an excessive amount of time! The patterns did show in those old black and white photos; but when we switched to color, the treated patterns looked as if they were white in the photographs. We use that process sparingly today; and instead of wetting, letting dry and wiping like we used to do, we use chalk for highlighting, which, of course, the photographer hates because of dust problems from that! One of my **former** photographers would see us unpacking Thistle and automatically inquire if we **really wanted to see the those thistles** this time! Photography lights cause Thistle to do a vanishing act, which is an act familiar to Thistle collectors. Our new photographer seems to have captured Thistle by placing the cake plate askew!

Green Thistle is even more sparse than pink except for the large fruit bowl that is practically a mirage in pink. I have owned the one pictured here for over 25 years, and I have only seen two others.

Thistle pieces have the same mould shapes as the thin Dogwood; there is no Thistle creamer or sugar known. The Thistle grill plate has the pattern on the edge only. Those plain centers scratched very easily; be aware of that problem should you locate a grill plate to scrutinize! Frankly, if you find one with a distinguishable pattern, buy it! Eventually, there'll be glass polishers available to the public to fix scratching.

If you find a thick butter dish, pitcher, tumbler, creamer, sugar, or other heavy moulded pieces with Thistle designs, they are new! These pieces are being made by Mosser Glass Company in Cambridge, Ohio. They are not a part of this pattern, but copies of a much older pattern glass. If you have a piece of Thistle not in the photograph, then you probably do not have a piece of MacBeth-Evans Thistle pattern; all seven pieces known to have been made by them are shown. Thistle patterns were made by many companies during America's rural heyday.

	Pink	Green
Bowl, 5½" cereal	28.00	30.00
Bowl, 10¼" large fruit	395.00	250.00
Cup, thin	25.00	28.00
Plate, 8" luncheon	20.00	22.00
Plate, 10¼" grill	25.00	30.00
Plate, 13" heavy cake	150.00	175.00
Saucer	10.00	10.00

TULIP DELL GLASS COMPANY, LATE 1930s–LATE 1940s

Color: Amethyst, turquoise, crystal, green.

Tulip is one of the newer collected patterns for which I have enjoyed finding new pieces. To my knowledge, no one has yet found a goblet like the one depicted in the ad on page 216. An amethyst decanter has been found with the Tulip stopper that is pictured in all three colors. This stopper stem is surrounded in cork. Since there is no catalog picture of the decanter to go by, a problem exists as to what the actual decanter looks like. The one found has a diamond optic design and a neck similar to the violin vase in the ad on page 216. I have it pictured for next time; hopefully some documentation will appear before then.

I borrowed a blue candy bottom from a collector in the Midwest to match my top. You can see the entire candy in blue below. I offered to sell him my candy top or buy his bottom at the same price. He chose to buy my top; so, I am looking again. At least you can now see it.

One style of candle holder is made from an ivy bowl (not a sherbet as the piece was previously thought to be). That ivy bowl (sherbet) is shown in the 1946 Montgomery Ward catalog with ivy growing in it. Have you ever seen the amber which I mistakenly listed and has since been copied in another book put out to compete with this one? I don't mind other books. I do mind my research being ripped off (mistakes and all) as someone else's work.

The juice tumbler (cigarette holder in ad) is 2¾" tall and holds three ounces while the whiskey is only 1¾" and holds one ounce.

The ad for Tulip shows no stippling on the pieces. Early in buying this pattern, I ignored some pieces without stippling; both styles are acceptable to collectors. I am finding about half with and half without. Personally, I prefer the stippled look.

I started buying Tulip about nine years ago, when I found nine green sugar bowls for $10.00. I couldn't turn them down at that price though I did not know whether there were collectors for it or not. I soon found out! Those sugars are often found in sets of four or more, making me believe they may also have been marketed as cream soups. I see about a dozen sugars for every creamer.

In buying Tulip, I have found that the scalloped rims have a tendency to have some damage. Most of the damage occurs **under the rim edge;** be sure to turn the piece over and check each of the pointed scallops. Many times a scallop or two will be absent and not show from the top side.

I have priced the crystal with the green since you will not see much of it. Crystal may be the rarest color!

	Amethyst, Blue	Crystal, Green
Bowl, oval, oblong, 13¼"	110.00	90.00
Candleholder, 3¾" (ivy bowl)	35.00	25.00
Candleholder, 5¼" base, 3" tall	55.00	35.00
Candy w/lid, ftd. (6" w/o lid)	135.00	100.00
Creamer	22.00	20.00
Cup	22.00	14.00
Decanter w/stopper	150.00	125.00
Ice tub, 4⅞" wide, 3" deep	95.00	65.00
Plate, 6"	10.00	9.00
Plate, 7¼"	15.00	10.00
Plate, 9"	38.00	32.00
Saucer	8.00	6.00
Sherbet, 3¾", flat (ivy bowl)	22.00	20.00
Sugar	22.00	20.00
Tumbler, 2¾" juice	28.00	22.00
Tumbler, whiskey	30.00	25.00

Room Accessories Introduce Accents of Color and Design to your Room Settings

EXCLUSIVE AT WARDS . . . three little words that mean a lot of individuality in both practical and purely ornamental accessories for your home. Words that tell of original designs made exclusively for Wards and to be found no other place. Look for them on these pages. . . .

(A) (B) GLASS BANJO ACCESSORIES. Matched bits of colorful whimsy for your home.

(A) GLASS BANJO BOTTLE. Complete with a metal bracket for hanging. Fill with ivy . . . to brighten your walls. In Turquoise or Amethyst. Abt. 12 in. high overall. (No Ivy.)
86 C 7148—Ship. wt. 2 lbs. *State color*. . $1.25

(B) GLASS BANJO ASHTRAY. Just like a real banjo with the neck hollowed out to hold a lighted cigarette with ease. In Turquoise or Amethyst. About 2⅞ by 5¼ in. long.
86 C 7146—Ship. wt. 1 lb. *State color*. . . . 55c

(C) MILK GLASS DOUBLE CRIMP VASE. Creamy White Victorian type Milk Glass with an edging of clear, crisp glass. Have a pair for your mantel. About 5½ inches high.
86 C 7403—Ship. wt. 2 lbs. 8 oz. $1.10

(D) MILK GLASS DOUBLE CRIMP BOWL. Victorian type Milk Glass . . . perfect for the table of today. Use it for either informal or the more formal flower arrangements. Graceful edge of clear glass. About 3¾ in. high.
86 C 7404—Ship. wt. 2 lbs. 12 oz. $1.10

(E) PANSY BASKET CANDY DISH. A border of white Milk Glass pansies form a dainty dish to hold candies or nuts. Abt. 4¼-in. diam.
86 C 7299—Ship. wt. 1 lb. 6 oz. 65c

(F) MILK GLASS DOUBLE CRIMP VASE. The perfect background for a gay bouquet. White Milk Glass with a fluted edge of clear glass. Vase is about 6½ in. high.
86 C 7402—Ship. wt. 2 lbs. 12 oz. $1.10

(G) (H) BENT GLASS SERVING PLATES. Matching plates for serving sandwiches, salads and snacks. Of Bent Glass with thin shadow lines on the back and a fruit pattern permanently fused into the overall design of the plates. Soap and water will not harm the Blue and Plum color design of each plate.

(G) BENT GLASS PLATE. An ample 16 inches in diameter. Matches (H) below.
86 C 7157—Ship. wt. 4 lbs. $3.25

(H) TWO-TIER BENT GLASS PLATE. Two trays, the top tray abt. 8-in. diam., the bottom tray abt. 12-in. diam. Metal rod and handle are rustproof. Matches (G) above.
86 C 7158—Ship. wt. 4 lbs. 8 oz. $4.75

(J) ROOSTER DISH. Reminder of Colonial days, this White Milk Glass Rooster that holds candy and nuts. Abt. 5¾ by 4¼ by 4 in. deep.
86 C 7298—Ship. wt. 1 lb. 8 oz. 60c

(K) HURRICANE LAMP. Friendly candlelight diffused through sparkling Cranberry glass on mantel or refectory table. Base of clear glass with six teardrop pendants, shade of Cranberry glass. Abt. 12¾ in. high.
86 C 7295—(No candle.) Ship. wt. 3 lbs. $1.95

(L) 5-PC. GLASS VANITY SET. Clear Glass accessories for your dressing table. Mirror is removable. Bottles are abt. 7¼ in. high, Jar abt. 3 in. high, Tray abt. 14¼ by 8⅜ in.
86 C 7401—Shipping weight 7 lbs. 8 oz.
5-piece Set. $1.95

(M) 3-PC. MILK GLASS CONSOLE SET. Fruit or flowers massed on your dining table, candlelight flickering on the deep bowl which holds them. Three pieces of White Milk Glass with an English Hobnail design. Bowl abt. 11⅞ by 4½ in. deep, each candle holder abt. 3¼ in. high. (No fruit, candles.)
86 C 7301—Ship. wt. 7 lbs. 3-pc. Set. . . . $2.95

(N) to (W) MATCHING GLASS TULIP ACCESSORIES. Gleaming glass in two distinctive colors hand molded into a collection of Tulip Accessories that are *Exclusive at Wards in Mail Order*. Each shining piece is embossed with the tulip motif and fire polished for brilliance. Choose either Turquoise or Amethyst or mix the two colors in the pieces you choose of these unusual Tulip Accessories . . .

(N) TULIP WALL BRACKET. The Green metal scroll bracket holds two small glass Tulip Design containers for ivy. Abt. 17½ in. long overall. Turquoise or Amethyst. (No ivy.)
86 C 7154—Ship. wt. 2 lbs. *State color*. . $1.95

(P) 16-PC. SET OF TULIP DISHES. Set a bright table with these glass Tulip Design dishes. Set consists of four 10½-in. Luncheon Plates, four 6-in. Salad Plates, four Cups, four Saucers. In Turquoise or Amethyst.
86 C 7155L—Set of 16 Dishes. Ship. wt. 20 lbs. *State color: Turquoise or Amethyst*. $8.95

(R) TULIP GOBLET. Stately glass footed goblet with the Tulip Design. About 7 in. high. In your choice of Turquoise or Amethyst.
86 C 7145—Ship. wt. 2 lbs. *State color*. . . . 65c

(T) TULIP SUGAR AND CREAMER. Of glass with Tulip Design. Both about 1⅞ in. high.
86 C 7156—Sugar and Creamer. Ship. wt. 2 lbs. *State color:* Turquoise or Amethyst. . $1.95

(U) TULIP CIGARETTE HOLDER. Individual size. Abt. 2¾ in. high. Tuquoise or Amethyst.
86 C 7152—Ship. wt. 1 lb. *State color*. . . . 50c

(V) (W) TULIP BOWL AND CANDLEHOLDERS. Something ever new can be done with flowers, fruit and this trio of glass Tulip Design pieces. Bowl is abt. 13 x 6¼ x 2¾ in. deep, each candleholder abt. 2 in. high. The cup-type candleholders are designed to hold tiny flowers as well as candles. Turquoise or Amethyst. (Flowers and candles not incl.)

(V) 86 C 7149—TULIP BOWL. Ship. wt. 4 lbs. *State color wanted*. $3.95

(W) 86 C 7150—PAIR OF TULIP CANDLEHOLDERS. Ship. wt. 2 lbs. *State color*. $1.95

444 WARDS

TWISTED OPTIC IMPERIAL GLASS COMPANY, 1927–1930

Colors: Pink, green, amber; some blue and Canary yellow.

All the pieces shown below belong to Twisted Optic. You can see an additional green piece of Twisted Optic under Spiral (page 203) placed there to help in differentiating these two confusing patterns. If you find a spiraling piece in some color besides pink or green, then it is most likely Twisted Optic or some pattern other than Hocking's. You should realize that many glass companies made twisting patterns besides Hocking and Imperial! Some smaller glass factories never issued catalogs and others were in business for so short a time that records disappeared if, indeed, they ever had any.

Twisted Optic's spirals go to the right and Spiral's go to the left!

Page 218 shows a photograph of Imperial's Canary color. This color is often mislabeled Vaseline. I was able to buy these pieces from a dealer who was selling a set, but with the pieces priced individually! I bought enough to illustrate this color and pattern. You should know that though powder jars and cologne bottles are in great demand due to so many collectors seeking only those items, the cologne bottle pictured here is U.S. Glass Milady pattern and not Twisted Optic. There is no Twisted Optic cologne even though I erroneously listed it. Milady certainly blends well with Twisted Optic, especially in Canary; but it was not made by Imperial.

	Blue, Canary Yellow	All Other Colors
Basket, 10", tall	95.00	60.00
Bowl, 4¾" cream soup	16.00	11.00
Bowl, 5" cereal	10.00	5.50
Bowl, 7" salad	15.00	10.00
Bowl, 9"	25.00	15.00
Bowl, 10½", console	35.00	20.00
Bowl, 11½", 4¼" tall	50.00	22.50
Candlesticks, 3" pr. (2 styles)	45.00	25.00
Candlesticks, 8", pr.	75.00	35.00
Candy jar w/cover, flat	60.00	30.00
Candy jar w/cover, flat, flange edge	70.00	35.00
Candy jar w/cover, ftd., flange edge	70.00	35.00
Candy jar w/cover, ftd., short, fat	85.00	45.00
Candy jar w/cover, ftd., tall	95.00	45.00
Creamer	12.50	7.50
Cup	10.00	4.00
Mayonnaise	40.00	20.00
Pitcher, 64 oz.		30.00

	Blue, Canary Yellow	All Other Colors
Plate, 6" sherbet	4.00	2.00
Plate, 7" salad	6.00	3.00
Plate, 7½" x 9", oval with indent	9.00	5.00
Plate, 8" luncheon	8.00	3.50
Plate, 10" sandwich	15.00	9.00
Powder jar w/lid	65.00	40.00
Preserve (same as candy w/slotted lid)		27.50
Sandwich server, open center hndl.	35.00	20.00
Sandwich server, two-hndl.	18.00	12.00
Saucer	4.00	2.00
Sherbet	10.00	6.00
Sugar	12.50	6.50
Tumbler, 4½", 9 oz.		6.00
Tumbler, 5¼", 12 oz.		8.00
Vase, 7¼", 2-hndl., rolled edge	65.00	35.00
Vase, 8", 2-hndl., fan	85.00	40.00
Vase, 8", 2-hndl., straight edge	85.00	35.00

"U.S. SWIRL" U.S. GLASS COMPANY, LATE 1920s

Colors: Pink, green, iridescent, and crystal.

"U.S. Swirl" is a pattern that receives little notoriety. Even though I named it years ago, no documentation has surfaced to indicate that it was ever named by U.S. Glass at all. I have only found one pink shaker and a butter dish in "U.S. Swirl" in the 12 years I have been searching. Probably very little pink was manufactured; or maybe there wasn't a complete line available in pink. I separated the colors by price due to demand for green outweighing that of pink. Occasionally, I see a few crystal sherbets. The 5⅜" tall comport is pictured behind the sherbet for size comparison. I know some collectors prefer I call it a martini or margarita glass, the newest use for compotes. (That's why Manhattan comports are so hard to find. Manhattan collectors are buying six or more for drinks instead of one for candy.) This "U.S. Swirl" comport is rarely found.

Several "U.S. Swirl" iridescent butter dishes have been discovered, but those and sherbets are the only pieces surfacing in that color. The tumbler listing 3⅝" conforms with the only known size of Aunt Polly and Cherryberry/Strawberry tumblers; but the 12 ounce tumbler has only been found in "U.S. Swirl." The footed piece in the back on the left is a vase, although it has been incorrectly called a tumbler at times.

"U.S. Swirl" has the plain butter bottom that is compatible with all the other patterns made by U.S. Glass. The butter dish in this pattern is the one that many Strawberry collectors have purchased over the years to borrow the bottom for their Strawberry tops. This plundering has stressed butters in this "U.S. Swirl" pattern, particularly in pink.

The smaller 1¾" deep, 8⅜," oval bowl in front of the 2¾" deep, oval bowl is seldom found; it may be rare!

	Green	Pink
Bowl, 4⅜" berry	5.50	6.50
Bowl, 5½", 1-hndl.	9.50	10.50
Bowl, 7⅞" large berry	15.00	16.00
Bowl, 8¼", oval (2¾" deep)	40.00	40.00
Bowl, 8⅜", oval (1¾" deep)	55.00	55.00
Butter and cover	120.00	120.00
Butter bottom	100.00	100.00
Butter top	20.00	20.00
Candy w/cover, 2-hndl.	27.50	32.00
Comport	30.00	20.00

	Green	Pink
Creamer	14.00	16.00
Pitcher, 8", 48 oz.	75.00	75.00
Plate, 6⅛" sherbet	2.50	2.50
Plate, 7⅞" salad	5.50	6.50
Salt and pepper, pr.	60.00	60.00
Sherbet, 3¼"	4.50	5.00
Sugar w/lid	35.00	35.00
Tumbler, 3⅝", 8 oz.	10.00	10.00
Tumbler, 4¾", 12 oz.	14.00	15.00
Vase, 6½"	25.00	20.00

"VICTORY" DIAMOND GLASS-WARE COMPANY, 1929–1932

Colors: Amber, pink, green; some cobalt blue and black.

After I mentioned that cobalt blue "Victory" was being spotted in the northeast, especially in Maine, in the last book, I have heard of other sets there. The latest two accumulations were in antique malls at very reasonable prices. Elsewhere, I see a blue piece now and then, but not in any large groupings.

Amber and black "Victory" are pictured below. That color combination seems to enhance each other. This combining of colors is catching on amongst collectors. The black with gold trim shows up better in the photo than the gold-trimmed amber. As with most black glass of this time, the pattern is on the back; you have to turn it over to see that the piece is "Victory" unless you can distinguish it from the indented edges. Collectors of black glass are more likely to own black "Victory" than Depression glass people, though they often appear with it in hand at shows not having a clue its an actual pattern with a name.

Sets of "Victory" can be completed in pink and green with a great deal of searching. Amber, cobalt blue, and black will take more hunting and some good fortune! It can be done even in today's market, but it will be expensive, at best.

The "Victory" gravy boat and platter are the most desirable pieces to own in any color. I have only seen one amber and one green set, but five cobalt blue ones. A green gravy and platter can be seen on the bottom of page 221.

The goblet, candlestick, cereal, soup, and oval vegetable bowls will keep you looking long and hard in all colors of "Victory." Right now, there are few collectors competing for these rare "Victory" pieces; it might be a good time to assemble a set in your selected color!

There are several techniques of ornamentation besides the 22K gold-trimmed pieces. There are floral decorations and even a black decorated design on pink and green that is rather Art Deco looking. I have spied more floral decorated console sets (bowl and candlesticks) than anything. I presume that complete sets of gold decorated pink and green can be found. The black pieces decorated with gold may only be found in luncheon or console sets.

	Amber, Pink, Green	Black, Blue
Bon bon, 7"	11.00	20.00
Bowl, 6½" cereal	14.00	40.00
Bowl, 8½" flat soup	20.00	60.00
Bowl, 9" oval vegetable	32.00	115.00
Bowl, 11", rolled edge	28.00	50.00
Bowl, 12" console	33.00	65.00
Bowl, 12½", flat edge	30.00	65.00
Candlesticks, 3", pr.	35.00	125.00
Cheese & cracker set, 12" indented plate & compote	40.00	
Comport, 6" tall, 6¾" diameter	15.00	
Creamer	15.00	50.00
Cup	9.00	33.00
Goblet, 5", 7 oz.	25.00	75.00
Gravy boat and platter	225.00	350.00
Mayonnaise set: 3½" tall, 5½" across, 8½" indented plate, w/ladle	42.00	100.00
Plate, 6" bread and butter	6.00	16.00
Plate, 7" salad	7.00	20.00
Plate, 8" luncheon	7.00	30.00
Plate, 9" dinner	20.00	55.00
Platter, 12"	30.00	85.00
Sandwich server, center hndl.	29.00	75.00
Saucer	4.00	12.00
Sherbet, ftd.	13.00	26.00
Sugar	15.00	50.00

VITROCK, "FLOWER RIM" HOCKING GLASS COMPANY, 1934–1937

Colors: White and white w/fired-on colors, usually red or green.

Vitrock was Hocking's headlong leap into the milk glass market. Today, platters, soup plates, and cream soups are pieces that are nearly impossible to find in Vitrock. If you locate a flat soup, you are usually wishing it has the Lake Como decoration. Lake Como was a decorated Vitrock pattern. I pictured a Lake Como soup with this pattern in the last edition, but I have been unable to locate a regular Vitrock flat soup. These are rarer than I previously thought. Vitrock was not a pattern per se, but a mid-1930s stark white color of Hocking's similar to Hazel Atlas' Platonite. There are many different patterns found on this very durable line, but collectors have adopted the decorated Lake Como and the "Flower Rim" dinnerware sets as patterns to collect.

Vitrock is mainly known for its kitchenware line of reamers, measuring cups, and mixing bowls. Notice that the Vitrock kitchenware items are also shown in this display of "The **NEW** Material" on page 223. This mid-1930s store display photograph was found in Anchor Hocking's files. Note the emphasis that Vitrock "Will not craze or check" on the display sign. Crazing was a major flaw for many **pottery** wares of the time.

I realize why those large Vitrock mixing bowls are so hard to find today. They retailed for a quarter which may have accounted for a half day's wage for a working man!

At the time, Vitrock competed with Hazel Atlas's Platonite; and by all indications today, Platonite won the battle!

You can see more Vitrock in my book *Kitchen Glassware of the Depression Years.* Some collectors are assembling patterns that cross other fields. This is a prime example of a pattern that fits into both collecting areas. Hazel Atlas did the same with their Platonite. It made perfect business sense to sell auxiliary items that matched your everyday dishes.

	White
Bowl, 4" berry	5.00
Bowl, 5½" cream soup	16.00
Bowl, 6" fruit	5.50
Bowl, 7½" cereal	6.00
Bowl, 9½" vegetable	15.00
Creamer, oval	6.00
Cup	4.00
Plate, 7¼" salad	2.50
Plate, 8¾" luncheon	5.00
Plate, 9" soup	30.00
Plate, 10" dinner	8.50
Platter, 11½"	33.00
Saucer	2.50
Sugar	6.00

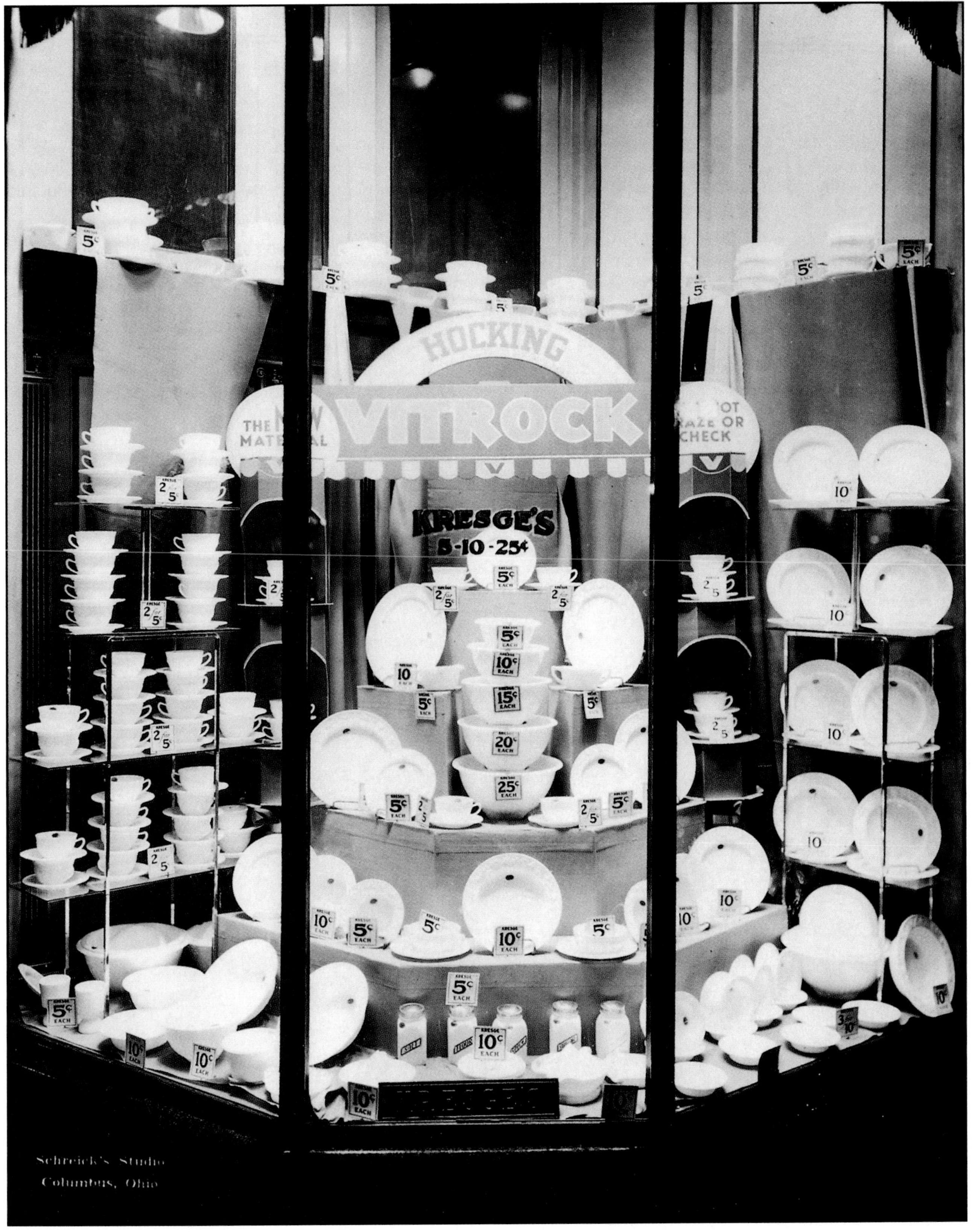
HOCKING
VITROCK
KRESGE'S
5-10-25¢
Schreick's Studio
Columbus, Ohio

WATERFORD, "WAFFLE" HOCKING GLASS COMPANY, 1938–1944

Colors: Crystal, pink; some yellow, Vitrock; forest green 1950s.

Crystal Waterford continues to sell very well. Availability and price have more to do with that than anything else. You can still find quantities of crystal, but pink is found a piece or two at a time. Most would like to **encounter** pink cereal bowls, a pitcher, or a butter dish sitting on a table or shelf for sale! Of these three pieces, the cereal is the most elusive. It has always been annoying to find, and worse, difficult to find **mint!** The inside rim is predictably damaged from stacking or use. A **little** roughness is typical; do not let that keep you from owning a hard-to-find piece. Because of the scalloped rim design, Waterford has been known to chip or flake.

There are some scarce crystal pieces. Cereal bowls, pitchers, and even water goblets are declining in number. Those shakers on the right in the top photograph were used by many restaurants through the 1960s which is why they are frequently seen today! There are two styles of sherbets. One sherbet has a scalloped top and base. It is not as commonly found and not as accepted as the plain edged one.

There is a Waterford "pretender" footed cup that is occasionally sold as a Waterford punch cup. This cup, and the larger lamps that are often displayed as Waterford, **are only similar** to Waterford. Waterford has a flattened **(not rounded)** "diamond" shape on each section of the design. There is also a large, pink pitcher with an indented, **circular design in each diamond** which is **not** Waterford. This pitcher was made by Hocking, but has more of a bull's-eye look. These pink pitchers with circular designs only sell for $35.00 and crystal for $20.00; do not pay Waterford prices for one!

A few pieces of Vitrock Waterford and some Dusty Rose and Springtime Green ash trays turn up occasionally; these sell near crystal prices. Examples of those rose and green colors can be seen in Oyster and Pearl on page 158. Forest green Waterford 13¾" plates were made in the 1950s promotion of Forest Green; these are usually found in the $30.00 range. Many of these have white sections sitting on them for a relish similar to those found in Manhattan. Some crystal has also been found trimmed in red. There is not enough of the red trim to collect a set piece by piece.

Advertising ash trays, such as the "Post Cereals" shown below, are selling for $20.00 to $25.00 depending upon the significance of the advertising on the piece! An advertisement for Anchor Hocking itself will bring $35.00 to $40.00.

Items listed below with Miss America shape in parentheses are Waterford patterned pieces with the same **mould shapes** as Miss America. You can see some of these in the seventh edition of this book or in the first *Very Rare Glassware of the Depression Years.*

Those yellow and amber goblets shown below are compliments of Anchor Hocking's photographer from items stored in their morgue. I have not seen yellow ones for sale, but amber ones sell for around $25.00.

	Crystal	Pink
* Ash tray, 4"	7.50	
Bowl, 4¾" berry	6.50	18.00
Bowl, 5½" cereal	19.00	38.00
Bowl, 8¼" large berry	14.00	25.00
Butter dish and cover	28.00	220.00
Butter dish bottom	6.00	30.00
Butter dish top	19.00	190.00
Coaster, 4"	4.00	
Creamer, oval	5.00	12.00
Creamer (Miss America shape)	35.00	
Cup	6.50	15.00
Cup (Miss America shape)		45.00
Goblets, 5¼", 5⅝"	16.00	
Goblet, 5½" (Miss America shape)	35.00	110.00
Lamp, 4", spherical base	26.00	
Pitcher, 42 oz., tilted, juice	24.00	
Pitcher, 80 oz., tilted, ice lip	36.00	150.00
Plate, 6" sherbet	3.00	7.00
Plate, 7⅛" salad	7.00	12.50

	Crystal	Pink
Plate, 9⅝" dinner	11.00	25.00
Plate, 10¼" handled cake	10.00	18.00
Plate, 13¾" sandwich	13.00	32.00
Relish, 13¾", 5-part	17.00	
Salt and pepper, 2 types	8.50	
Saucer	3.00	6.00
Sherbet, ftd.	5.00	18.00
Sherbet, ftd., scalloped base	5.00	
Sugar	5.00	12.50
Sugar cover, oval	10.00	30.00
Sugar (Miss America shape)	35.00	
Tumbler, 3½", 5 oz. juice (Miss America shape)		95.00
Tumbler, 4⅞", 10 oz., ftd.	14.00	25.00

* With ads $15.00 – $20.00

WINDSOR, "WINDSOR DIAMOND" JEANNETTE GLASS COMPANY, 1936–1946

Colors: Pink, green, crystal; some Delphite, amberina red, and ice blue.

Distinctive crystal Windsor items continue to be discovered that are not found in pink or green. The one-handled candle stick and 10½" pointed edge tray are a couple that come to mind. There are many collectors of colored Windsor, but fewer collect crystal. Color was discontinued about 1940, but crystal pieces were made as late as 1946. Redesigned moulds for the Windsor butter, creamer, and sugar were later conveyed to Holiday when that pattern was introduced in 1947. There are two styles of sugars and lids. One is shaped like Holiday and has no lip for the lid to rest upon; the pink sugar on page 227 represents the second style with lip. The pink sugar and lid shaped like Holiday are hard to find.

Relish trays can be found with or without tab (closed) handles. Pictured below are green relish trays with tab handles; the large one holds two sizes of crystal relishes without the tabs. Trays without handles commonly appear in crystal, but pink trays without handles are seldom found! Two styles of sandwich plates were made. The normally found one is 10¼" and has open handles. The newly discovered tray is 10" and has closed handles.

Green Windsor tumblers are elusive. The water tumbler (which is commonly found in pink) is scarce. As often happened during this time, an unusual amount of mould roughness is found on seams of tumblers; and Windsor tumblers have an inclination to chip on the protruding sides. The diamond pattern juts outward, making the sides an easy target for chips and flakes. Check these seams cautiously before you buy! There are color variations in green; be conscious of that if you see a piece that looks darker than you are used to seeing! It might be!

The pink 13⅝" plate is often found as an underliner tray for a beverage set with a pitcher and six water tumblers. That may have been a premium item since so many pitchers and water tumblers are available today. Green pitcher and tumbler sets do not experience this abundance.

The 10½ " pointed edge bowl is rarely seen in pink, but the hard-to-find 5" pointed edge bowl is pictured on the far right of page 227. The large bowl in crystal, along with the comport, make up a punch bowl and stand. The upended comport fits inside the base of the bowl to keep it from sliding. In recent years, there have been newly made comports in crystal and with sprayed-on, multicolor that have a beaded edge. That recently made crystal comport will not work as a punch stand because the beaded edge will not fit inside the base of the bowl.

A new style pink ash tray and a tab-handled berry bowl can be seen in the *Very Rare Glassware of the Depression Years, Second Series.* While looking there, check out the **blue** Windsor butter dish! In the Fifth Series of that book, there is an oval, **handled, four-footed** bowl pictured. Was some worker playing around at the factory?

Windsor always brings a feeling of satisfaction when it comes up on my computer screen! Adam starts the book, Windsor ends the writing about patterns. There are still Reproductions and new patterns to write, but the light is shining at the end of the tunnel! As I wrote this two years ago, I was past my birthday; but this time, I should be finished in time to actually celebrate the double nickel!

	Crystal	Pink	Green
* Ash tray, 5¾"	13.50	42.00	45.00
Bowl, 4¾" berry	4.00	10.00	12.00
Bowl, 5", pointed edge	6.00	30.00	
Bowl, 5" cream soup	7.00	24.00	29.00
Bowls, 5⅛, 5⅜" cereal	8.50	22.00	25.00
Bowl, 7⅛", three legs	9.00	30.00	
Bowl, 8", pointed edge	18.00	60.00	
Bowl, 8½" large berry	10.00	22.00	22.00
Bowl, 9", 2-hndl.	10.00	22.00	25.00
Bowl, 9½" oval vegetable	7.00	22.00	30.00
Bowl, 10½" salad	15.00		
Bowl, 10½", pointed edge	30.00	135.00	
Bowl, 12½" fruit console	28.00	110.00	
Bowl, 7" x 11¾", boat shape	20.00	38.00	40.00
Butter dish (two styles)	28.00	60.00	95.00
Cake plate, 10¾", ftd.	8.50	25.00	25.00
Candleholder, one hndl.	15.00		
Candlesticks, 3", pr.	25.00	85.00	
Candy jar and cover	20.00		
Coaster, 3¼"	4.00	15.00	20.00
Comport	10.00		
** Creamer	5.00	14.00	16.00
Creamer (shaped as "Holiday")	7.50		
** Cup	4.00	10.00	12.50
Pitcher, 4½", 16 oz.	26.00	125.00	
*** Pitcher, 6¾", 52 oz.	17.00	33.00	55.00
Plate, 6" sherbet	2.50	5.00	8.00
Plate, 7" salad	4.50	20.00	25.00

	Crystal	Pink	Green
** Plate, 9" dinner	8.00	25.00	25.00
Plate, 10" sandwich, closed hndl.		25.00	
Plate, 10½", pointed edge	10.00		
Plate, 10¼" sandwich open hndl.	6.00	18.00	20.00
Plate, 13⅝" chop	14.00	35.00	42.00
Platter, 11½" oval	12.00	22.00	22.00
**** Powder jar	15.00	60.00	
Relish platter, 11½", divided	12.00	225.00	
Salt and pepper, pr.	16.00	40.00	50.00
Saucer (ice blue $15.00)	2.50	5.00	6.00
Sherbet, ftd.	3.50	14.00	15.00
Sugar & cover	12.00	30.00	33.00
Sugar & cover (like "Holiday")	15.00	125.00	
Tray, 4", square, w/hndl.	5.00	10.00	12.00
Tray, 4", square, w/o hndl.	10.00	50.00	
Tray, 4⅛" x 9", w/hndl.	4.00	10.00	16.00
Tray, 4⅛" x 9", w/o hndl.	12.00	60.00	
Tray, 8½" x 9¾", w/hndl.	6.50	24.00	35.00
Tray, 8½" x 9¾", w/o hndl.	15.00	95.00	
** Tumbler, 3¼", 5 oz.	10.00	25.00	32.00
** Tumbler, 4", 9 oz. (red 55.00)	7.00	20.00	28.00
Tumbler, 5", 12 oz.	10.00	33.00	50.00
Tumbler, 4⅝", 11 oz.	9.00		
Tumbler, 4", ftd.	8.00		
Tumbler, 5", ftd., 11 oz.	11.00		
Tumbler, 7¼", ftd.	18.00		

* Delphite – $45.00 ** Blue – $65.00 *** Red – $450.00 **** Yellow – $175.00; Blue – $185.00

REPRODUCTIONS

NEW "ADAM" PRIVATELY PRODUCED OUT OF KOREA THROUGH ST. LOUIS IMPORTING COMPANY

ONLY THE ADAM BUTTER DISH HAS BEEN REPRODUCED!

The reproduction Adam butter dish is finally off the market as far as I can determine. Identification of the reproduction is easy.

Top: Notice the veins in the leaves.

New: Large leaf veins do not join or touch in center of leaf.

Old: Large leaf veins all touch or join the center vein.

A further note about the original Adam butter dish: the veins of all the leaves at the center of the design are very clear cut and precisely moulded; in the new, these center leaf veins are very indistinct — and almost invisible in one leaf of the center design.

Bottom: Place butter dish bottom upside down for observation. Square it to your body.

New: Four (4) arrowhead-like points line up in northwest, northeast, southeast, and southwest directions of compass. There are very bad mould lines and a very glossy light pink color on the butter dishes I examined; but these have since been somewhat improved. However, the points still head in the wrong directions!

Old: Four (4) arrowhead-like points line up in north, east, south, and west directions of compass.

NEW "AVOCADO" INDIANA GLASS COMPANY Tiara Exclusives Line, 1974 – 1980s

Colors: Pink, frosted pink, yellow, blue, red, amethyst, and green.

In 1979 a green Avocado pitcher was produced. It was darker than the original green and was a limited hostess gift item. Yellow pieces are all recently made! Yellow was never made originally!

The old pink color Indiana made was a delicate, attractive pink. The new tends to be more orange than the original color. The other colors shown pose little threat since none of those colors were made originally.

I understand that Tiara sales counselors told potential customers that their newly made glass was collectible because it was made from old moulds. I don't share this view. I feel it's like saying that since you were married in your grandmother's wedding dress, you will have the same happy marriage for the 57 years she did. All you can truly say is that you were married in her dress. I think all you can say about the new Avocado is that it was made from the old moulds. **Time, scarcity,** and **people's whims** determine collectibility in so far as I'm able to determine it. It's taken nearly 50 years or more for people to turn to collecting Depression glass — and that's done, in part, because **everyone** remembers it; they had some in their home at one time or another; it has universal appeal. Who is to say what will be collectible in the next 50 years. If we knew, we could all get rich!

If you like Tiara products, then of course buy them; but don't do so **depending** upon their being collectible just because they are made in the image of the old! You have an equal chance, I feel, of going to Las Vegas and **depending** upon getting rich at the blackjack table.

NEW "CAMEO"

Colors: Green, pink, cobalt blue (shakers); yellow, green, and pink (children's dishes).

I hope you can still see how very weak the pattern is on this reproduction shaker. It was originally made by Mosser Glass Company in Ohio, but is now being made overseas. Also, you can see how much glass remains in the bottom of the shaker; and, of course, the new tops all make this easy to spot at the market. These were to be bought wholesale at around $6.00 but did not sell well. An **importer** made shakers in pink, cobalt blue, and a terrible green color. These, too, are weakly patterned! They were never originally made in the blue, but **beware of pink!**

Children's dishes in Cameo pose no problem to collectors since they were **never made originally.** These, also made by Mosser, are scale models of the larger size. This type of production I have no quarrel with since they are not made to dupe anyone. There are over 50 of these smaller pieces; thus, if you have a piece of glass that looks like a smaller (child's) version of a larger piece of Cameo, then you probably have a newly manufactured item!

NEW "ADAM"

NEW "AVOCADO"

NEW "CHERRY BLOSSOM"

Colors: Pink, green, blue, Delphite, cobalt, red, and iridized colors.

Please use information provided only for the piece described. Do not apply the information on the tumbler for the pitcher, etc. Realize that with various importers now reproducing glass, there are more modifications than I can possibly scrutinize for you. Know your dealer and HOPE he knows what he is doing!

Due to all the altered reproductions of the same pieces over and over, please understand this is only a guide as to what you should look for when buying! We've now seen some reproductions of those reproductions! All the items pictured on the next page are easy to spot as reproductions once you know what to look for with the possible exception of the 13" divided platter pictured in the center. It's too heavy, weighing 2¾ pounds, and has a thick ⅜" of glass in the bottom; but the design isn't too bad! The edges of the leaves aren't smooth; but neither are they serrated like old leaves.

There are many differences between old and new scalloped bottom, AOP Cherry pitchers. The easiest way to tell the difference is to turn the pitcher over. The branch crossing the bottom of my old Cherry pitchers **looks** like a branch. It's knobby and gnarled and has several leaves and cherry stems directly attached to it. One variation of the new pitcher just has a bald strip of glass cutting the bottom of the pitcher in half. Further, the old Cherry pitchers have a plain glass background for the cherries and leaves in the bottom of the pitcher. In the new pitchers, there's a rough, filled in, straw-like background. You see **no plain glass.**

As for the new tumblers, the easiest way to tell old from new is to look at the ring dividing the patterned portion of the glass from the plain glass lip. The old tumblers have three indented rings dividing the pattern from the plain glass rim. The new has only one. Again, the pattern at the bottom of the new tumblers is brief and practically nonexistent in the center curve of the glass bottom. The pattern, what there is, mostly hugs the center of the foot.

2 handled tray — old: 1⅞ lb.; $\frac{3}{16}$" glass in bottom; leaves and cherries east/west from north/south handles **(some older trays were rotated so this is not always true);** leaves have real spine and serrated edges; cherry stems end in triangle of glass. new: 2⅛ lb.; ¼" glass in bottom; leaves and cherries north/south with the handles; canal type leaves (but uneven edges; cherry stem ends before canal shaped line).

cake plate — new: color too light pink, leaves have too many parallel veins that give them a "feathery" look; arches at plate edge don't line up with lines on inside of the rim to which the feet are attached.

8½" bowl — new: crude leaves with smooth edges; veins in parallel lines.

cereal bowl — new: wrong shape, looks like 8½" bowl, small 2" center. old: large center, 2½" inside ring, nearly 3½" if you count the outer rim before the sides turn up.

plate — new: center shown close up; smooth edged leaves, fish spine type center leaf portion; weighs 1 pound plus; feels thicker at edge with mould offset lines clearly visible. old: center leaves look like real leaves with spines, veins, and serrated edges; weighs ¾ pound; clean edges; no mould offset.

cup — new: area in bottom left free of design; canal centered leaves; smooth, thick top to cup handle (old has triangle grasp point).

saucer — new: offset mould line edge; canal leaf center.

The Cherry child's cup (with a slightly lopsided handle) having the cherries hanging upside down when the cup was held in the right hand appeared in 1973. After I reported this error, it was quickly corrected by re-inverting the inverted mould. These later cups were thus improved in design but slightly off color. The saucers tended to have slightly off center designs, too. Next came the "child's butter dish" that was never made by Jeannette. It was essentially the child's cup without a handle turned upside down over the saucer and having a little glob of glass added as a knob for lifting purposes.

Pictured are some of the colors of butter dishes made so far. Shaker reproductions were introduced in 1977 and some were dated '77 on the bottom. Shortly afterward, the non-dated variety appeared. How can you tell new shakers from old — should you get the one in a million chance to do so?

First, look at the tops. New tops could indicate new shakers. Next, notice the protruding edges beneath the tops. **In the new they are squared off juts rather than the nicely rounded scallops on the old** (which are pictured under Cherry Blossom pattern). The design on the newer shakers is often weak in spots. Finally, notice how far up inside the shakers the solid glass (next to the foot) remains. The newer shakers have almost twice as much glass in that area. They appear to be ¼ full of glass before you ever add the salt!

In 1989, a new distributor began making reproduction glass in the Far East. He made shakers in cobalt blue, pink, and a hideous green, that is no problem to spot! These shakers are similar in quality to those made before. However, the present pink color is good; yet the quality and design of each batch could vary greatly. Realize that **only two original pairs of pink Cherry shakers have ever been found** and those were discovered before any reproductions were made in 1977!

Butter dishes are naturally more deceptive in pink and green since those were the only original colors. The major flaw in the new butter is that there is **one band** encircling the bottom edge of the butter top; there are **two bands** very close together along the skirt of the old top.

NEW "FLORAL" IMPORTING COMPANY OUT OF GEORGIA

The important news in Floral is that reproduction shakers are now being found in pink, red, cobalt blue, and a dark green color. Cobalt blue, red, and the dark green Floral shakers are of little concern since they were never made in these colors originally. The green is darker than the original green, but not as deep as Forest green. The pink shakers are not only a very good pink, but they are also a very good copy. There are lots of minor variations in design and leaf detail to someone who knows glassware well; but I have always tried to pick out a point that anyone can use to ascertain legitimacy. There is one easy way to tell the Floral reproductions. Take off the top and look at the threads where the lid screws onto the shaker. On the old there are a **pair** of parallel threads on each side or a least a pair on one side which end right before the mold seams down each side. The new Floral has one continuous line thread which starts at one side and continues around the shaker until it ends above the beginning line on the other side. There is approximately one inch of overlapped thread making two lines for that inch; but the whole thread is one continuous line and not two separate ones as on the old. No other Floral reproductions have been made as of May 1999.

NEW "FLORENTINE" NO. 1 IMPORTING COMPANY OUT OF GEORGIA

Although a picture of a reproduction shaker is not shown, I would like for you to know of its existence.

Florentine No. 1 shakers have been reproduced in pink, red, and cobalt blue. There may be other colors to follow. I only have examined one reproduction shaker, and it is difficult to know if all shakers will be as badly molded as this is. I can say by looking at this one shaker that there is little or no design on the bottom. No red or cobalt blue Florentine No. 1 shakers have ever been found; so those are no problem. The pink is more difficult. I compared this one to several old pairs. The old shakers have a major open flower on each side. There is a top circle on this blossom with three smaller circles down each side. The seven circles form the outside of the blossom. The new blossom looks more like a strawberry with no circles forming the outside of the blossom. This repro blossom looks like a poor drawing! Do not use the Floral thread test for the Florentine No. 1 shakers, however. It won't work for Florentine although these are made by the same importing company out of Georgia.

NEW "FLORENTINE" NO. 2 IMPORTING COMPANY OUT OF GEORGIA

A reproduced footed Florentine No. 2 pitcher and footed juice tumbler appeared in 1996. First to surface was a cobalt blue set that alerted knowledgeable collectors that something was strange. Next, sets of red, dark green, and two shades of pink began to be seen at the local flea markets. All these colors were dead giveaways since the footed Florentine No. 2 pitcher was never made in any of those shades.

The new pitchers are approximately ¼" shorter than the original and have a flatter foot as opposed to the domed foot of the old. The mold line on the lip of the newer pitcher extends ½" below the lip while only ⅜" below on the original. All of the measurements could vary over time with the reproductions and may even vary on the older ones. The easiest way to tell the old from the new, besides color, is by the handles. The new handles are ⅞" wide, but the older ones were only ¾" wide. That ⅛" seems even bigger than that when you set them side by side as shown below.

The juice tumbler differences are not as apparent; but there are two. The old juice stands 4" tall and the diameter of the base is 2⅛". The reproduction is shorter and smaller in base diameter. It is only 3$^{15}/_{16}$" tall and 2" in diameter. These are small differences, I know; but color is the most telling discrepancy!

NEW "MADRID" CALLED "RECOLLECTION" Currently being made.

I hope you have already read about Recollection Madrid on page 114. Indiana Glass made Madrid in teal after making it in **blue, pink, and crystal.** This light teal color was never made originally; so there is no problem of it being confused with old! The teal was sold through all kinds of outlets ranging from better department stores to discount catalogs. In the past couple of years we have received several ads stating that this is genuine Depression glass made from old moulds. None of this is made from old glass moulds unless you consider 1976 old. Most of the pieces are from moulds that were never made originally.

The light blue was a big seller for Indiana according to reports I am receiving around the country. It is a brighter, more fluorescent looking blue than the soft, original color. More and more of it is turning up in antique malls. Buy it if you like it, just don't pay antique prices for it!

Look at the picture below! Only the cup, saucer, and oval vegetable were ever made in old Madrid. The new grill plate has one division splitting the plate in half, but the old had three sections. A goblet or vase was never made. The vase is sold with a candle making it a hurricane lamp. The heavy tumbler was placed on top of a candlestick to make this vase/hurricane lamp. That candlestick gets a workout. It was attached to a plate to make a pedestal cake stand and to a butter dish to make a preserve stand. That's a clever idea, actually. You would not believe the mail spawned by these two pieces!

The shakers are short and heavy and you can see both original styles pictured on page 115. The latest item I have seen is a heavy 11 oz. flat tumbler being sold in a set of four or six called "On the Rocks." The biggest giveaway to this newer pink glass is the **pale, washed out** color.

The only concerns in the new pink pieces are the cups, saucers, and oval vegetable bowl. These three pieces were made in pink in the 1930s. None of the others shown were ever made in the 1930s in pink; so realize that when you see the butter dish, dinner plate, soup bowl, or sugar and creamer. These are new items! Once you have learned what this washed-out pink looks like by seeing these items for sale, the color will be a clue when you see other pieces.

The least difficult piece for new collectors to tell new from old is the candlestick. The new ones all have **three raised ridges inside** to hold the candle more firmly. All old ones do not have any inside ridges. You may even find new candlesticks in black.

NEW "MAYFAIR" IMPORTING COMPANY

Colors: Pink, green, blue, cobalt (shot glasses), 1977; pink, green, amethyst, cobalt blue, red (cookie jars), 1982; cobalt blue, pink, amethyst, red, and green (odd shade), shakers 1988; green, cobalt, pink, juice pitchers, 1993.

Only the pink shot glass need cause any concern to collectors because that glass wasn't made in any other color originally. At first glance, the color of the newer shots is often too light pink or too orange. Dead giveaway is the stems of the flower design, however. In the old that stem branched to form an **"A"** shape at the bottom; in the new, you have a single stem. Further, in the new design, the leaf is hollow with the veins moulded in. In the old, the leaf is moulded in and the veining is left hollow. In the center of the flower on the old, dots (anther) cluster entirely to one side and are rather distinct. Nothing like that occurs in the new design.

As for the cookie jars, at cursory glance the base of the cookie has a very indistinct design. It will feel smooth to the touch, it's so faint. In the old cookie jars, there's a distinct pattern that feels like raised embossing to the touch. Next, turn the bottom upside down. The new bottom is perfectly smooth. The old bottom contains a **1¾" mould circle rim** that is raised enough to catch your fingernail in it. There are other distinctions as well; but that is the **quickest** and **easiest** way to tell old from new.

In the Mayfair cookie lid, the new design (parallel to the straight side of the lid) at the edge curves gracefully toward the center "V" shape (rather like bird wings in flight); in the old, that edge is a flat straight line going into the "V" (like airplane wings sticking straight out from the side of the plane as you face it head on).

The green color of the cookie, as you can see from the picture, is not the pretty, yellow/green color of true green Mayfair. It also **doesn't glow** under black light as the old green does; so, that is a simple test for green.

NEW "MAYFAIR"

The corner ridges on the old shaker rise half way to the top and then smooth out. The new shaker corner ridges rise to the top and are quite pronounced. The measurement differences are listed below, but the diameter of the opening is the critical and easiest way to tell old from new!

	OLD	NEW
Diameter of opening	$\frac{3}{4}$"	$\frac{5}{8}$"
Diameter of lid	$\frac{7}{8}$,"	$\frac{3}{4}$"
Height	$4\frac{1}{16}$"	4"

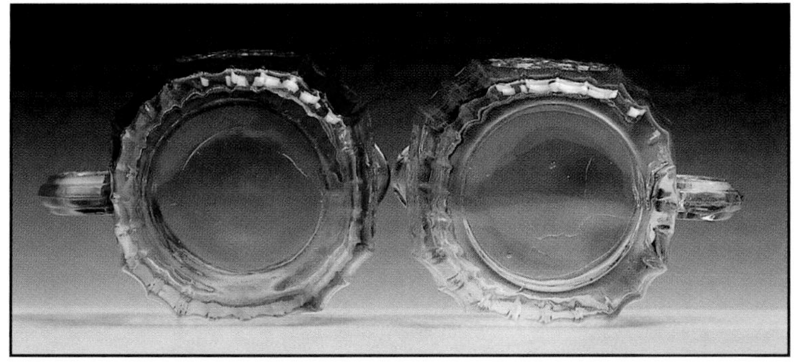

OLD **NEW**

Mayfair juice pitchers were reproduced in 1993. The old pitchers have a distinct mould circle on the bottom that is missing on the newly made ones. This and the oddly applied handles on the repros make these easily spotted! The blue pitcher is the old one in the photos.

OLD **NEW**

NEW "MISS AMERICA"

Colors: Crystal, green, pink, ice blue, red amberina, cobalt blue.

Miss America cobalt creamers and sugars are smaller than the originals; Miss America was **not made in cobalt** in olden days. Other colors have followed. These creamer and sugars are poorly made. There are many bubbles in the glass of the ones I have seen.

The reproduction butter dish in Miss America design is probably the best of the newer products; yet there are three, diverse differences to be found between the original butter top and the newly made ones. Since the expense of the butter dish lies in the top, it seems more beneficial to investigate it. **There is a new importer who is making reproductions of the reproductions.** Unfortunately, these newer models deviate greatly from one batch to the next. The only obvious thing I have seen on these butters is how the top knob sticks up away from the butter caused by a **longer than usual stem at the knob.** The paragraph in bold below explains the best way to tell old from new!

Pick up the top of the new dish and feel up inside it. If the butter top knob is filled with glass so that it is convex (curved outward), the dish is new; the old inside knob area is concave (curved inward).

Finally, from the underside, look through the top toward the knob. In the original butter dish you would see a perfectly formed multi-sided star; in the newer version, you see distorted rays with no visible points.

Shakers have been made in green, pink, cobalt blue, and crystal. The latest copies of **shakers are becoming more difficult to distinguish from the old!** The new distributor's copies are creating havoc with new collectors and dealers alike. **The measurements given below for shakers do not hold true for all the latest reproductions.** It is impossible to know which generation of shaker reproductions that you will encounter, so you have to be careful on these! Know your dealer and **if the price is too good to be true,** there is likely a good reason! **It's new!**

New shakers most likely will have new tops; but since some old shakers have been given new tops, that isn't conclusive at all. Unscrew the lid. Old shakers have a very neatly formed ridge of glass on which to screw the lid. It overlaps a little and has rounded off ends. Old shakers stand 3⅜" tall without the lid. **Most new** ones stand 3¼" tall. Old shakers have almost a forefinger's depth inside (female finger) or a fraction short of 2½". **Most new** shakers have an inside depth of 2", about the second digit bend of a female's finger. (I'm doing finger depths since most of you will carry those with you to the flea market, rather than a tape measure). In men, the old shaker's depth covers my knuckle; the new shaker leaves my knuckle exposed. **Most new** shakers simply have more glass on the inside of the shaker — something you can spot from 12 feet away! The **hobs are more rounded** on the newer shaker, particularly **near the stem and seams;** in the old shaker these areas remained pointedly sharp!

New Miss America tumblers have ½" of glass in the bottom, have a smooth edge on the bottom of the glass with no mould rim, and show only **two distinct** mould marks on the sides of the glass. Old tumblers have only ¼" of glass in the bottom, have a distinct mould line rimming the bottom of the tumbler, and have **four distinct** mould marks up the sides of the tumbler.

New Miss America pitchers (without ice lip only) are all perfectly smooth rimmed at the top edge above the handle. All old pitchers that I have seen have a **"hump"** in the top rim of the glass above the handle area, rather like a camel's hump. The very bottom diamonds next to the foot in the new pitchers "squash" into elongated diamonds. In the old pitchers, these get noticeably smaller, but they retain their diamond shape.

NEW "ROYAL LACE" IMPORTING COMPANY

Colors: cobalt blue.

The first thing you notice about the reproduced pieces is the extra dark, vivid cobalt blue color! It is not the soft cobalt blue originally made by the Hazel Atlas. So far, only the cookie jar, juice, and water tumblers have been made as of May 1999.

The original cookie jar lid has a mould seam that bisects the center of the pattern on one side, and runs across the knob and bisects the pattern on the opposite side. There is no mould line at all on the reproduction.

There are a multitude of bubbles and imperfections on the bottom of the new cookie jar that I am examining. The bottom is poorly moulded and the pattern is extremely weak. Original bottoms are plentiful anyway; learn to recognize the top and it will save you money!

As for tumblers, the first reproduction tumblers had plain bottoms without the four-pointed design which makes these simple to distinguish. The new juice tumbler has a bottom design, but it is as large as the one on the water tumbler and covers the entire bottom of the glass. Originally, this design was very small and did not encompass the whole bottom as does this reproduction. Additionally, there are design flaws on both size tumblers that stand out. The four ribs between each of the four designs on the side of the repro tumblers protrude far enough to catch your fingernail. The original tumblers have a very smooth, flowing design that you can only feel. The other distinct flaw is a semi-circular design on the rim of the glass above those four ribs. Originally these were very tiny on both tumblers with five oval leaves in each. There are three complete diamond-shaped designs in the new tumblers with two being doubled diamonds (diamond shapes within diamonds); and the semi-circular design almost touches the top rim! There's at least an ⅛" of glass above the older "fan."

Also, on the bottom of the tumblers, the four flower petal center designs in the old is open-ended leaving ⅛" of open glass at the tip of each petal. In the new version, these ends are closed, causing the petals to be pointed on the end.

NEW "SHARON" Privately Produced 1976...(continued page 238)

Colors: Blue, dark green, light green, pink, cobalt blue, opalescent blue, red, burnt umber.

A blue Sharon butter turned up in 1976 and turned my phone line to liquid fire! The color was Mayfair blue — a fluke and dead giveaway as far as real Sharon is concerned. The original mastermind of reproductions did not know his patterns very well and mixed up Mayfair and Sharon! (He admitted that when I talked to him!)

When Sharon butters are found in colors similar to the old pink and green, you can immediately tell that the new version has more glass in the top where it changes from pattern to clear glass, a thick, defined ring of glass as opposed to a thin, barely defined ring of glass in the old. The knob of the new dish tends to stick up more. In the old butter dish there's barely room to fit your finger to grasp the knob. The new butter dish has a sharply defined ridge of glass in the bottom around which the top sits. The old butter has such a slight rim that the top easily scoots off the bottom.

In 1977 a cheese dish appeared having the same top as the butter and having all the flaws inherent in that top which were discussed in detail above. However, the bottom of this dish was all wrong. It was about half way between a flat plate and a butter dish bottom, **bowl** shaped; and it was very thick, giving it an awkward appearance. The real cheese bottom was a **salad plate** with a rim of glass for holding the top inside that rim. These round bottom cheese dishes are but a parody of the old and are easily spotted.

REPRODUCTIONS (Continued)

NEW "SHARON" (Continued)

Some of the latest reproductions in Sharon are a too-light pink (other colors are being made) creamer and sugar with lid. They are pictured with the "Made in Taiwan" label. These retail for around $15.00 for the pair and are also easy to spot as reproductions. I'll just mention the most obvious differences. Turn the creamer so you are looking directly at the spout. In the old creamer the mould line runs dead center of that spout; in the new, the mould line runs decidedly to the left of center spout.

On the sugar, the leaves and roses are "off" but not enough to describe it to new collectors. Therefore, look at the center design, both sides, at the stars located at the very bottom of the motif. A thin leaf stem should run directly from that center star upward on both sides. In this new sugar, the stem only runs from one; it stops way short of the star on one side; or look inside the sugar bowl at where the handle attaches to the bottom of the bowl; in the new bowl, this attachment looks like a perfect circle; in the old, its an upside down "v" shaped teardrop.

As for the sugar lid, the knob of the new lid is perfectly smooth as you grasp its edges. The old knob has a **mould seam running mid circumference** (equator). You could tell these two lids apart blindfolded!

While there is a slight difference between the height, mouth opening diameter, and inside depth of the old Sharon shakers and those newly produced, I won't attempt to upset you with those sixteenths and thirty-seconds of an inch of difference. It is safe to say that in physical appearance, they are very close. However, when documenting design, they're miles apart.

The old shakers have true appearing roses. The flowers really look like roses. On the new shakers, the roses appear as poorly drawn circles with wobbly concentric rings. The leaves are not as clearly defined on the new shakers as the old. However, forgetting all that, in the old shakers, the first design you see below the lid is a rose bud. It's angled like a rocket shooting off into outer space with three leaves at the base of the bud (where the rocket fuel would burn out). In the new shakers, this "bud" has become four paddles of a windmill. It's the difference between this and this .

Candy dishes have been made in pink, green, cobalt blue, red, and opaque blue that goes to opalescent. These candy jars are among the easiest items to discern old from new. Pick up the lid and look from the bottom side. On the old there is a 2" circle ring knob below the knob; on the new, that ring of glass below the knob is only ½". This shows from the top also but it is difficult to measure with the knob in the center. There are other major differences, but this one will not be mould corrected easily. The bottoms are also simple to distinguish. The **base diameter of the old is 3¼"** and the new only 3". On the example I have, quality of the new is rough, poorly shaped and moulded; but I do not know if that will hold true for all reproductions of the candy. I hope so!

Collectible Glassware from the 40s, 50s, 60s...

Fifth Edition

by Gene Florence

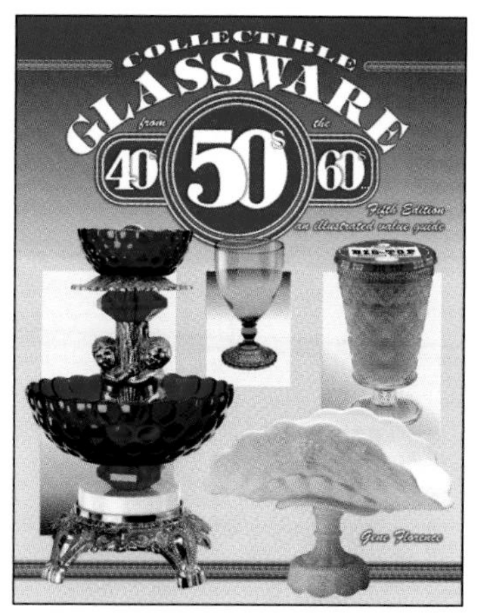

Covering collectible glassware made after the Depression era, this is the only book available that deals exclusively with the mass-produced and handmade glassware from the 40s, 50s, and 60s, features many new original company catalog pages and seven new patterns that have been requested by collectors – making a total of 88 patterns from Anniversary to Yorktown, with many of the most popular Fire-King patterns in between. Each pattern is alphabetically listed, all known pieces in each pattern are described and priced, and gorgeous color photographs showcase both common and very rare pieces.

ISBN: 1-57432-139-0

#5357 • 8½ x 11 • 240 pgs. • HB • **$19.95**

Florence's Glassware Pattern Identification Guide

by Gene Florence

Gene Florence's Glassware Pattern Identification Guide is a great companion for his other books. It includes most every pattern featured in his other price guides, as well as many more — over 400 patterns in all. A gorgeous close-up photograph of a representative piece of each pattern shows great detail to make identification easy. Florence provides the names, the company which made the glass, dates of production, and even colors available. This new guide is the ideal reference for all glass collectors and dealers, as well as the novice, and will be a great resource for years to come. No values.

ISBN: 1-57432-045-9

#5042 • 8½ x 11 • 176 Pgs. • PB • **$18.95**

A Publication I recommend:

DEPRESSION GLASS DAZE

The Original National Depression glass newspaper

Depression Glass Daze, the original, national monthly newspaper dedicated to the buying, selling and collecting of colored glassware of the 20s and 30s. We average 60 pages each month, filled with feature articles by top-notch columnists, readers' "finds," club happenings, show news, a china corner, a current listing of new glass issues to be aware of and a multitude of ads! You can find it in the DAZE! Keep up with what's happening in the dee gee world with a subscription to the DAZE. Buy, sell or trade from the convenience of your easy chair.

Name __________

Street __________

City __________ State ______ Zip ______

☐ 1 Year - $21.00 ☐ Check Enclosed ☐ Please bill me

☐ Mastercard ☐ Visa

(Foreign subscribers - Please add $1.00 per year)

Card No. __________ Exp. Date ______

Signature __________

Send to: D.G.D., Box 57GF, Otisville, MI 48463-0008

Please allow 30 days